CLASSIC ESSAYS ON
THE CULTURE OF CITIES

Edited by

RICHARD SENNETT
Brandeis University

PRENTICE-HALL, INC., ENGLEWOOD CLIFFS, NEW JERSEY

Printed in the United States of America

ISBN: 0-13-135194-X

Library of Congress Catalog Card Number: 71-77533

10

PRENTICE-HALL INTERNATIONAL, INC., *London*
PRENTICE-HALL OF AUSTRALIA, PTY. LTD., *Sydney*
PRENTICE-HALL OF CANADA, LTD., *Toronto*
PRENTICE-HALL OF INDIA PRIVATE LIMITED, *New Delhi*
PRENTICE-HALL OF JAPAN, INC., *Tokyo*

For Max and Pierre

CONTENTS

ONE

THE CLASSIC SCHOOLS
OF URBAN STUDIES

AN INTRODUCTION
Richard Sennett

The essays in this book are the first modern explorations of what it means to live in a city; they are also the greatest essays on city culture yet written. Almost all of these works were composed between 1900 and the Second World War, but they belong together not simply because they share a common epoch or a common reputation. Most of the writers of these pieces worked with each other in sequence, and out of this personal contact has come a common body of themes, a step-by-step expression of certain ideas, that continues to dominate the way we understand the urban cultures of today.

Urban studies is a very recent field of study, yet cities are one of the oldest artifacts of civilized life. The reason for this is that up to the time of the Industrial Revolution, the city was taken by most social thinkers to be the image of society itself, and not some special, unique form of social life. In the ancient world this identification occurred in the writings of Aristotle, Plato, and Augustine; during the reemergence of city life in the late Middle Ages it could be found in the work of Machiavelli; during the 18th century this merging of city and society was powerfully stated in the social theory of Rousseau. Occasionally the city was treated as a special society, in the work of the 17th-century philosopher Jean Bodin, for instance, but the authority of the greater social theorists overwhelmed the view of those who felt as did Bodin. Thus, until quite recently, the field of urban studies had no real meaning of its own; the city was taken to be the mirror of a broader reality, more appropriate as a focus of thought.

This identification of society and city changed during the Industrial Revolution of the last two centuries because the cities themselves changed. They became immensely larger than anything known since the time of Rome, and their growth came not from within, through internal population change, but from without, as a result of agricultural changes that either encouraged or, in fewer cases, forced men of the countryside to move to town. This human migration, unsettling in itself, was conjoined to a new means of labor by which the experience of time, motion, and human relatedness became altered in men's lives. This new labor cannot simply be identified with the growth of "the factory" or of "capitalism," for extensive factory systems had existed in the medieval towns and Renaissance cities, and the process of orderly capital formation was more institutionalized, more coherently understood, in 14th-century Venice than in 19th-century Manchester. Something tangled and complex was involved in these industrial cities, something to be explored as a problem of itself, something that could not be understood by the use of a few easy labels or categories.

This was the task the writers in this book set themselves. It may be asked why it was their generation, at the opening of our own century, who performed this labor, and not the people who, 75 to 100 years earlier, first felt the brunt of the urban transformation. There was in fact a great deal of documentary evidence and discussion of the city by the people initially caught in its grip: in England the reports of commissions on child labor and factory conditions were read with concern by wide sections of the public; in France, the reshaping of Paris by Baron Haussmann in the middle of the century produced great debate; in America, the evils of the European factory cities were closely watched and the sylvan experiments of Lowell or Waltham offered up as a solution to the degradation of urban life in the Old World.

But holding sway over all these particular discussions and experiments was what Karl Polanyi has called the "grand idea" of the 19th-century intellectuals, that all these urban traits could be related in one way or another to society as a huge market place in which individuals or groups struggled with each other for gain. This system, generating the social conditions of cities, was thought to be perfectly clear as an idea, and useful new knowledge would be gained, supposedly, in discovering the good and evil of the system in practice.

It is the sway of the mechanical idea of a market economy generating urban social conditions that the writers in this book were the first to attack. They felt it was too simple and reduced away the complexity of experience that occurred in a city. Significantly, none of these new thinkers challenged the rightness or wrongness of the market idea as such, but rather sought to show that the economic life of the city was shaped in part by, or had at least a symbiotic relation to, noneconomic conditions peculiar only to urban areas. In this way, these classic urban theorists established themselves by enlarging the genera, the creative forces, that men understood to have produced the specific conditions of city culture.

This enlarging of the genera of social life helps explain why the essays in this book are so broad in the phenomena they treat. The generality was a breath of freedom for these men; it was the way in which they could tear down the rigid simplicities of thought that had made previous theories of city conditions sterile.

The classic urban writers fall into two schools of research. The first school was a German one, centered in Heidelberg and Berlin; its members were Max Weber, Georg Simmel, and a little later, Oswald Spengler. All wrote in the first quarter of the century. The second school grew up at the University of Chicago in the 1920s, where most of its members remained active until after the Second World War; the leaders of this Chicago School were Robert Park, Louis Wirth, and Ernest Burgess, of whom Park and Wirth appear in this volume. While all three called themselves sociologists, their intellectual influence at the university spread widely, and one of the notable conjunctions it effected was in the theoretical work of an anthropologist, Robert Redfield, whose urban essays appear as the conclusion of this volume. Redfield's ideas were both a summation of the work of the German and Chicago schools and a transition into the thinking about cities current today, thinking that still largely revolves, as elaboration or dispute, around the work done by all these men.

The German School

The first modern effort in urban studies, Max Weber's *The City*, appeared in 1905. The subject was a new one for him, and he also treated it in a way unlike anything before written on cities. Weber's work on the city is difficult to read, yet its difficulties, which are reflected in the impossibly abstract language of the book, say a great deal about the intentions of the author.

Weber was in his own life torn between being a man of action, committed to practical goals and specific ethical standards, and being a scientist, committed to a "value-free" description of society; in his

scholarly work the moralist, the man committed to living in the
world, is always present but hidden, so that what seems to be description is in· fact critique. Weber's abstract language is one way
the writer defends against this committment in himself, makes it
possible to write as an observer without acknowledging directly the
ethical implications of his ideas. Weber deals with the tension between
observation and judgement also by arguing through implication; he
presents the materials of a human situation in such a way that certain conclusions inevitably follow, yet will not commit himself in
print to drawing them. This tension may seem perverse, and perhaps
is; yet Weber's work has an enormous power in spite of itself, if the
reader is patient and unhurried.

   The sources of Weber's thinking on the city, as distinct from
his immense knowledge about cities, are surprising. One would think
he would have absorbed and dealt with the writings of Tonnies and
Durkheim, sociologists of his era who were beginning to uncover the
effect of urban factors on seemingly unrelated aspects of social life,
though neither formulated an urban theory as such. Weber took a
route different from theirs, however, in that he sought to describe
not how cities could lead to a sense of isolation and lostness in men,
but rather under what conditions cities could be positive and creative
influences on men's common lives. That he sought this kind of city in
the past rather than the present is the cornerstone of Weber's critique
of modern urban life. The reasons why Weber turned to the past for
a description of creative cities are more complicated, and depend in
part on his definition of a city and in part on how he believed this
definition could be explored.

   Weber's concept of a city is clearest if we define a word that
stands close to it, the term "cosmopolitan." A human settlement
could be called cosmopolitan if, in the same place, a variety of styles
of life and different sorts of individuals could coexist. Weber trans-
posed this definition to the nature of the city itself: the city is that
social form which permits the greatest degree of individuality and uniqueness in each of its actual occurrences in the world. To define
the city is not to describe one style of life, but one set of social
structures that can produce a multitude of concretely different styles
of life. The city is therefore the set of social structures that encourage
social individuality and innovation, and is thus the instrument of
historical change.

This may seem an innocuous definition, but was at the time quite striking. Lord Bryce, after touring the industrial cities of America at the end of the 19th century, commented that the main differences between them were that some were made of brick and some were made of wood. The reaction of Europeans to the industrial cities developing in their own cultures was much the same: these industrial places had no character of their own; they were all cut out of the uniform mold, the impersonality, spawned by the giant factories and office bureaucracies in the metropolis.

In this light, Weber's study of the city was a bold undertaking, for he assumed that the modern cities did not articulate and express the real possibility of "the city" as a culture. He looked at the cities of his day as primitive and undeveloped institutions, rather than, as as many of his contemporaries believed, the products of a long and complex line of historical development. The rational and bureaucratic forces underlying modern capitalism might be complex and sophisticated processes, Weber argued, but they had produced a retrograde urban environment. Unlike the Marxists of his day, Weber did not believe historical developments occurred in a rigid, directional sequence; the forces of industrial growth, by his reasoning, had produced a state of affairs less civilized than that to be found in the cities of the late Middle Ages.

Weber's ideas were developed through a means as unique as his definition of the city itself. What we have called here a definition of city life, Weber called an "ideal-typical" condition of the city, by which he meant a state of urban life that most nearly fulfilled the social capacities inherent in this organization of human settlement. This "ideal-typical" condition supposes that it is possible to make a rational description of a social phenomenon, like a city, but the rational discourse is built out of the language of history.

As Weber used this method of argument, the building blocks of a rational theory of society come out of history, out of what men have actually experienced, not out of hypotheses or constructs that belong to a particular thinker alone. The subtlety of this approach is that it attempts something broader than a historical description of social phenomena. The materials of men's experience, their history, are to be used to build a model of social life connected by the rational links between historical materials; in this way, very large structures in society could be given a logical form, apart from their chronological relationship in time. By the ideal-typical method, bureaucracies in medieval Europe could be compared to those of ancient China, the city-states of Greece compared to the republics of Renaissance Italy, and so on. The meaning was in the logical comparison of composite social pictures; reason was to be used as a tool to bring out depths in historical experience that would not emerge if the observer's vision were narrowly limited to the historical material in sequence.

Using this method, Weber located an urban form, in the late Middle Ages in the Low Countries, and slightly later in the early Renaissance cities of Italy, that seemed most nearly to typify those conditions of city structure which bred rich, diverse urban styles of life. It was in the contrast of these cities to the cities of modern-day Europe that Weber hoped to show, not what should be changed or how change should occur, but what was now missing, what richness was possible within the city's borders.

Georg Simmel was a friend and younger colleague of Max Weber, one of the first to appreciate the greatness of Weber's work. Weber in his turn spent much effort, out of his faith in Simmel's powers, in trying to have Simmel appointed to a good university post; since Simmel was Jewish, he had a difficult time in the school system of Germany and was never fully accorded the honors that Weber and others sought for him.

Intellectually, Weber and Simmel shared a conception of the structures forming the modern Western city, but Simmel disagreed with Weber's explanation of how the city came into being; in addition, Simmel saw in these urban forms of the modern age the possibility for a new and complex civilized life.

Simmel, like Weber, believed that cities could be described in an "ideal-typical" form, but the elements of this description would be psychological, not structural, as in Weber's description of urban markets, families, and laws. For Simmel, the inescapable fact of urban life of all kinds was the feeling of being overwhelmed, the feeling that there was too much around one in a city to be dealt with. This excess of psychic stimulation, as Simmel called it, led men to try to defend themselves by not reacting emotionally to the people around them in a city; for Simmel this meant they would try not to react as whole human beings with distinct identities.

As a defense against the complexities of urban life, men tried to live, in Simmel's account, in a nonemotional, reasoned, functional relationship to other men; this defense was to break life into separate, neat compartments in order to be in control over each one separately. If men were in a city to try to mesh such realms of their lives as their families, their work, and their friends, they would be destroyed, Simmel argued, by compounding the complexities in each one of these realms within an urban milieu.

The market economy and the office and factory bureaucracies were the apotheosis of this fragmentation process, for in these socioeconomic forms the urbanite was most shielded from acting with other men as a full, emotional human being, most directed toward human contact in purely functional and rational forms. And since the threat of overstimulation was great in all the mammoth cities of Simmel's time, he argued that it was no accident that they should all appear so uniform; the market exchange and the office were the impersonal means suitable in all of them as a defense against the psychic disintegration of being overwhelmed.

Thus Simmel arrived at a portrait much like Weber's of the characteristics of modern city life: the impersonality, the faceless bureaucracies, the rational market processes. But Simmel believed these traits were the product of an urban condition social-psychological in its nature, while Weber believed they were the product of the confluence of economic and noneconomic forces called modern capitalism. Simmel also saw a possibility for life in these modern cities that Weber's indirect argument never approached.

Simmel's description of the psychological mechanism that goes into effect whenever large numbers of people live together assumed that there is a selfhood, a human identity, which tries to protect itself in the process. But this self, this emotional being, is not an insulated, otherworldly sphere that can live untouched by the defense mechanisms established in response to the city. The process of building defenses against the city inevitably molds the identity of the man doing the building. The great subtlety of Simmel's thinking was that he did not reduce this connection between the outer city world and the inner emotional world to a single form: there is no necessity for alienated spirits to arise in men whose day-to-day lives are functional and impersonal; the emotional lives of men need not wither because they have little outlet in ordinary affairs. These things could come to pass, but the city condition could lead as well to something different: a specially urban, specially civilized kind of human freedom.

Simmel believed that a man could, in a complex city, come to free his spirit from his acts, that is, come to understand that "who I am" is not simply "what I do ordinarily." There is something ironic in a persecuted Jewish intellectual giving this most Christian of ideas its first modern form in terms of city life, yet for Simmel the emotionless and functional qualities of most contacts in the city are powerful forces driving men to look for a more transcendent order of life, powerful forces to free men from making the circle of their routine acts the circle also of their feelings and intellectual horizons. Because the routine of life in the city is a defensive act, the person defending himself could believe that his own selfhood lay in the capacity to defend, to rise above mundane, emotionless things, and to live a life apart from them.

What Simmel envisioned, concretely, was that a man could learn in a city not to feel tied to his job, or his family, or his friends, but finally to turn in on himself for sustenance and growth, the way a monk would meditate. It is an open issue in Simmel's essay whether this freedom will prevail or whether men will become dispirited by the routine of their daily lives, but at least Simmel was willing to explore what good the great, impersonal metropolises of his and of our time could serve. Unlike almost all other writers during and since his day, Simmel was a visionary of the real world, not a visionary of the past or of some utopia to be established in the unknown future. He had the courage to look at routine and impersonality in order to see what could be made of it.

The final German theorist in this book, Oswald Spengler, was not a personal friend of either Weber or Simmel, nor a deep student of their work. Yet his writings on the city have a surprising affinity to certain of Weber's and Simmel's ideas, and his own thinking was later to influence the young American, studying with Simmel in Germany before the war, who was to found the Chicago School of Urban Studies.

Spengler believed that the stages of city development indicated the stages of civilized life as a whole in Western cultures. In this belief, he diverged sharply from the thinkers at the turn of the century like Weber and Simmel who were trying to specify unique features of the city as a social form. Further, the stages of civilized growth Spengler envisioned the city to embody were cyclical; the rise and fall of city cultures had a clear pattern which indicated the stages of growth and decay in society.

But Spengler parted ways with earlier thinkers by setting the course of urban growth inversely to the healthy growth of society, beyond a certain point. The large cities of his own time Spengler believed were a cancer, drawing off the sources of vigor and energy to be found in those less routinized, more brutal times when country and town were of equal strength. Soon, he prophesied, the giant metropolitan cultures of the present day should meet the fate of Rome, so that the cities would be destroyed in some apocalyptic war, and the society would revert to a barbaric agricultural life. Then the whole cycle of urban growth would reinstitute itself, civilized life would return, again become overcivilized at the point where the city overpowers the country, and collapse once more.

His major work, *Decline of the West*, derives its title from Spengler's belief that Western city culture had, by the early 20th century, become overripe; yet the cycle of urbanism was applicable, Spengler said, to other, non-Western cultures. For in all cases, cities of a certain size would corrupt their inhabitants by overinstitutionalizing the processes of human interchange, by making them routine and unemotional. This was also a possibility Simmel foresaw in the development of very large cities; but Spengler's notion of corruption was closest to the characterless cities of the modern world as they figured in Weber's account.

Spengler believed that every culture, Western and non-Western alike, formulated a "folk spirit" in its early agrarian phases, a spirit that gave the culture a particular identity; the growth of the massive city gradually obliterated this cultural character by encouraging a sense of individuality and separateness in the members of the city. Thus it comes about, Spengler argued, that all great cities are the same, though they spring out of radically different cultures, and that this sameness is a sign of their sickness and imminent collapse. The balance between town and country, which Weber believed critical in establishing the vigor of the Renaissance culture, was to Spengler the key to the health of all developing societies.

Spengler's argument may seem a flaccid, enormous generality, and indeed became so when perverted during the Nazi era in Germany. Yet cyclical accounts in which the city figures in some way as a symbol of growth or decline have deep roots in our culture; the Roman historian Polybius made a powerful argument along these lines;

there are some hints of this connection in the work of Herder, the 18th-century German writer who was one of the first to speak of a "folk-spirit;" and since Spengler's time the linking of city growth to the cyclical development of culture has been powerfully expressed in the writings of the English historian Arnold Toynbee and the American urbanist Lewis Mumford. What is so annoying about this cyclical idea in Spengler's essay, I believe, is that it was presented as a metaphor without a process; that is, the sense of the cycle was conveyed without a clear idea of the steps by which a large city could install separatism and isolated individualism in the place of common cultural character. One of the great achievements of the Chicago School taking form at the time Spengler wrote was to specify such evolution in concrete terms of migration to cities and the internal structure within the city itself.

This problem in Spengler's writing on the city identifies an assumption about the city found as well in the work of Weber and Simmel, an assumption which the Chicago School did a great deal to clarify. Weber, Simmel, and Spangler all assumed the characteristics of city culture—the large impersonal bureaucracies, the rule of rational exchange and rational law, the lack of warm personal contact between city men—to be qualities that pertain to the city *as a whole*. The enterprise of all three writers was directed toward defining city culture as a unitary phenomenon, by contrasting it to other kinds of social entities.

The first members of the Chicago School set out in an opposite way to deal with the city: they asked questions about the internal character of the city, about how the different parts of the city functioned in relation to each other, about the different kinds of experience to be had within the same city at the same point in time. This second generation of urbanists took the city as a world in itself, and sought to define what the city was in terms of the relations between the parts in this world; their effort was thus a new departure from the Germans in that, during the early phases of the Chicago School, no searching attempt was made to understand the city through its relations to the social forms that lay beyond it. Only in the last phases of the Chicago School, in the work of Robert Redfield, was the insight of the wider social bearing of the city, as explored by the Germans, to be combined with the knowledge of the internal workings of the city developed by the first researchers of the city at the University of Chicago.

The Chicago School

Despite this difference, the themes in the work of the Chicago urbanists Robert Park, Louis Wirth, Ernest Burgess, and Robert Redfield were those of the earlier German generation, themes now thrown into greater focus and detail. Because of this continuity, urban studies as a discipline has been fortunate in achieving coherence over the course of time, while other areas of social study have become fragmented. These themes fall into two large groupings: What are the noneconomic forces that work to create the "culture" of the city? What are the possibilities for free choice and innovation in the culture of the city? In addition to these common concerns, Robert Redfield, working in conjunction with Milton Singer, arrived at a means of describing the evolution of cities that resolved a confusion prevading both the German and earlier Chicago School writers on the nature of the evolution of the city form itself.

The Chicago School began to take form after the First World War when a young journalist-turned-sociologist, Robert Park, attracted to the University of Chicago two other scholars in the then novel field of city culture, Ernest Burgess and Louis Wirth. Park had done his doctoral work in Germany, at the University of Heidelberg, before the war, and there had been much influenced by the lectures of Georg Simmel. The first fruit of this work was an article of Park's appearing in 1916, "The City: Some Suggestions for the Study of Human Behavior in the Urban Environment"; this landmark in the development of urban studies has influenced the course of urban research in America and Europe ever since.

Park in this article set out to understand the city both as a place and as a "moral order." He belived that the city could be described in such a way that its functional, tangible character would ultimately reveal the cultural and ethical possibilities for life in it. What Park called the "ecology" of the city, the way it was internally divided and operative, was not to be simply a map of where things were and how they worked; rather, Park wanted to discover how these physical vessels shape the emotional, human experience of city men.

This is a more subtle undertaking than it first appears, for Park assumed that psychic and moral conditions of living in a city would reflect themselves in physical ways—in how space was used, in the patterns of human motion and transport, and so on. Park assumed, in other words, that a culture could be manifest directly through its tangible artifacts, and that the city must therefore have an organic character which writers like Spengler, contrasting the "organic manifestation" of the farm or village to the disembodied society of the city, had previously denied it.

Park's idea was a suggestion as to where research on the tangible, immediate aspects of city life could lead. This organic picture, unfortunately, was achieved by few of Park's many students, so that most ecological work during and since his time has produced dry and anesthetic studies of urban conditions that reveal little of what is experienced in the actual conduct of life. But among some of Park's disciples the humane intent of his original formulation has been realized, notably in the theoretical essays of Louis Wirth and Robert Redfield, and in the concrete researches today of such Chicago urbanists as Donald Bogue.

We have seen that Simmel and Spengler both used the concept of a division of labor to describe the way in which city men lived in a fragmented and specialized relation to each other; the force urging on this division of labor was the desire for rational efficiency in performing tasks—rationality apart from, or as a defense against, the emotional relations involved in social acts. The writers of the Chicago School, notably Park and Wirth, were to show how this "force for rationality" was expressed in the physical arrangement of the city itself, how the geography of the place was the concrete expression of the division of labor and the fragmenting of social roles.

Because we are today so familiar with this geographical condition of the city, where business district, ghetto slum, are distinct each one from the others, it is hard to imagine that any other kind of urban form could exist, or that the description of such a functional geography could have been a discovery. Actually, this ecology is unique to the industrial city. The geographical separation of house and factory, place to live and place to work, was unknown to the late medieval cities of northern Europe, or the Renaissance city-state of Italy. As late as the middle of the last century, in the rebuilding of Paris, living quarters could be planned themselves to include all units from rich to poor in the same place.

The segmentalization Park and Wirth sought to describe was therefore a new physical artifact of industrial cities, in which the efficient use of land and distribution of population was based on the concentration of homogeneously functional units in the same physical territory. It was this condition, Park and Wirth thought, that would make the city a cluster of separate worlds, but where each one would be all of a piece within its own boarders.

For Park, this kind of physical-functional separation had an immence impact on the way behavior could be controlled in the city, and thus determined the freedom of behavior and expression possible in the city. This concern for city freedom set Park apart from those of his students, like Louis Wirth, who explored the response of urban people to fragmentation in their lives in terms of paths of communication and power in the city, through such limited groups as voluntary organizations. Park's emphasis on the freedom possible for men in cities as a consequence of the division of labor was rather in line with the concerns of his own teacher, Georg Simmel.

Where Simmel believed city men could become free by transcending the routine of city life, by forming an "I" that was greater and apart from any of the emotionless daily acts that "I" performs, Park went a step further; he asked what it would mean for the control of human behavior if all the activities of daily life were broken up into small, routine parts in which men were not emotionally involved. His answer was that in such a city, no one of the parts would have the power, or the total desire, to dictate the acts of any other, beyond what was necessary to preserve functional relations between the two. This was because the people who under one rubric might be considered a coherent social segment would not uniformly remain as a group defined by another measure: if the Swedes, for instance, belonged to twenty different occupations in a city, with cross-loyalities to each, no one could organize the Swedes as a group to achieve one particular occupational goal, like supporting a printers' strike; in the same way, the guild organization of workers, so common in the medieval and pre-industrial cities of Europe, could not survive the fragmenting of loyalties within each worker in the industrial city as he comes to have at the same time a number of different and often conflicting interests in his various social roles.

The outcome of these crossed loyalties was, Park believed, the impossibility of enforcing uniform standards of behavior in the city,

even though most of the city's people might have similar codes of conduct, without the use of violent force. Thus the possibility for what Park
called a "moral" range of deviant behavior would be very great in
cities, no one nonviolent agency being able to limit nonconformers.
But for a man to innovate, to free himself from old cultural restrictions
is, exactly, not to conform. Thus Park saw the city as the medium for the
emergence of free men, whose personal development could transcend
general societal standards, whose innovations could provide the basis
for historical change in urban society itself.

This urban freedom, as envisioned by Park, is sharply opposed
to Simmel's concept of liberty in the city. The freedom Park envisioned
was *behavioral*, and involved the capacity of men to express themselves
through acts unlike, and unrestrained by, the community as a whole.
The liberty Simmel envisioned does not suppose this condition of social
deviance; it was instead a transcendental, inner activity of searching
out a sense of selfhood beyond petty routine, routine Simmel took to
be an ineradicable condition of metropolitan life. Where Park's free
urban man is an innovator, a deviant, Simmel's free urban man is
more like a monk.

Further, where Simmel's notion of a free urban man makes it in-
nately impossible to point him out by the nature of his acts, and so directly study what his life is like, Park's concept of freedom clearly shows
where the tangle signs of the condition could be found throughout
the city: in the patterns of deviance which define the city's moral order.

A reader who has absorbed the ideas of Park will sense immeliately
the direction of thought in the essays of Louis Wirth, though Wirth
emphasized a different result of the urban fragmentation process than
Park. Wirth was a disciple in the best sense of the word; he was not a
highly orginial thinker, but he was creative in his capacity to develop
an idea, once germinated, into all of its logical possibilities. Wirth
made a great contribution, in particular, trying to envision the ways
in which the division of labor as an urban phenomenon would influence
the relations of urban economics, urban land use, urban labor patterns,
and urban political structures to each other; from this pattern of inter-
relation he sought to understand how the fragments communicated and
influenced each other. What was suggested in previous accounts of division of labor was spelled out in great theoretical detail in Wirth,
so that the process of urban specialization received for the first time a
coherent and disciplined presentation.

To my mind, the most interesting essays to come out of the Chicago School are those by Robert Redfield. His work deepened that of his collegues by showing how their views of the modern city were based on assumptions about the lives of nonurban, or what Redfield called "folk," societies. Together with a younger colleague, Milton Singer, Redfield went on to show how the difference between urban and folk societies were related to the evolution of the city form itself. In this way, Redfield was able to unite the explorations of the internal character of the city made by the early Chicago urbanists with the work of the German School on the city in the larger realm of society and social development.

Redfield's method of analysis was much like that of Max Weber: both used composite pictures of societies, "ideal-types," in order to build a rational discourse out of not necessarily rational historical materials. The special ideal-type Redfield was interested in was a picture of village or rural societies that could stand as a direct opposite to all that Park and Wirth had ascribed to the city. The essence of this folk culture was that all men could participate in the same way in society; nothing was so specialized that only a few people would be directly involved in it, since the scale of life was small in the sense that men knew each other as people, not as special performers with only functional relations to each other. Redfield brought his immense knowledge of anthropology to bear on tracing out how such an unsegmented society would affect religion, the exercise of power, and kin groups. In each case, his intent was to show what happened when men acted as full emotional beings, that is, when the principle of division of labor and roles was absent from their lives. In making this comparison, Redfield brought the enterprise of urban studies back to the generally comparative approach of Weber and Spengler; both urban and folk cultures, in Redfield's schema, were to acquire their reality by virtue of their differences.

Redfield took this simple idea as the cornerstone of an elaborate, sophisticated description of what happens to men as they come to be urbanized. Passage from folk to urban society was Redfield believed, a two-stage process, the first a kind of halfway structural absorption into the city, the second an internal change of attitude in the mind of the new urbanite. The kind of urbanization Redfield envisioned was a teleological one; that is, the move from folk to urban cultures was a process with a definite beginning and a definite end. This teleogical approach is similar to the method of Max Weber in that both men assumed there was some final and definable condition of life that could be called urban.

But Redfield, with his colleague Singer, went a step beyond Weber by arguing that once this process of urbanization had been fully achieved, further development to the nature of the city itself could occur. What the city does to people and the nature of the city as a formal structure were separate forces to Redfield and Singer. The forms of the city were themselves in evolution, and the evolution is onto-logical; that is, there is a process of development, but toward no clear end. The typing of cities in the Redfield-Singer article was to illustrate the kinds of stages through which cities might pass, although no one of these stages would be final. Thus, during or after the time a people experienced the defined passage from folk culture to urban culture in a teleological way, the cities themselves were freely developing histori-cally.

This may seem an unnecessarily abstract description of city life, but in fact these ideas made clear a puzzle in city culture that previous writers could not resolve: how, if the city is a special kind of society, can it evolve without losing the marks of its specialness?

Weber believed that in fact there were certain conditions under which the development of the city meant the decline of the special marks of city life; the industrial cities of the modern world were his prime examples, for most people had come to live in them, yet they had no character of their own.

Redfield and Singer, unlike Weber, believed that cities could in-nately possess the power of growing without losing their special char-acter because they existed in two dimensions at the same time. In one dimension, the teleological one, their character was fixed, in the trans-forming of folk culture into urban culture; in another dimension, the functional relations of the city to other elements of society, left the city itself free to change its form as the culture in which it exist-ed changed. Redfield and Singer believed there was nothing inevitable, and thus unfree, in these larger relations; there was only an inevitable change on the people who came from another culture into the sway of the city itself.

By resolving this problem, Redfield and Singer came to a much stronger picture of the city as the agent of social change than did Spengler; instead of being the harbinger of unceasing, regular patterns of growth and decline, the city becomes the medium by which a regular rhythm of human change is combined with the free evolution of social life. If this Idea is joined to Park's notion of how innovators within the city are free, there emerges a comprehensive portrait of the means by which the people in a city have a definite character, and yet a real freedom, just as their city has an identifiable structure and yet the capacity to change.

There is one common quality to all these essays, and that concerns their relevance to the turbulent search for a decent social order in the cities of our own time.

By a strange twist of events, as more and more people come to be concerned about creating just and humane urban life, the work of the professionals in urban studies has become increasingly removed, and in fact irrelevant, to the new search for values. The field of urban studies is now plagued by a kind of superstitious belief in scientific purity of research, as though, like Faust, if we had perfect and pure knowledge the world around us would suddenly change. As a human discipline, urban studies shows all the signs of rapidly dying out. The emotional perspective of the essayists in this book, for all the generality of their ideas, are probably the only guides to the conduct of modern urban life on a moral plane, apart from a few modern writers like Lewis Mumford, that are relevant to renewing a sense of freedom and vitality in our cities. Despite the sweep and abstractness of the first great urban schools, their members were in earnest is conveying to other men what human values are destroyed, preserved, or generated in the city. I believe there is therefore nothing out of date about these essays, for they are the works that still speak most directly to our search now for a city life not merely to be endured but to be prized.

TWO

THE GERMAN SCHOOL

THE NATURE OF THE CITY
Max Weber

Economic Character of the City: Market Settlement

The many definitions of the city have only one element in common: namely that the city consists simply of a collection of one or more separate dwellings but is a relatively closed settlement. Customarily, though not exclusively, in cities the houses are built closely to each other, often, today, wall to wall. This massing of elements interpenetrates the everyday concept of the "city" which is thought of quantitatively as a large locality. In itself this is not imprecise for the city often represents a locality and dense settlement of dwellings forming a colony so extensive that personal reciprocal acquaintance of the inhabitants is lacking. However, if interpreted in this way only very large localities could qualify as cities; moreover it would be ambiguous, for various cultural factors determine the size at which "impersonality" tends to appear. Precisely this impersonality was absent in many historical localities possessing the legal character of cities. Even in contemporary Russia there are villages comprising many thousands of inhabitants which are, thus, larger than many old "cities" (for example, in the Polish colonial area of the German East) which had only a few hundred inhabitants. Both in terms of what it would include and what it would exclude size alone can hardly be sufficient to define the city.

Economically defined, the city is a settlement the inhabitants of which live primarily off trade and commerce rather than agriculture.

Reprinted with permission of The Macmillan Company from *The City* by Max Weber. Edited and translated by Don Martindale and Gertrude Neuwirth. Copyright © 1958 by The Free Press, a Corporation.

First published in *Archiv für Sozialwissenschaft und Sozialpolitik,* Vol. 47, p. 621 ff. 1921). Last edition: *Wirtschaft und Gesellechaft* (Tübingen: J. C. B. Mohr, 1956) Vol. 2, p. 735 ff.—All the notes in this translation are those of the editors.

However, it is not altogether proper to call all localities "cities" which are dominated by trade and commerce. This would include in the concept "city" colonies made up of family members and maintaining a single, practically hereditary trade establishment such as the "trade villages" of Asia and Russia. It is necessary to add a certain "versatility" of practiced trades to the characteristics of the city. However, this in itself does not appear suitable as the single distinguising characteristic of the city either.

Economic versatility can be established in at least two ways by the presence of a feudal estate or a market. The economic and political needs of a feudal or princely estate can encourage specialization in trade products in providing a demand for which work is performed and goods are bartered. However, even though the *oikos* of a lord or prince is as large as a city, a colony of artisans and small merchants bound to villein services is not customarily called a "city" even though historically a large proportion of important "cities" originated in such settlements.[1] In cities of such origin the products for a prince's court often remained a highly important, even chief, source of income for the settlers.

The other method of establishing economic versatility is more generally important for the "city"; this is the existence in the place of settlement of a regular rather than an occasional exchange of goods. The market becomes an essential component in the livelihood of the settlers. To be sure, not every "market" converted the locality in which it was found into a city. The periodic fairs and yearly foreign-trade markets at which traveling merchants met at fixed times to sell their goods in wholesale or retail lots to each other or to consumers often occured in places which we would call "villages."

Thus, we wish to speak of a "city" only in cases where the local inhabitants satisfy an economically substantial part of their daily wants in the local market, and to an essential extent by products which the local market, and to an essential extent by products which the local population and that of the immediate hinterland produced for sale in the market or acquired in other ways. In the meaning employed here the "city" is a market place. The local market forms the economic center of the colony in which, due to the specialization in economic products,

[1]For the place of the household or oikos-economy cf. Max Weber, *General Economic History*, trans. Frank H. Knight (Glencoe: The Free Press, 1950) pp. 48, 58, 124 ff., 131, 146, 162 and Johannes Hase Broek, *Griechische Wirtschaftsgeschichte* (Tübingen: J. C. B. Mohr, 1931) pp. 15, 24, 27, 29, 38, 46, 69, 284.

both the nonurban population and urbanites satisfy their wants for articles of trade and commerce. Wherever it appeared as a configuration different from the country it was normal for the city to be both a lordly or princely residence as well as a market place. It simultaneously possessed centers of both kinds, *oikos* and market and frequently in addition to the regular market it also served as periodic foreign markets of traveling merchants. In the meaning of the word here, the city is a "market settlement."

Often the existence of a market rests upon the concessions and guarantees of protection by a lord of prince. They were often interested in such things as a regular supply of foreign commercial articles and trade products, in tolls, in moneys for escorts and other protection fees, in market tarriffs, and taxes from law suits. However, the lord of prince might also hope to profit from the local settlement of tradesmen and merchants capable of paying taxes and, as soon as the market settlement arose around the market, from land rents arising therefrom. Such opportunities were of especial importance to the lord of prince since they represented chances for monetary revenues and the increase in his treasure of precious metal.

However, the city could lack any attachment, physical or otherwise, to a lordly or princely residence. This was the case when it originated as a pure market settlement at a suitable intersection point (*Umschlageplatz*)[2] where the means of transportation were changed by virtue of concession to nonresident lords or princes or usurpation by the interested parties themselves. This could assume the form of concessions to entrepreneurs—permitting them to lay out a market and recruit settlers for it. Such capitalistic establishment of cities was especially frequent in medieval frontier areas, particularly in East, North, and Central Europe. Historically, though not as a rule, the practice has appeared throughout the world.

Without any attachment to the court of a prince or without princely concessions, the city could arise through the association of foreign invaders, naval warriors, or commercial settlers or, finally, native parties interested in the carrying trade. This occurred frequently in the early Middle Ages. The resultant city could be a pure market place. However, it is more usual to find large princely or patrimonial

[2]Charles H. Cooley's theory of transportation took the break in communication either physical or economic as the most critical of all factors for the formation of the city.

households and a market conjoined. In this case the eminent household as one contact point of the city could satisfy its want either primarily by means of a natural economy (that is by villein service or natural service or taxes place upon the artisans and merchants dependent on it) or it could supply itself more or less secondarily by barter in the local market as that market's most important buyer. The more pronounced the latter relation the more distinct the market foundation of the city looms and the city ceases by degrees to be a mere appendaged market settlement alongside the *oikos*. Despite attachment to the large household it then became a market city. As a rule the quantitative expansion of the original princely city and its economic importance go hand in hand with an increase in the satisfaction of wants in the market by the princely household and other large urban households attached to that of the prince as courts of vassals or major officials.

Types of Consumer and Producer City

Similar to the city of the prince, the inhabitants of which are economically dependent upon the purchasing power of noble households, are cities in which the purchasing power of the other larger consumers, such as rentiers, determines the economic opportunities of resident tradesmen and merchants. In terms of the kind and source of their incomes such larger consumers may be of quite varied types. They may be officials who spend their legal and illegal income in the city, or lords or other political power holders who spend their non-urban land rents or politically determined incomes there. In either of these cases the city closely approximates the princely city for it depends upon patrimonial and political incomes which supply the purchasing power of large consumers. Peking was a city of officials; Moscow, before suspension of serfdom, was a land-rent city.

Different in principle are the superficially similar cities in which urban land-rents are determined by traffic monopolies of landed property. Such cities originate in the trade and commerce consolidated in the hands of an urban aristocracy. This type of development has always been widespread: it appeared in Antiquity; in the Near East until the Byzantine Empire; and in the Middle Ages. The city that emerges is not economically of a rentier type. It is, rather, a merchant or trade city the rents of which represent a tribute of acquisitors to the owners of houses. The conceptual differentiation of this case from the one in which rents are not determined by tributary obligations to monopolists but by nonurban sources, should not obscure the inter-relation in the past of both forms. The large consumers can be rentiers spending their business incomes (today mainly interest on bonds, dividends or shares) in the city. Whereupon purchasing power rests on capitalistically conditioned monetary rentier sources as in the city of Arnheim. Or purchasing power can depend upon state pensions or other state rents as appears in a "pensionopolis" like Weibaden. In all similar cases one may describe the urban form as a consumer city, for the presence in residence of large consumers of special economic character is of decisive economic importance for the local tradesmen and merchants.

A contrasting form is presented by the producer city. The increase in population and purchasing power in the city may be due, as for example in Essen or Bochum, to the location there of factories, manufactures, or home-work industries supplying outside territories—thus representing the modern type. Or, again, the crafts and trades of the locality may ship their goods away as in cities of Asiatic, Ancient, and Medieval types. In either case the consumers for the local market are made up of large consumers if they are residents and/or entrepreneurs, workers and craftsmen who form the great mass, and merchants and benefactors of land-rent supported indirectly by the workers and craftsmen.

The trade city and merchant city are confronted by the consumer city in which the purchasing power of its larger consumers rests on the retail for profit of foreign products on the local market (for example, the woolen drapers in the Middle Ages), the foreign sale for profit of local products or goods obtained by native producers (for example, the herring of the Hansa), or the purchase of foreign products and their sale with or without storage at the place to the outside (intermediate commercial cities). Very frequently a combination or all these economic activities occured: the *commenda* and *societas maris* implied that a *tractator* (traveling merchant) journeyed to Levantine markets with products purchased with capital entrusted to him by resident capitalists.[3] Often the tractator travelled entirely

[3]Weber, *General Economic History*, pp. 205, 206 and W. Silberschmidt, *Die Commenda in ihrer Frühesten Entwicklung* (1884).

in ballast. He sold these products in the East and with the proceeds he purchased oriental articles brought back for sale in the local market. The profits of the undertaking were then divided between *tractator* and capitalist according to prearranged formulas.

The purchasing power and tax ability of the commercial city rested on the local economic establishment as was also the case for the producers' city in contrast to the consumers' city. The economic opportunities of the shipping and transport trade and of numerous secondary wholesale and retail activities were at the disposal of the merchants. However the economic activity of these establishments was not entirely executed for the local retail trade but in substantial measure for external trade. In principle, this state of affairs was similar to that of the modern city, which is the location of national and international financiers or large banks (London, Paris, Berlin) or of joint stock companies or cartels (Duesseldorf). It follows that today more than ever before a predominant part of the earnings of firms flow to localities other than the place of earning. Moreover, a growing part of business proceeds are not consumed by their rightful receivers at the metropolitan location of the business but in suburban villas, rural resorts of international hotels. Parallel with these developments "city-towns" or city-districts consisting almost exclusively of business establishments are arising.

There is no intention here of advancing the further casuistic distinctions required by a purely economic theory of the city. Moreover, it hardly needs to be mentioned that actual cities nearly always represent mixed types. Thus, if cities are to be economically classified at all, it must be in terms of their prevailing economic component.

Relation of the City to Agriculture

The relation of the city to agriculture has not been clear-cut. There were and are "semi-rural cities" (*Ackerburgerstaedte*), localities which while serving as places of market traffic and centers of typically urban trade, are sharply separated from the average city by the presence of a broad stratum of resident burghers satisfying a large part of their food needs through cultivation and even producing food for sale. Normally the larger the city the less the opportunity for urban residents to dispose of acreage in relation to their food needs at the same time without controlling a self-sufficient pasture and wood lot in the manner of the village. Cologne, the largest German city in the Middle Ages, almost completely lacked the *Allmende* (commons) from the beginning though the commons was not absent from any normal village of the time. Other German and foreign medieval cities at least placed considerable pastures and woods at the disposal of their burghers.

The presence of large acreages accessible to the urbanite is found more frequently as one turns attention to the South or back toward Antiquity. While today we justly regard the typical "urbanite" as a man who does not supply his own food need on his own land, originally the contrary was the case for the majority of typical ancient cities. In contrast to the medieval situation, the ancient urbanite was quite legitimately characterized by the fact that a *kleros, fundus* (in Israel: *chelek*) which he called his own, was a parcel of land which fed him.[4] The full urbanite of antiquity was a semi-peasant.

In the Medieval period, as in Antiquity, agricultural property was retained in the hands of merchant strata. This was more frequently the case in the south than in the north of Europe. In both medieval and ancient city-states agricultural properties, occasionally of quite exorbitant size, were found widely scattered, either being in the possession of eminent individual citizen landlords. Examples politically dominated by municipal authorities of powerful cities or are supplied by the Cheronesic domination of the Miltiades or the political or lordly estates of medieval aristocratic families, such as the Genoese Grimaldi, in the provinces or overseas.

As a general rule interlocal estates and the sovereign rights of individual citizens were not the objects of an urban economic policy. However, mixed conditions at times arose such that according to the circumstances estates were guaranteed to individuals by the city. In the nature of the case this only occurred when the individuals whose estates were guaranteed by the city belonged to the most powerful patricians. In such cases the estate was acquired and maintained through indirect help of civic power which in turn might share in its economic and political usufruct. This was frequently the case in the past.

[4]Pöhlmann, *Aus Altertum und Gegenwart,* p. 124 ff.; Weber, *General Economic History,* p. 328; Weber, *Ancient Judaism* (Glencoe: The Free Press, 1952), p. 465.

The relation of the city as agent of trade and commerce to the land as producer of food comprises one aspect of the "urban economy" and forms a special "economic stage" between the "household economy" on the one hand and the "national economy" on the other.[5] When the city is visualized in this manner, however, politico-economic aspects are conceptually fused with pure economic aspects and conceived as forming one whole. The mere fact that merchants and tradesmen live crowded together carrying on a regular satisfaction of daily needs in the market does not exhaust the concept of the "city." Where only the satisfaction of agricultural needs occurs within closed settlements and where—what is not identical with it—agricultural production appears in relation to nonagricultural acquisition, and when the presence or absence of markets constitutes the difference, we speak of trade and commercial localities and of small market-towns, but not of cities. There were, thus, hidden noneconomic dimensions in the phenomena brought under review in the previous sections. It is time to expand the concept of the "city" to include extra-economic factors.

The Politico-Administrative Concept of the City

Beside possessing an accumulation of abodes the city also has an economic association with its own landed property and a budget of receipts and expenditure. Such an economic association may also appear in the village no matter how great the quantitative differences. Moreover, it was not peculiar to the city alone, at least in the past, that it was both an economic and a regulatory association. Trespass restrictions, pasture regulations, the prohibition of the export of wood and straw, and similar regulations are known to the village, constituting an economic policy of the association as such.

The cities of the past were differentiated only by the kinds of regulations which appeared. Only the objects of political economic regulation on behalf of the association and the range of characteristic measures embraced by them were peculiar. It goes without saying that measures of the "urban economic policy" took substantial account of the fact that under the transportation conditions of the time the majority of all inland cities were dependent upon the agri-

[5]Weber has in mind distinctions introduced by Gustav Schmoller.

cultural resources of the immediate hinterland. As shown by the grain policies of Athens and Rome this was true for maritime cities. In a majority, not all, of urban trades areas, opportunity was provided for the natural "play of the market." The urban market supplied the normal, not the sole, place for the exchange of products, especially food.

Account also must be taken of the fact that production for trade was predominantly in the form of artisan technology organized in specialized small establishments. Such production operated without or with little capital and with strictly limited numbers of journeymen who were trained in long apprenticeships. Such production was economically in the form of wage worker as price work for customers. Sale to the local retailers was largely a sale to customers.

The market conditions of the time were the kind that would naturally emerge, given the above facts. The so-called "urban economic policy" was basically characterized by its attempt to stabilize the conditions of the local urban economy by means of economic regulations in the interest of permanently and cheaply feeding the masses and standardizing the economic opportunities of tradesmen and merchants. However, as we shall see, economic regulation was not the sole object of the urban economic policy nor, when it historically appears, was it fully developed. It emerges only under the political regime of the guild. Finally it can not be proved to be simply a transitional stage in the development of all cities. In any case, the urban economic policy does not represent a universal stage in economic evolution.

On the basis of customer relations and specialized small establishments operating without capital, the local urban market with its exchange between agricultural and nonagricultural producers and resident merchants, represents a kind of economic counterpart to barter as against systematically divided performances in terms of work and taxes of a specialized dependent economy in connection with the *oikos*, having its basis in the accumulation and integration of work in the manor, without exchange occurring inside. Following out the parallel: the *regulation* (urban economic policy) of the exchange and production conditions in the city represent the counterpart to the *organization* (traditional and feudalcontractual) of activities united in the economy of the *oikos*.

The very fact that in drawing these distinctions we are led to use the concepts of an "urban economic area" and "urban area," and "urban authority," already indicates that the concept of the "city" can and must be examined in terms of a series of concepts other than the purely economic categories so far employed. The additional concepts required for analysis of the city are political. This already appears in the fact that the urban economic policy itself may be the work of a prince to whom political dominion of the city with its inhabitants belongs. In this case when there is an urban economic policy it is determined *for* the inhabitants of the city not *by* them. However even when this is the case the city must still be considered to be a partially autonomous association, a "community" with special political and administrative arrangements.

The economic concept previously discussed must be entirely separated from the political-administrative concept of the city. Only in the latter sense may a special *area* belong to the city. A locale can be held to be a city in a political-administrative sense though it would not qualify as a city economically. In the Middle Ages there were areas legally defined as "cities" in which the inhabitants derived 90 percent or more of their livelihood from agriculture, representing a far larger fraction of their income then that of the inhabitants of many localities legally defined as "villages."

Naturally, the transition from such semi-rural cities to. consumers', producers', or commercial cities is quite fluid. In those settlements which differ administratively from the village and are thus dealt with as cities only one thing, namely, the kind of regulations of land-owning, is customarily different from rural land-owning forms. Economically such cities are differentiated by a special kind of rent situation presented in urban real estate which consists in house owner-ship to which land ownership is accessory. The position of urban real estate is connected administratively with special taxation principles. It is bound even more closely to a further element decisive for the political-administrative concept of the city and standing entirely outside the purely economic analysis, namely, the fortress.

Fortress and Garrison

It is very significant that the city in the past, in Antiquity and the Middle Ages, outside as well as within Europe, was also a special fortress or garrison. At present this property of the city has been entirely lost, but it was not universal even in the past. In Japan, for example, it was not the rule. Administratively one may, with Rathgen,[6] doubt the existence of cities at all. In contrast to Japan, in China every city was surrounded with a gigantic ring of walls. However, it is also true that many economically rural localities which were not cities in the administrative sense, possessed walls at all time. In China such places were not the seat of state authorities.

In many Mediterranean areas such as Sicily a man living outside the urban walls as a rural worker and country resident is almost unknown. This is a product of century-long insecurity. By contrast in old Hellas the Spartan polis sparkled by the absence of walls, yet the property of being a "garrison-town" was met. Sparta despised walls for the very reason that it was a permanent open military camp.

Though there is still dispute as to how long Athens was without walls, like all Hellenic cities except Sparta it contained in the Acropolis a castle built on rock in the same manner as Ekbantama and Persepolis which were royal castles with surrounding settlements. The castle or wall belonged normally to Oriental as well as to ancient Mediterranean and ordinary medieval cities.

The city was neither the sole nor oldest fortress. In desputed frontier territory and during chronic states of war, every village fortified itself. Under the constant danger of attack in the area of the Elbe and Oder Rivers Slavic settlements were fortified, the national form of the rural village seems early to have been standardized in the form of the "hedge-enclosed" circular area with a single entrance which could be locked and through which at night cattle were driven to the central protection of the village area. Similarly, walled hill retreats were diffused throughout the world from Israelite East Jordan to Germanic territories. Unarmed persons and cattle took refuge within in times of danger. The so-called cities of Henry I in the German East were merely systematically established fortresses of this sort.

In England during the Anglo-Saxon period a "burgh" (borough) belonged to each shire whose name it took. Guard and garrison duty as the oldest specifically "civic" obligations were attached to certain

---

[6]Karl Rathgen, "Gemeindefinanzen" in *Verein für Sozialpolitik* (Leipzig: Duncker & Humblot, 1908–10) and *Allgemeine Verfassungs und Verwaltungsgeschichte* (Leipzig: Huebner, 1911).

persons of pieces of land. When in normal times such fortresses were occupied, guards or vassals were maintained as a permanent garrison and paid in salaries or in land. There were fluid transitions from the permanently garrisoned fortress to the Anglo-Saxon burgh, the "garrison-city," in the sense of Maitland's theory, with a "burgess" as inhabitants. The burgess received its name from its political position which like the legal nature of its civic land and house property was determined by the duty of maintaining and guarding the fortress.

However, historically neither the palisaded village nor the emergency fortification are the primary forerunners of the city fortress, which was, rather, the manorial castle. The manorial castle was a fortress occupied by the lord and warriors subordinated to him as officials or as a personal following, together with their families and servants.

Military castle construction is very old, doubtlessly older than the chariot and military use of the horse. Like the war chariot the importance of the castle was determined by the development of knightly and royal warfare. In old China of the classic songs, in India of the Vedas, in Egypt and Mesopotamia, in Canaan, in Israel at the time of the Song of Deborah, in Greece during the period of the Homeric epics, and among the Etruscans, Celts, and Irish, the building of castles and the castle-principality were diffused universally. Old Egyptian sources speak of castles and their commanders and it may be assumed that they originally accommodated just as many small princes. From old documents it can be inferred that in Mesopotamia the development of the provincial kingships was preceded by a castle-dwelling princedom such as existed in Western India at the time of the oldest *Gathas*. The castle was certainly universally dominant in Northern India on the Ganges during the time of political disintegration. In this last instance, the old Kshatriyas whom the sources show to be peculiarly sandwiched between the king and nobility, were obviously princes.

In the period of Christianization, castle construction was pressed in Russia. It appears also during the dynasty of Thutmose in Syria at the time of the Israelite confederation (Abimelech). Old Chinese literature also provides irrefutable evidence of its original occurrence. The Hellenic and Asia Minor sea-castle was as universally diffused as piracy. There must have been an interim period of especially deep pacification to allow the Cretan unfortified places to arise in the place of the castle. In this area later castles like the Decelia,[7] so important in the Peloponnesian Wars, were originally fortresses of noble families. The medieval development of a politically independent gentry opened with the *castelli* in Italy. In Northern Europe the independence of the vassals was also bound up with enormous castle construction as established by Below.[8] Even in modern times individual deputyship in Germany has been dependent upon possession by the family of a castle, even if only the meager ruins of one. Disposal of a castle originally signified military dominion over the country. The only question was: In whose hands? It could be in the hands of the individual lords, or confederations of knights, or of a ruler who could depend on the trustworthiness of his vassals, ministers, or officers.

The City as the Fusion of Fortress and Market

In the first stage of its development into a special political form the fortified city was incorporated in or dependent upon a castle, the fortress of a king, noblemen, or association of knights. Such nobles either resided in the fortress themselves or maintained a garrison of mercenaries, vassals, or servants therein. In Anglo-Saxon England the right to possess a "haw," a fortified house in a "burgh," was bestowed as a privilege on certain landowners of the surrounding countryside. In Antiquity and in Medieval Italy the city-house of the nobleman was held in addition to his rural castle. The inhabitants or residents adjoining the castle, sometimes all, sometimes special strata, were bound as citizens (burgess) to the performance of certain military duties such as building and repair of the walls, guard duty, defense service and, at times, other military services such as communication and supply for the urban military noble. In this instance the burgher is a member of his estate because, and insofar, as, he participates in the military association of the city.

Maitland[9] has worked this out with especial clarity for England. The houses of the "burgh" were in the possession of people having

<hr />

[7]Hill commanding the pass between Pentelicus and Poenes occupied by the Spartans in 413.

[8]Georg Below, *Der deutsche Staat des Mittelalters* (Leipzig: Zuelle & Meyer, 1914); *Territorium und Stadt* (München: R. Oldenberg, 1900).

[9]Frederic William Maitland, *The Charters of the Borough of Cambridge* (Cambridge: University Press, 1901) and *The Court Law* (London: Quaritsch, 1891).

the duty of maintaining the fortification. This contrasts with the village. Alongside royal or aristocratically guaranteed market place appears military jurisdiction. The politically oriented castle and economically oriented market with the market area of the towns at times simultaneously serving both functions, again drill field and assembly area of the army and the place of pacific economic exchange on the other, often stand in plastic dualism beside one another.

The military drill field and economic market are not everywhere spatially separated. The Attic *pnyx* was a much later development then the *agora* which originally served the economic traffic as well as political and religious activities. On the other hand in Rome from ancient times the *comitium* and *campus martius* were separated from the economic *fora* as in the Middle Ages the *piazza del campo* at Siena (a tournament place still used today as a place for holding races between the wards of the city), as the front of the municipal place, is distinct from the *mercato* at the rear. Analogously in Islamic cities the *kasbeh*, the fortified camp of the warriors, was spatially separated from the bazaar. In Southern India the political city of notable men appears separately alongside the economic city.

The relation between the garrison of the political fortress and the civil economic population is complicated but always decisively important for the composition of the city. Wherever a castle existed artisans came or were settled for the satisfaction of manorial wants and the needs of the warriors. The consumption power of a prince's military household and the protection it guaranteed attracted the merchants. Moreover the lord was interested in attracting these classes since he was in position to procure money revenues through them either by taxing commerce or trade or participating in it through capital advances. At times the lord engaged in commerce on his own, even monopolizing it. In maritime castles as shipowner or ruler of the port the lord was in a position to procure a share in piratical or peacefully won seaborne profits. His followers and vassals resident in the place were also in position to profit whether he voluntarily gave them permission or, being dependent on their good will, was forced to do so.

The evidences of the participation of the ancient city lords in commercial activities are many. Vases from old Hellenic cities like Cyrene picture the king weighing goods (*silphion*). In Egypt at the beginning of histroical time a commercial fleet of the Lower-Egyptian

Pharaoh is reported. Widely diffused over the world, but especially in maritime "cities" where the carrying trade was easily controlled, the economic interest of resident military families flourished beside the monopoly of the castle chieftain, as a result of their own participation in commercial profits. Their capacity to participate in the civic economy often shattered the monopoly (if it existed) of the prince. When this occured the prince was considered only to be *primus inter pares* in the ruling circle or even simply as equal. The ruling circle comprised the urban sibs domiciled through landed property and deriving capital from some form of peaceful commerce, especially the *commenda* capital in the Middle Ages, or from personal participation in piracy or sea war. Often the prince was elected for short times and in any case he was decisively limited in power. In ancient maritime cities since Homer's time yearly municipal councils gradually appeared. Quite similar formations often occur in the early Middle Ages. In Venice they formed a counterbalance to the doges though with very different leadership positions depending on whether a royal count or vicomte or bishop or someone else was lord of the city. Equivalent developments also appear in other typical commercial cities.

Thus in early Antiquity and in the Middle Ages the urban commercial capitalists, the financiers of commerce, the specific notable persons of the city, have to be separated in principle from the domiciled holders of commercial "establishments," the merchants proper. To be sure the strata often blended into each other. However, with this we already anticipate later explanations.

In the hinterland, shipping points, terminals, crossings of rivers, and caravan routes (for example, Babylon) could become locations of similar developments. At times competition arose between the priest of the temple, and priestly lord of the city, for temple districts of famous gods offered sacred protection to inter-ethnic elements. Such areas could provide locations for politically unprotected commerce. Thus a city-like settlement, economically supplied by temple revenues, could attach itself to the temple district in a manner similar to the princely city with its tributes to the prince.

Individual cases varied depending on the extent to which the prince's interest in monetary revenues predominated in the granting of privileges for merchandising and manufacturing independent of the lordly household and taxed by the lord. On the other hand, the lord could be interested in satisfying his own needs hence in acting in ways strengthening his own powers and monopolizing trade in his own hands. When attracting foreigners by offering special privileges the lord also had to take into consideration the interests and "established" ability (which was also important for himself) of those already resident, who were dependent on his political protection or manorial supplies.

To this variety of possible development must be added the effects of the political-militaristic structure of the dominating group within which the founding of the city or its development occurred. We must consider the main antitheses in city development arising therefrom.

Association and Status Peculiarities of the Occidental City

Neither the "city," in the economic sense, nor the garrison, the inhabitants of which are accoutred with special political-administrative structures, necessarily constitute a "community." An urban "community," in the full meaning of the word, appears as a general phenomenon only in the Occident. Exceptions occasionally were to be found in the Near East (in Syria, Phoenicia, and Mesopotamia) but only occasionally and in rudiments. To constitute a full urban community a settlement must display a relative predominance of trade-commercial relations with the settlement as a whole displaying the following features: (1) a fortification; (2) a market; (3) a court of its own and at least partially autonomous law. (4) a related form of association; and (5) at least partial autonomy and autocephaly, thus also an administration by authorities in the election of whom the burghers participated.

In the past, rights such as those which define the urban community were normally privileges of the estates. The peculiar political properties of the urban community appeared only with the presence of a special stratum, a distinct new estate. Measured by this rule the "cities" of the Occidental Middle Ages only qualify in part as true cities: even the cities of the eighteenth century were genuine urban communities only in minor degree. Finally measured by this rule, with possible isolated exceptions, the cities of Asia were not urban communities at all even though they all had markets and were fortresses.

All large seats of trade and commerce in China and most of the small ones were fortified. This was true also for Egyptian, Near East-

ern, and Indian centers of commerce and trade. Not infrequently
the large centers of trade and commerce of those countries were
also separate jurisdictional districts. In China, Egypt, the Near East,
and India the large commercial centers have also been seats of large
political associations—a phenomenon not characteristic of Medieval
Occidental cities, especially those of the North. Thus, many, but not
all of the essential elements of the true urban community were at
hand. However, the possession by the urbanites of a special sub-
stantive or trial law or of courts autonomously nominated by them
were unknown to Asiatic cities. Only to the extent that guilds or castes
(in India) were located in cities did they develop courts and a
special law. Urban location of these associations was legally incidental.
Autonomous administration was unknown or only vestigial.

If anything, even more important than the relative absence of
autonomous administration, the appearance in the city of an association of urbanites in contradiction to the countryman was also found
only in rudiments. The Chinese urban dweller legally belonged to his
family and native village in which the temple of his ancestors stood
and to which he conscientiously maintained affiliation. This is similar
to the Russian village-comrade, earning his livelihood in the city but
legally remaining a peasant. The Indian urban dweller remained a
member of the caste. As a rule urban dwellers were also members of
local professional associations, such as crafts and guilds of specific
urban location. Finally they belonged to administrative districts such
as the city wards and street districts into which the city was divided
by the magisterial police.

Within the administrative units of the city, wards and street
districts, urban dwellers had definite duties and even, at times, rights
as well. In the attempt to secure peace, city or street districts could
be made liturgically responsible collectively for the security of persons
or other police purposes. It was possible thus for them to be formed
into communities with elected official or hereditary elders. This occured
in Japan where one or more civil-administrative body (Machi-Bugyo)
was established as superior to self-administered street communities.
However, a city law similar to that of Antiquity or the Middle Ages
was absent. The city as corporate *per se* was unknown. Of course,
eventually the city as a whole formed a separate administrative district as in the Merovingian and Carolingian Empires, but as was still
the case in the Medieval and Ancient Occident, the autonomy and

participation of the inhabitants in local administration were out of the question. As a matter of fact, local individual participation in self-administration was often more strongly developed in the country than in the relatively large commercially organized city. In the village, for example, in China, in many affairs the confederation of elders was practically all-powerful and the Pao-Chia[10] was dependent on them, even though this was not legally expressed. Also in India the village community had nearly complete autonomy in most significant circumstances. In Russia the mir enjoyed nearly complete autonomy until bureaucratization under Alexander III. In the whole of the Near Eastern world the "elders" (in Israel, *sekenim*)[11] originally of family and later chiefs of noble clans were representatives and administrators of localities and the local court. This could not occur in the Asiatic city because it was usually the seat of a high official or prince and thus under the direct supervision of their bodyguards. However, the city was a princely fortress and administered by royal officials (in Israel, *sarim*)[12] who retained judicial power.

In Israel the dualism of officials and elders can be traced in the royal period. Royal officials everywhere triumphed in bureaucratic kingdoms. Such royal bureaucrats were not all-powerful but subject to public opinion often to an astonishing degree. As a rule the Chinese official was quite powerless against local associations when they united in a particular case. At every serious united opposition of the clans and local associations the Chinese official lost his position. Obstruction, boycott, closing of shops, and strikes of artisans and merchants in response to oppression were a daily occurrence, setting limits on power of officials. However, such limits on official power were of a completely indeterminate kind.

In China and India the guilds and other professional associations had competencies with which the officials had to reckon. The chairman of the local associations often exercised extensive coercive powers even against third parties. However all their powers involved only special competencies of particular association in particular questions of concrete group interest. Moreover, there was ordinarily no joint association representing a community of city burghers *per se*, even

[10]Even until recent times every ten families constituted a "pao" formally under a headman. A hundred families constituted a "Chia" under a "Pao Chia" also called "Ti Pao". We read Pao-Chia for Taotai.

[11]Weber, *Ancient Judaism*, p. 16.

[12]*Ibid*, p. 18.

the concept of such a possibility is completely lacking. Citizenship as a specific status quality of the urbanite is missing. In China, Japan, and India neither urban community nor citizenry can be found and only traces of them appear in the Near East.

In Japan the organization of estates was purely feudal. The *samurai* (mounted) and *kasi* (unmounted) ministerial officials confronted the peasant (*no*) and the merchants and tradesmen who were partly united in professional associations. However, here too, the concepts of a "citizenry" and an "urban community" are absent. This was also true in China during the feudal period. After the feudal period in China a bureaucratic administration of literati qualified for office in terms of examinations leading to academic degrees confronted the illiterate strata among whom appeared economically privileged guilds of merchants and professional associations. But in this period in China, too, the ideas of an "urban citizenry" and "urban community" are missing. This was true even though in China as well as in Japan the professional associations were self-administered. Moreover while the villages were self-administered the cities were not. In China the city was a fortress and official seat of imperial authorities in a sense completely unknown in Japan.

The cities of India were royal seats or official centers of royal administration as well as fortresses and market places. Guilds of merchants and castes largely coinciding with professional associations were present, enjoying considerable autonomy especially with respect to their own legal competence and justice. Nevertheless, the hereditary caste system of Indian society with its ritualistic segregation of the professions, excluded the emergence of a citizenry and urban community. And though there were numerous castes and subcastes of traders and artisans they cannot be taken together and equated with the Occidental burgher strata. Nor was it possible for the commercial and artisan castes of India to unite in a form corresponding to the medieval urban corporations, for caste estrangement hindered all inter-caste fraternization.

To be sure in India during the period of the great salvation-religions, guilds appeared with hereditary elders (*schreschths*) uniting in many cities into an association. As residues from this period there are, at present, some cities (Allahabad) with a mutual urban *schreschth* (elder) corresponding to the occidental mayor. Moreover, in the period before the great bureaucratic kingdoms there were

some politically autonomous cities in India ruled by a patriciate recruited from families supplying elephants to the army. Later this
phenomenon almost completely disappeared. The triumph of ritualistic
caste estrangement shattered the guild associations and royal bureaucracies in alliance with the Brahmans swept away, except for
vestiges, such trends toward a citizenry and urban community in
Northwestern India.

In Near Eastern Egyptian antiquity the cities were fortresses
and official administrative centers with royal market privileges. However, in the period of the dominion of the great kingdom they lacked
autonomy, community organizations, and a privileged citizen estate.
In Egypt during the Middle Empire office feudalism existed; in the
New Empire a bureaucratic administration of clerks appeared. "Civic
privileges" were bestowed on feudal or prebendal office holders in localities comparable to the privileges of bishops in old Germany.
However, civic rights were not bestowed on an autonomous citizenry
and even the beginnings of a "city patriciate" have not been found.

In contrast to the complete absence of a citizenry in ancient
Egypt were the phenomena in Mesopotamia, Syria, and especially
Phoenicia, where at an early period typical city-kingdoms emerged
at intersection points of sea and caravan traffic. Such civic kingdoms
were of intensified sacred-secular character. They were also typified
by the rising power of patrician families in the "city-house" (*bitu*
in the Tel-el-Amarna tablets) in the period of charioteering.[13] In the
Canaanite city an association of chariot-fighting knights possessing urban residences appeared. This knighthood kept the peasant farmers
in a state of debt servitude and clientship as in the case of the
early Hellenic polis. It was obviously similar in Mesopotamia where
the "patrician" as a landowning full burgher economically qualified
for war service is separated from the peasant. Immunities and privileges of this stratum were chartered by the king. However, with the
mounting military power of the government this also disappeared.
Politically autonomous cities and a burgher stratum of Occidental
type are as little to be found in Mesopotamia as is a special urban
law alongside royal law.

Only in Phoenicia did the landed patriciate engaging in commerce
with its capital manage to maintain its dominion over the city state.
However, the coins of the time *am Sor* and *am Karthadast* in Tyre

[13]Weber, *Ancient Judaism*, p. 14 f.

and Carthage hardly indicate the presence of a ruling "demos" and if such was ever the case it was only at a later time. Thus a true citizenry only partly developed. In Israel, Judah became a city-state but the elders (*sekenim*) who in the early period governed the administration as chieftains of patrician sibs were thrust into the background by the royal administration. The *gibborim* (knights) became royal attendants and soldiers. In contrast to the countryside, the royal *sarim* (officials) ruled in the large cities. Only after the exile did the community (*kahal*) or fellowship (*cheber*) appear as an institution on a confessional basis under the rule of priestly families.[14]

Nevertheless, all these phenomena indicate that here on the coasts of the Mediterranean Sea and on the Euphrates appeared the first real analogies of a civic development equivalent to that of Rome at the time of the reception of the Gens Claudia. The city is ruled by a patriciate resident in the city with powers resting on monetary wealth primarily won in commerce and secondarily invested in landed property, debt slaves, and war slaves.[15] The military power of the urban patriciate was a product of its training for knightly warfare, a training often spent in feuds against one another. The patricians were inter-locally diffused and united with the king or *schofeten* or *sekenim* as *primus inter pares*. Such a patriciate like the Roman nobility with consuls was threatened by the tyranny of the charismatic war king relying upon recruited bodyguards (Abimelech, Jepthah, David). Prior to the Hellenic period this stage of urban development was nowhere permanently surpassed.

Obviously such a patriciate also dominated in cities of the Arabian coast during the period of Mohammed, remaining in existence in those Islamic cities where the autonomy of the city and its patriciate was not completely destroyed as in the larger state. Under Islamic rule ancient oriental conditions were often preserved, whereupon a labile ratio of autonomy between urban families and princely officials appears. Resident city families enjoyed a position of power resting on wealth from urban economic opportunities and invested in land and slaves. Without formal legal recognition the princes and their

[14]*Ibid.*, p. 385 f.
[15]In all these areas in the early period enslavement for debt appears and debt slaves are found alongside slaves captured in battles—battles at times being actually slave raids.

officials had to take account of the power of the patriciate in the same manner that the Chinese Pao Chia had to take account of the obstruction of clan elders of the villages and merchant and professional associations. However, the city was not thereby necessarily formed into an independent association. Often the contrary occurred, as may be exemplified.

Arabian cities like Mecca were settlements of clans such as remained typical in the Middle Ages to the threshold of the present. Snouck Hurgronje[16] has proven that the city of Mecca was surrounded by the *bilad* representing lordly property of an individual *dewis* of sibs descending from Ali—such were the *hasnaidic* and other noble sibs. The *bilad* was occupied by peasants, clients, and protected Bedouins. *Bilads* were often intermixed. A *dewis* was any sib one ancestor of which was once a sherif. Since 1200 the sherif himself belonged without exception to the Alidic family *Katadahs*. Legally the sherif should have been installed by the governor of the caliph (who was often unfree and once, under Harun al Rashid, was a Berber slave). However in reality the sherif was chosen from the qualified family by election of the chieftains of the *dewis* who were resident in Mecca. For this reason as well as the fact that residence in Mecca offered opportunities to exploit pilgrims, the heads of the class (*emirs*) lived in the city. Between them at times alliances obtained with agreements for preserving the peace and establishing quotas for dividing chances for gain. Such alliances were terminable at any time, dissolution signaling the start of a feud inside and outside the city. Slave troops were employed in such feuds and the defeated group was exiled from the city. However, despite defeat the community of interest between hostile families as against outsiders led to observance of the courtesy of sparing the goods and lives of members of the families and clientele of the exiles. Such courtesies were observed under the threat of general mutiny of one's own partisans.

In modern times the city of Mecca recognizes the following official authorities: (1) On paper the collegiate administrative council (*Medschlis*) installed by the Turks appears as the authority, (2) In fact the Turkish governor is the effective authority, occupying the position of protector (in former times usually the ruler of Egypt), (3) authority is shared by the four *cadis* of the orthodox rights who are

[16]Snouck Hurgronje, *Mekka in the Latter Part of the 19th Century* (London: Luzac, 1931).

always noble men of Mecca, the most eminent (*schafitic*) for centuries being nominated from one family by the sherif or proposed by the protector, (4) The sherif simultaneously is head of the urban corporation of nobles, (5) The guilds, especially the cicerones, followed by the butchers, corn merchants and others, (6) The city ward with its elders is partly autonomous. These authorities competed with each other in many ways without fixed competences. A party to a legal suit selected the authority appearing most favorable or whose power against the accused seemed to be the most strong. The governor was unable to prevent an appeal to the *cadi* who competed with him in all matters of ecclesiastical law. The sherif was held to be the proper authority of the natives especially in all matters concerning the Bedouins and caravans of pilgrims. The governor was dependent on the willingness of the sherif to cooperate. Finally, here as in other Arabic areas, particularly in the cities, the cooperation of the nobility was decisive for the effectiveness of authority.

In the ninth century a development reminiscent of Occidental circumstances occurred when with the flight of the Tuluniden and Deschafariden, in Mecca the position of the richest guilds, that of the butchers and corn merchants, held the balance of power. However, it was still unconditionally true at the time of Mohammed that only the noble *koreischitic* families were militarily and politically important, thus, a government by guilds never arose. Slave troops sustained by profit-shares of resident urban families continually sustained their power. In a similar manner, in medieval Italian cities power continually tended to glide into the hands of the knightly families as wielders of military power.

The idea of an association which could unite the city into a corporate unit was missing in Mecca. This furnished its characteristic difference from the ancient polis and the early medieval Italian commune. However, when all is said and done, this Arabic condition—of course omitting specific Islamic traits or replacing them by Christian counterparts—may be taken to typify the period before the emergence of the urban community association. It is also typical for Occidental commercial sea cities.

So far as sound information extends, in Asiatic and Oriental settlements of an urban economic character, normally only extended families and professional associations were vehicles of communal actions. Communal action was not the product of an urban burgher stratum as such. Transitions, of course, are fluid but precisely the largest settlement at times embracing hundreds of thousands even millions of inhabitants displays this very phenomenon. In medieval Byzantine Constantinople the representatives of urban districts were leaders of party divisions who financed circus races (as is still the case for the horse race of Siena). The Nika revolt under Justinian was a product of such local cleavages of the city. Also in Constantinople, from the time of the Islamic Middle Ages until the sixteenth century, only merchants, corporations, and guilds appear as representatives of the interests of the burghers beside purely military associations such as the *Janitscharen* and *Sipahis* and the religious organizations of the *Ulemas* and *Dervishes*. However, in sixteenth century Constantinople there is still no city representation. Similarly in late Byzantine Alexandria, beside the power of the patricians, relying upon the support of very sturdy monks, and the competitive power of the governor relying on a small garrison there was no militia for particular city districts. Within the districts of the city only the circus parties of rival "greens" and "blues" represented the leading organizations.

THE METROPOLIS AND MENTAL LIFE
Georg Simmel

The deepest problems of modern life derive from the claim of the individual to preserve the autonomy and individuality of his existance in the face of overwhelming social forces, of historical heritage, of external culture, and of the technique of life. The fight with nature which primitive man has to wage for his *bodily* existence attains in this modern form its latest transformation. The eighteenth century called upon man to free himself of all the historical bonds in the state and in religion, in morals and in economics. Man's nature, originally good and common to all, should develop unhampered. In addition to more liberty, the nineteenth century demanded the functional specialization of man and his work; this specialization makes one individual incomparable to another, and each of them indispensable to the highest possible extent. However, this specialization makes each man the more directly dependent upon the supplementary activities of all others. Nietzsche sees the full development of the individual conditioned by the most ruthless struggle of individuals; socialism believes in the suppression of all competition for the same reason. Be that as it may, in all these positions the same basic motive is at work: the person resists to being leveled down and worn out by a social technological mechanism. An inquiry into the inner meaning of specifically modern life and its products, into the soul of the cultural body, so to speak, must seek to solve the equation which structures like the metropolis set up between the individual and the super-individual contents of life. Such an inquiry must answer the question of how the personality accommodates itself in the adjustments to external forces. This will be my task today.

Translated by H. H. Gerth with the assistance of C. Wright Mills. Reprinted with permission of The Macmillan Company from *The Sociology of Georg Simmel* edited by Kurt Wolff. Copyright 1950 by The Free Press.

The psychological basis of the metropolitan type of individuality consists in the *intensification of nervous stimulation* which results from the swift and uninterrupted change of outer and inner stimuli. Man is a differentiating creature. His mind is stimulated by the difference between a momentary impression and the one which preceded it. Lasting impressions, impressions which differ only slightly from one another, impressions which take a regular and habitual course and show regular and habitual contrasts—all these use up, so to speak, less consciousness than does the rapid crowding of changing images, the sharp discontinuity in the grasp of a single glance, and the unexpectedness of onrushing impressions. These are the psychologial conditions which the metropolis creates. With each crossing of the street, with the tempo and multiplicity of economic, occupational, and social life, the city sets up a deep contrast with small town and rural life with reference to the sensory foundations of psychic life. The metropolis exacts from man as a discriminating creature a different amount of consciousness than does rural life. Here the rhythm of life and sensory mental imagery flows more slowly, more habitually, and more evenly. Precisely in this connection the sophisticated character of metropolitan psychic life becomes understandable—as over against small town life which rests more upon deeply felt and emotional relationships. These latter are rooted in the more unconscious layers of the psyche and grow most readily in the steady rhythm of uninterrupted habituations. The intellect, however, has its locus in the transparent, conscious, higher layers of the psyche; it is the most adaptable of our inner forces. In order to accommodate to change and to the contrast of phenomena, the intellect does not require any shocks and inner upheavals; it is only through such upheavals that the more conservative mind could accommodate to the metropolitan rhythm of events. Thus the metropolitan type of man—which, of course, exists in a thousand individual variants—develops an organ protecting him against the threatening currents and discrepancies of his external environment which would uproot him. He reacts with his head instead of his heart. In this an increased awareness assumes the psychic prerogative. Metropolitan life, thus, underlies a heightened awareness and a predominance of intelligence in metropolitan man. The reaction to metropolitan phenomena is shifted to that organ which is least sensitive and quite remote from the depth of the personality. Intellectuality is thus seen to preserve subjective life against the overwhelming power of metropolitan life, and intellectuality branches out in many directions and is integrated with numerous discrete phenomena.

The metropolis has always been the seat of the money economy. Here the multiplicity and concentration of economic exchange gives an importance to the means of exchange which the scantiness of rural commerce would not have allowed. Money economy and the dominance of the intellect are intrinsically connected. They share a matter-of-fact attitude in dealing with men and with things; and, in this attitude, a formal justice is often coupled with an inconsiderate hardness. The intellectually sophisticated person is indifferent to all genuine individuality, because relationships and reactions result from it which cannot be exhausted with logical operations. In the same manner, the individuality of phenomena is not commensurate with the pecuniary principle. Money is concerned only with what is common to all: it asks for the exchange value, it reduces all quality and individuality to the question: How much? All intimate emotional relations between persons are founded in their individuality, whereas in rational relations man is reckoned with like a number, like an element which is in itself indifferent. Only the objective measurable achievement is of interest. Thus metropolitan man reckons with his merchants and customers, his domestic servants and often even with persons with whom he is obliged to have social intercourse. These features of intellectuality contrast with the nature of the small circle in which the inevitable knowledge of individuality as inevitably produces a warmer tone of behavior, a behavior which is beyond a mere objective balancing of service and return. In the sphere of the economic psychology of the small group it is of importance that under primitive conditions production serves the customer who orders the good, so that the producer and the consumer are acquainted. The modern metropolis, however, is supplied almost entirely by production for the market, that is, for entirely unknown purchasers who never personally enter the producer's actual field of vision. Through this anonymity the interests of each party acquire an unmerciful matter-of-factness; and the intellectually calculating economic egoisms of both parties need not fear any deflection because of the imponderables of personal relationships. The money economy dominates the metropolis; it has displaced the last survivals of domestic production and the direct barter of goods; it minimizes, from day to day, the amount of work ordered by customers. The matter-of-fact attitude is obviously so intimately interrelated with the money economy, which is dominant in the metropolis, that nobody can say whether the intellectualistic mentality first promoted the money economy or whether the latter determined the former. The metropolitan way of life is certainly the most fertile soil for this reciprocity, a point which I shall document merely by citing the dictum of the most eminent English constitutional historian: through the whole course of English history, London has never acted as England's heart but often as England's intellect and always as her moneybag.

In certain seemingly insignificant traits, which lie upon the surface of life, the same psychic currents characteristically unite. Modern mind has become more and more calculating. The calculative exactness of practical life which the money economy has brought about corresponds to the ideal of natural science: to transform the world into an arithmetic problem, to fix every part of the world by mathematical formulas. Only money economy has filled the days of so many people with weighing, calculating, with numerical determinations, with a reduction of qualitative values to quantitative ones. Through the calculative nature of money a new precision, a certainty in the definition of identities and differences, an unambiguousness in agreements and arrangements has been brought about in the relations of life-elements—just as externally this precision has been effected by the universal diffusion of pocket watches. However, the conditions of metropolitan life are at once cause and effect of this trait. The relationships and affairs of the typical metropolitan usually are so varied and complex that without the strictest punctuality in promises and services the whole structure would break down into an inextricable chaos. Above all, this necessity is brought about by the aggregation of so many people with such differentiated interests, who must integrate their relations and activities into a highly complex organism. If all clocks and watches in Berlin would suddenly go wrong in different ways, even if only by one hour, all economic life and communication of the city would be disrupted for a long time. In addition an apparently mere external factor: long distances, would make all waiting and broken appointments result in an ill-afforded waste of time. Thus, the technique of metropolitan life is unimaginable without the most punctual integration of all activities and mutual relations into a stable and impersonal time schedule. Here again the general conclusions of this entire task of reflection become obvious, namely, that from each point on the surface alone—one may drop a sounding into the depth of the psyche so that all the most banal external-

ities of life finally are connected with the ultimate decisions concerning
the meaning and style of life. Punctuality, calculability, exactness are
forced upon life by the complexity and extension of metropolitan existence and are not only most intimately connected with its money economy and intellectualistic character. These traits must also color the contents of life and favor the exclusion of those irrational, instinctive,
sovereign traits and impulses which aim at determining the mode of
life from within, instead of receiving the general and precisely schemati-
zed form of life from without. Even though soverign types of personality, characterized by irrational impulses, are by no means impossible
in the city, they are, nevertheless, opposed to typical city life. The passionate hatred of men like Ruskin and Nietzsche for the metropolis is
understandable in these terms. Their natures discovered the value of
life alone in the unschematized existence which cannot be defined with
precision for all alike. From the same source of this hatred of the metropolis surged their hatred of money economy and of the intellectualism of modern existence.

The same factors which have thus coalesced into the exactness
and minute precision of the form of life have coalesced into a structure
of the highest impersonality; on the other hand, they have promoted a
highly personal subjectivity. There is perhaps no psychic phenomeon
which has been so unconditionally reserved to the metropolis as has
the blasé attitude. The blasé attitude results first from the rapidly changing and closely compressed contrasting stimulations of the nerves.
From this, the enhancement of the metropolitan intellectuality, also,
seems originally to stem. Therefore, stupid people who are not intellectually alive in the first place usually are not exactly blasé. A life in
boundless pursuit of pleasure makes one blasé because it agitates the
nerves to their strongest reactivity for such a long time that they finally
cease to react at all. In the same way, through the rapidity and contra-
dictoriness of their changes, more harmless impressions force such violent responses, tearing the nerves so brutally hither and thither that
their last reserves of strength are spent; and if one remains in the same
milieu they have no time to gather new strength. An incapacity thus
emerges to react to new sensations with the appropriate energy. This
constitutes that blasé attitude which, in fact, every metropolitan child
shows when compared with children of quieter and less changeable
milieus.

This physiological source of the metropolitan blasé attitude is joined by another source which flows from the money economy. The essence of the blasé attitude consists in the blunting of discrimination. This does not mean that the objects are not perceived, as is the case with the half-wit, but rather that the meaning and differing values of things, and thereby the things themselves, are experienced as insubstantial. They appear to the blasé person in an evenly flat and gray tone; no one object deserves preference over any other. This mood is the faithful subjective reflection of the completely internalized money economy. By being the equivalent to all the manifold things in one and the same way, money becomes the most frightful leveler. For money expresses all qualitative differences of things in terms of "how much?" Money, with all its colorlessnesss and indifference, becomes the common denominator of all values; irreparably it hollows out the core of things, their individuality, their specific value, and their incomparability. All things float with equal specific gravity in the constantly moving stream of money. All things lie on the same level and differ from one another only in the size of the area which they cover. In the individual case this coloration, or rather discoloration, of things through their money equivalence may be unnoticeably minute. However, through the relations of the rich to the objects to be had for money, perhaps even through the total character which the mentality of the contemporary public everywhere imparts to these objects, the exclusively pecuniary evaluation of objects has become quite considerable. The large cities, the main seats of the money exchange, bring the purchasability of things to the fore much more impressively than do smaller localities. That is why cities are also the genuine locale of the blasé attitude. In the blasé attitude the concentration of men and things stimulate the nervous system of the individual to its highest achievement so that it attains its peak. Through the mere quantitative intensification of the same conditioning factors this achievement is transformed into its opposite and appears in the peculiar adjustment of the blasé attitude. In this phenomenon the nerves find in the refusal to react to their stimultion the last possibility of accommodating to the contents and forms of metropolitan life. The self-preservation of certain personalities is brought at the price of devaluating the whole objective world, a devaluation which in the end unavoidably drags one's own personality down into a feeling of the same worthlessness.

Whereas the subject of this form of existence has to come to terms with it entirely for himself, his self-preservation in the face of the large city demands from him a no less negative behavior of a social nature.

This mental attitude of metropolitans toward one another we may designate, from a formal point of view, as reserve. If so many inner reactions were responses to the continuous external contacts with innumerable people as are those in a small town, where one knows almost everybody one meets and where one has a positive relation to almost everyone, one would be completely atomized internally and come to an unimaginable psychic state. Partly this psychological fact, partly the right to distrust which men have in the face of the touch-and-go elements of metropolitan life, necessitates our reserve. As a result of this reserve we frequently do not even know by sight those who have been our neighbors for years. And it is this reserve which in the eyes of the small-town people makes us appear to be cold and heartless. Indeed, if I do not deceive myself, the inner aspect of this outer reserve is not only indifference but, more often than we are aware, it is a slight aversion, a mutual strangeness and repulsion, which will break into hatred and fight at the moment of a closer contact, however caused. The whole inner organization of such an extensive communicative life rests upon an extremely varied hierarchy of sympathies, indifferences, and aversions of the briefest as well as of the most permanent nature. The sphere of indifference in this hierarchy is not as large as might appear on the surface. Our psychic activity still responds to almost every impression of somebody else with a somewhat distinct feeling. The unconscious, fluid, and changing character of this impression seems to result in a state of indifference. Actually this indifference would be just as unnatural as the diffusion of indiscriminate mutual suggestion would be unbearable. From both these typical dangers of the metropolis, indifference and indiscriminate suggestibility, antipathy protects us. A latent antipathy and the preparatory stage of practical antagonism effect the distances and aversions without which this mode of life could not at all be led. The extent and the mixture of this style of life, the rhythm of its emergence and disappearance, the forms in which it is satisfied—all these, with the unifying motives in the narrower sense, form the inseparable whole of the metropolitan style of life. What appears in the metropolitan style of life directly as dissociation is in reality only one of its elemental forms of socialization.

This reserve with its overtone of hidden aversion appears in turn as the form or the cloak of a more general mental phenomenon of the metropolis: it grants to the individual a kind and an amount of personal freedom which has no analogy whatsoever under other conditions. The metropolis goes back to one of the large developmental tendencies of social life as such, to one of the few tendencies for which an approximately universal formula can be discovered. The earliest phase of social formations found in historical as well as in contemporary social structures is this: a relatively small circle firmly closed against neighboring, strange, or in some way antagonistic circles. However, this circle is closely coherent and allows its individual members only a narrow field for the development of unique qualities and free, self-responsible movements. Political and kinship groups, parties and religious associations begin in this way. The self-preservation of very young associations requires the extablishment of strict boundaries and a centripetal unity. Therefore they cannot allow the individual freedom and unique inner and outer development. From this stage social development proceeds at once in two different, yet corresponding, directions. To the extent to which the group grows—numerically, spatially, in significance and in content of life—to the same degree the group's direct, inner unity loosens, and the rigidity of the original demarcation against others is softened through mutual relations and connections. At the same time, the individual gains freedom of movement, far beyond the first jealous delimitation. The individual also gains a specific individuality to which the division of labor in the enlarged group gives both occasion and necessity. The state and Christianity, guilds and political parties, and innumerable other groups have developed according to this formula, however much, of course, the special conditions and forces of the respective groups have modified the general scheme. This scheme seems to me distinctly recognizable also in the evolution of individuality within urban life. The small-town life in Antiquity and in the Middle Ages set barriers against movement and relations of the individual toward the outside, and it set up barriers against individual independence and differentiation within the individual self. These barriers were such that under them modern man could not have breathed. Even today a metropolitan man who is placed in a small town feels a restriction similar, at least, in kind. The smaller the circle which forms our milieu is, and the more restricted those relations to others are which dissolve the boundaries of the individual, the more anxiously the circle guards the achievements, the conduct of life, and the outlook of the individual, and the more readily a quantitative and qualitative specialization would break up the framework of the whole little circle.

The ancient *polis* in this respect seems to have had the very character of a small town. The constant threat to its existence at the hands of enemies from near and afar effected strict coherence in political and military respects, a supervision of the citizen by the citizen, a jealousy of the whole against the individual whose particular life was suppressed to such a degree that he could compensate only by acting as a despot in his own household. The tremendous agitation and excitement, the unique colorfulness of Athenian life, can perhaps by understood in terms of the fact that a people of incomparably individualized personalities struggled against the constant inner and outer pressure of a de-individualizing small town. This produced a tense atmosphere in which the weaker individuals were suppressed and those of stronger natures were incited to prove themselves in the most passionate manner. This is precisely why it was that there blossomed in Athens what must be called, without defining it exactly, "the general human character" in the intellectual development of our species. For we maintain factual as well as historical validity for the following connection: the most extensive and the most general contents and forms of life are most intimately connected with the most individual ones. They have a preparatory stage in common, that is, they find their enemy in narrow formations and groupings the maintenance of which places both of them into a state of defense against expanse and generality lying without and the freely moving individuality within. Just as in the feudal age, the "free" man was the one who stood under the law of the land, that is, under the law of the largest social orbit, and the unfree man was the one who derived his right merely from the narrow circle of a feudal association and was excluded from the larger social orbit—so today metropolitan man is "free" in a spiritualized and refined sense, in contrast to the pettiness and prejudices which hem in the small-town man. For the reciprocal reserve and indifference and the intellectual life conditions of large circles are never felt more strongly by the individual in their impact upon his independence than in the thickest crowd of the big city. This is because the bodily proximity and narrowness of space makes the mental distance only the more visible. It is obviously only the obverse of this freedom if, under certain circumstances, one nowhere feels as lonely and lost as in the metropolitan crowd. For here as elsewhere it is by no means necessary that the freedom of man be reflected in his emotional life as comfort.

It is not only the immediate size of the area and the number of persons which, because of the universal historical correlation between the enlargement of the circle and the personal inner and outer freedom, has made the metropolis the locale of freedom. It is rather in transcending this visible expanse that any given city becomes the seat of cosmopolitanism. The horizon of the city expands in a manner comparable to the way in which wealth develops; a certain amount of property increases in a quasi-automatical way in ever more rapid progression. As soon as a certain limit has been passed, the economic, personal, and intellectual relations of the citizenry, the sphere of intellectual predominance of the city over its hinterland, grow as in geometrical progression. Every gain in dynamic extension becomes a step, not for an equal, but for a new and larger extension. From every thread spinning out of the city, ever new threads grow as if by themselves, just as within the city the unearned increment of ground rent, through the mere increase in communication, brings the owner automatically increasing profits. At this point, the quantitative aspect of life is transformed directly into qualitative traits of character. The sphere of life of the small town is, in the main, self-contained and autarchic. For it is the decisive nature of the metropolis that its inner life overflows by waves into a far-flung national or international area. Weimar is not an example to the contrary, since its significance was hinged upon individual personalities and died with them; whereas the metropolis is indeed characterized by its essential independence even from the most eminent individual personalities. This is the counterpart to the independence, and it is the price the individual pays for the independence, which he enjoys in the metropolis. The most significant characteristic of the metropolis is this functional extension beyond its physical boundaries. And this efficacy reacts in turn and gives weight, importance, and responsibility to metropolitan life. Man does not end with the limits of his body or the area comprising his immediate activity. Rather is the range of the person constituted by the sum of effects emanating from him temporally and spatially. In the same way, a city consists of its total effects which extend beyond its immediate confines. Only this range is the city's actual extent in which its existence is expressed. This fact makes it obvious that individual freedom, the logical and historical complement of such extension, is not to be understood only in the negative sense of mere freedom of mobility and elimination of prejudices and petty philistinism. The essential point is that the particularity and incomparability, which ultimately every human being possesses, be somehow expressed in the working-out of a way of life. That we follow the laws of our own nature —and this after all is freedom—becomes obvious and convincing to ourselves and to others only if the expressions of this nature differ from the expressions of others. Only our unmistakability proves that our way of life has not been superimposed by others.

Cities are, first of all, seats of the highest economic division of labor. They produce thereby such extreme phenomena as in Paris the remunerative occupation of the *quatorzième*. These are persons who identify themselves by signs on their residences and who are ready at the dinner hour in correct attire, so that they can be quickly called upon if a dinner party should consist of thirteen persons. In the measure of its expansion, the city offers more and more the decisive conditions of the division of labor. It offers a circle which through its size can absorb a highly diverse variety of services. At the same time, the concentration of individuals and their struggle for customers compel the individual to specialize in a function from which he cannot be readily replaced by another. It is decisive that city life has transformed the struggle with nature for livelihood into an inter-human struggle for gain, which here is not granted by nature but by other men. For specialization does not flow only from the competition for gain but also from the underlying fact that the seller must always seek to call forth new and differentiated needs of the lured customer. In order to find a source of income which is not yet exhausted, and to find a function which cannot readily be displaced, it is necessary to specialize in one's services. This process promotes differentiation, refinement, and the enrichment of the public's needs, which obviously must lead to growing personal differences within this public.

All this forms the transition to the individualization of mental and psychic traits which the city occasions in proportion to its size. There is a whole series of obvious causes underlying this process. First, one must meet the difficulty of asserting his own personality within the dimensions of metropolitan life. Where the quantitative increase in importance and the expense of energy reach their limits, one seizes upon qualitative differentiation in order somehow to attract the attention of the social circle by playing upon its sensitivity for differences. Finally, man is tempted to adopt the most tendentious peculiarities, that is, the specifically metropolitan extravagances of mannerism, caprice, and preciousness. Now, the meaning of these extravagances does not at all lie in the contents of such behavior, but rather in its form of "being different," of standing out in a striking manner and thereby attracting attention. For many character types, ultimately the only means of saving for themselves some modicum of self-esteem and the sense of filling a position is indirect, through the awareness of others. In the same sense a seemingly insignificant factor is operating, the cumulative effects of which are, however, still noticeable. I refer to the brevity and scarcity of the inter-human contacts granted to the metropolitan man, as compared with social intercourse in the small town. The temptation to appear "to the point," to appear concentrated and strikingly characteristic, lies much closer to the individual in brief metropolitan contacts than in an atmosphere in which frequent and prolonged association assures the personality of an unambiguous image of himself in the eyes of the other.

The most profound reason, however, why the metropolis conduces to the urge for the most individual personal existence—no matter whether justified and successful—appears to me to be the following: the development of modern culture is characterized by the preponderance of what one may call the "objective spirit" over the "subjective spirit." This is to say, in language as well as in law, in the technique of production as well as in art, in science as well as in the objects of the domestic environment, there is embodied a sum of spirit. The individual in his intellectual development follows the growth of this spirit very imperfectly and at an ever increasing distance. If, for instance, we view the immense culture which for the last hundred years has been embodied in things and in knowledge, in institutions and in comforts, and if we compare all this with the cultural progress of the individual during the same period—at least in high status groups—a frightful disproportion in growth between the two becomes evident. Indeed, at some points we notice a retrogression in the culture of the individual with reference to spirituality, delicacy, and idealism. This discrepancy results essentially rom the growing division of labor. For the division of labor demands from the individual an ever more one-sided accomplishment, and the greatest advance in a one-sided pursuit only to a frequently means dearth to the personality of the individual. In any case, he can cope less and less with the overgrowth of objective culture. The individual is reduced to a negligible quantity, perhaps less in his consciousness in his practice and in the totality of his obscure emotional states that are derived from this practice. The individual has become a mere cog in an enormous organization of things and powers which tear from his hands all progress, spirituality, and value in order to transform them from their subjective from into the form of a purely objective life. It needs merely to be pointed out that the metropolis is the genuine arena of this culture which outgrows all personal life. Here in buildings and educational institutions, in the wonders and comforts of space-conquering technology, in the formations of community life, and in the visible institutions of the state, is offered such an overwhelming fullness of crystallized and impersonalized spirit that the personality, so to speak, cannot maintain itself under its impact. On the one hand, life is made infinitely easy for the personality in that stimulations, interests, uses of time and consciousness are offered to it from all sides. They carry the person as if in a stream, and one needs hardly to swim for oneself. On the other hand, however, life is composed more and more of these impersonal contents and offerings which tend to displace the genuine personal colorations and incomparabilities. This results in the individual's summoning the utmost in uniqueness and particularization, in order to preserve his most personal core. He has to exaggerate this personal element in order to remain audible even to himself. The atrophy of individual culture through the hypertrophy of objective culture is one reason for the bitter hatred which the preachers of the most extreme individualism, above all Nietzsche, harbor against the metropolis. But it is, indeed, also a reason why these preachers are so passionately loved in the metropolis and why they appear to the metropolitan man as the prophets and saviors of his most unsatisfied yearnings.

If one asks for the historical position of these two forms of individualism which are nourished by the quantitative relation of the metropolis, namely, individual independence and the elaboration of individuality itself, then the metropolis assumes an entirely new rank order in the history of the spirit. The eighteenth century found the individual in oppressive bonds which had become meaningless—bonds of a political, agrarian, guild, and religious character. They were restraints which, so to speak, forced upon man an unnatural form and outmoded, unjust inequalities. In this situation the cry for liberty and equality arose, the belief in the individual's full freedom of movement in all social and intellectual relationships. Freedom would at once permit the noble substance common to all to come to the fore, a substance which nature had deposited in every man and which society and history had only deformed. Besides this eighteenth-century ideal of liberalism, in the nineteenth century, through Goethe and Romanticism, on the one hand, and through the economic division of labor, on the other hand, another ideal arose: individuals liberated from historical bonds now wished to distinguish themselves from one another. The carrier of man's values is no longer the "general human being" in every individual, but rather man's qualitative uniqueness and irresplaceability. The external and internal history of our time takes its course within the struggle and in the changing entanglements of these two ways of defining the individual's role in the whole of society. It is the function of the metropolis to provide the area for this struggle and its reconciliation. For the metropolis presents the peculiar conditions which are revealed to us as the opportunities and the stimuli for the development of both these ways of allocating roles to men. Therewith these conditions gain a unique place, pregnant with inestimable meanings for the development of psychic existence. The metropolis reveals itself as one of those great historical formations in which opposing streams which enclose life unfold, as well as join one another with equal right. However, in this process the currents of life, whether their individual phenomena touch us sympathetically or antipathetically, entirely transcend the sphere for which the judge's attitude is appropriate. Since such forces of life have grown into the roots and into the crown of the whole of the historical life in which we, in our fleeting existence, as a cell, belong only as a part, it is not our task either to accuse or to pardon, but only to understand.*

---

*The content of this lecture by its very nature does not derive from a citable literature. Argument and elaboration of its major cultural-historical ideas are contained in my *Philosophie des Geldes* (The Philosophy of Money; München und Leipzig: Duncker und Humblot, 1900).

THE SOUL OF THE CITY
Oswald Spengler

About the middle of the second millennium before Christ, two worlds lay over against one another on the Aegean Sea. The one, darkly groping, big with hopes, drowsy with the intoxication of deeds and sufferings, ripening quietly towards its future, was the Mycenaean. The other, gay and satisfied, snugly ensconced in the treasures of an ancient Culture, elegant, light, with all its great problems far behind it, was the Minoan of Crete.

We shall never really comprehend this phenomenon, which in these days is becoming the center of research-interest, unless we appreciate the abyss of opposition that separates the two souls. The man of those days must have felt it deeply, but hardly "cognized" it. I see it before me: the humility of the inhabitant of Tiryns and Mycenae before the unattainable *esprit* of life in Cnossus, the contempt of the well-bred of Cnossus for the petty chiefs and their followers, and withal a secret feeling of superiority in the healthy barbarians, like that of the German soldier in the presence of the elderly Roman dignitary.

How are we in a position to know this? There are several such moments in which the men of two Cultures have looked into one another's eyes. We know more than one "Inter-Culture" in which some of the most significant tendencies of the human soul have disclosed themselves.

As it was (we may confidently say) between Cnossus and Mycenae, so it was between the Byzantine court and the German chieftains who, like Otto II, married into it—undisguised wonder on the part of the knights and counts, answered by the contemptuous astonishment of a refined somewhat pale and tired Civilization at that bearish morning vigour of the German lands which Scheffel has described in *Ekkehard.*[1]

In Charlemagne the mixture of a primitive human spirituality, on the threshold of its awakening, with a superposed Late intellectuality, becomes manifest. Certain characteristics of his rulership would lead us to name him the Caliph of Frankistan, but on his other side he is but the chief of a Germanic tribe; and it is the mingling of the two that makes him symbolic, in the same way as the form of the Aachen palace-chapel—no longer mosque, not yet cathedral. The Germanic-Western pre-Culture meanwhile is moving on, but slowly and underground, for that sudden illumination which we most ineptly call the Carolingian Renaissance is a ray from Baghdad. It must not be overlooked that the period of Charles the Great is an episode of the surface, ending, as accidentals do end, without issue. After 900, after a new deep depression, there begins something really new, something having the telling force of a Destiny and the depth that promises duration. But in 800 it was the sun of the Arabian Civilization passing on from the world-cities of the East to the countryside of the West. Even so the sunshine of Hellenism had spread to the distant Indus.[2]

That which stands on the hills of Tiryns and Mycenae is *Pfalz* and *Burg* of root-Germanic type. The palaces of Crete—which are not kings' castles, but huge cult-buildings for a crowd of priests and priestesses—are equipped with megalopolitan—nay, Late-Roman—luxury. At the foot of those hills were crowded the huts of yeomen and vassals, but in Crete (Gournia, Hagia Triada) the excavation of towns and villas has shown that the requirements were those of high civilization, and the building technique that of a long experience, accustomed to catering for the most pampered taste in furniture and wall decoration, and familiar with lighting, water circulation, staircases, and suchlike problems.[3] In the one, the plan of the house is a strict life-symbol; in the other, the expression of a refined utilitarianism. Compare the Kamares vases and the frescoes of smooth stucco with everything that is genuinely Mycenaean—they are, through and through, the product of an industrial art, clever and empty, and not of any grand and deep art of heavy,

[1]Published 1857. **English translation, 1872.**—*Tr.*

[2]Without Alexander, and even before him, for Alexander neither kindled nor spread that light; he did not lead, but followed its path to the East.

[3]See G. Glotz's recent work *La Civilisation égéene,* 1923 (English translation, 1927).—*Tr.*

clumsy, but forceful symbolism like that which in Mycenae was ripening towards the geometrical style. It is, in a word, not a style but a taste.[4] In Mycenae was housed a primitive race which chose its sites according to a soil value and facilities for defence, whereas the Minoan population settled in business foci, as may be observed very clearly in the case of Philakopi on Melos which was established for the export trade in obsidian. A Mycenaean palace is a promise, a Minoan something that is ending. But it was just the same in the West about 800—the Frankish and Visigothic farms and manor-houses stretched from the Loire to the Ebro, while south of them lay the Moorish castles, villas, and mosques of Cordova and Granada.

It is surely no accident that the peak of this Minoan luxury coincides with the period of the great Egyptian revolution, and particularly the Hyksos time (1780—1580 B.C.).[5] The Egyptian craftsmen may well have fled in those days to the peaceful islands and even as far as the strongholds of the mainland, as in a later instance the Byzantine scholars fled to Italy. For it is axiomatic that the Minoan Culture is a part of the Egyptian, and we should be able to realize this more fully were it not that the part of Egypt's art-store which would have been decisive in this connection—*viz.*; what was produced in the Western Delta— has perished from damp. We only know the Egyptian Culture in so far as it flourished on the dry soil of the south, but it has long been admitted as certain that the center of gravity of its evolution lay elsewhere.

It is not possible to draw a strict frontier between the late Minoan and the young Mycenaean art. Throughout the Egyptian-Cretan world we can observe a highly modern fad for these alien and primitive things, and vice versa the war-band kings of the mainland strongholds stole or bought Cretan *objets d'art* wherever and however they could come by them, admiring and imitating—even as the style of the Migrations, once supposed to be, and prized as, proto-German, borrows the whole of its form-language from the East.[6] They had their palaces and tombs built and decorated by captive or invited craftsmen. The "Treasure-house" (Tomb) of Atreus in Mycenae, therefore, is exactly analogous to the tomb of Theoderich at Ravenna.

In this regard Byzantium itself is a marvel. Here layer after layer

[4]This is now recognized by art-research; cf. Salis, *Die Kunst der Griechen* (1919), pp. 3, *et seq.*;H. Th. Bosser, *Alt-Kreta* (1921), introduction.
[5]D. Fimmen, *Die kretisch-mykenische Kultur* (1921), p. 210.
[6]Dehio, *Gesch. d. deutsch. Kunst* (1919), pp. 16, *et seq.*

has to be carefully separated. In 326 Constantine, rebuilding on the ruins of the great city destroyed by Septimus Severus, created a *Late Classical cosmopolis* of the first rank, into which presently streamed hoary Apollinism from the West and youthful Magism from the East. And long afterwards again, in 1096, it is a *Late Magian* cosmopolis, confronted in its last autumn days with spring in the shape of Godfrey of Bouillon's crusaders, whom that clever royal lady Anna Comnena[7] portrays with contempt. As the easternmost of the Classical West, this city bewitched the Goths; then, a millennium later, as the northernmost of the Arabian world, it enchanted the Russians. And the amazing Vasili Blazheny in Moscow (1554), the herald of the Russian pre-Culture, stands "between styles," just as, two thousand years before, Solomon's Temple had stood between Babylon the Cosmopolis and early Christianity.

II

Primeval man is a *ranging* animal, a being whose waking-consciousness restlessly feels its way through life, all microcosm, under no servitude of place or home, keen and anxious in its senses, ever alert to drive off some element of hostile Nature. A deep transformation sets in first with agriculture—for that is something *artificial*, with which hunter and shepherd have no touch. He who digs and ploughs is seeking not to plunder, but to *alter* Nature. To plant implies, not to take something, but to produce something. *But with this, man himself becomes plant*— namely, as a peasant. He roots in the earth that he tends, the soul of man discovers a soul in the countryside, and a new earthboundness of being, a new feeling, pronounces itself. Hostile Nature becomes the friend; earth becomes *Mother* Earth. Between sowing and begetting, harvest and death, the child and the grain, a profound affinity is set up. A new devoutness addresses itself in chthonian cults to the fruitful earth that grows up along with man. And as completed expression of this life-feeling, we find everywhere the *symbolic shape of the farmhouse*, which in the disposition of the rooms and in every line of external form tells up about the blood of its inhabitants. The peasant's dwelling is the great symbol of settledness. It is itself plant, thrusts its roots deep into its "own" soul.[8] It is *property* in the most sacred sense of

[7]Dieterich, *Byzant, Charakterköpfe*, pp. 136, *et seq.*
[8]Even admitting within itself the animals of its fields.—*Tr.*

the word. The kindly spirits of hearth and door, floor and chamber—Vesta, Janus, Lares and Penates—are as firmly fixed in it as the man himself.

This is the condition precedent of every Culture, which itself in turn grows up out of a mother-landscape and renews and intensifies the intimacy of man and soil. What his cottage is to the peasant, that the town is to the Cultureman. As each individual house has its kindly spirits, so each town has its tutelary god or saint. The town, too, is a plantlike being, as far removed as a peasantry is from nomadism and the purely microcosmic. Hence the development of a high form-language is linked always to a landscape. Neither an art nor a religion can alter the site of its growth; only in the Civilization with its giant cities do we come again to despise and disengage ourselves from these roots. Man as civilized, as *intellectual nomad,* is again wholly microcosmic, wholly homeless, as free *intellectually* as hunter and herdsman were free sensually. *"Ubi bene, ibi patria"* is valid *before* as well as *after* a Culture. In the not-yet-spring of the Migrations it was a Germanic yearning—virginal, yet already maternal—that searched the South for a home in which to nest its future Culture. Today, at the end of this Culture, the rootless intellect ranges over all landscapes and all possibilities of thought. But between these limits lies the time in which a man held a bit of soil to be something *worth dying for.*

It is a conclusive fact—yet one hitherto never appreciated—that all great Cultures are town-Cultures. Higher man of the Second Age is a town-tied animal. Here is the real criterion of "world-history" that differentiates it with utter sharpness from man's history—*world-history is the history of civic man.* Peoples, states, politics, religion, all arts, and all sciences rest upon *one* prime phenomenon of human being, the town. As all thinkers of all Cultures themselves live in the town (even though they may reside bodily in the country), they are perfectly unaware of what a bizarre thing a town is. To feel this we have to put ourselves unreservedly in the place of the wonder-struck primitive who for the first time sees this mass of stone and wood set in the landscape, with its stone-enclosed streets and its stone-paved squares—a domicile, truly, of strange forms and strangely teeming with men!

But the real miracle is the birth of the *soul* of a town. A mass-soul of a wholly new kind—whose last foundations will remain hidden from us for ever—suddenly buds off from the general spirituality of its Culture. As soon as it is awake, it forms for itself a visible body. Out of the rustic group of farms and cottages, each of which has its own history, arises a totality. And the whole lives, breathes, grows, and acquires a face and inner form and history. Thenceforward, in addition to the individual house, the temple, the cathedral, and the palace, the town-figure itself becomes a unit objectively expressing the form-language and style-history that accompanies the Culture throughout its life-course.

It goes without saying that what distinguishes a town from a village is not size, but the presence of a soul. Not only in primitive conditions, such as those of central Africa, but in Late conditions too—China, India, and industrialized Europe and America—we find very large settlements that are nevertheless not to be called cities. They are centers of landscape; they do not inwardly form worlds in themselves. They have no soul. Every primitive population lives wholly as peasant and son of the soil—the being "City" does not exist for it. That which in externals develops from the village is not the city, but the market, a mere meeting-point of rural life-interests. Here there can be no question of a separate existence. The inhabitant of a market may be a craftsman or a tradesman, but he lives and thinks as a peasant. We have to go back and sense accurately what it means when out of a primitive Egyptian or Chinese or Germanic village—a little spot in a wide land—a city comes into being. It is quite possibly not differentiated in any outward feature, but spiritually it is *a place from which the countryside is henceforth regarded, felt, and experienced as "environs,"* as something different and subordinate. From now on there are two lives, that of the inside and that of the outside, and the peasant understands this just as clearly as the townsman. The village smith and the smith in the city, the village headman and the burgomaster, live in two different worlds. The man of the land and the man of the city are different essences. First of all they feel the difference, then they are dominated by it, and at last they cease to understand each other at all. Today a Brandenburg peasant is closer to a Sicilian peasant than he is to a Berliner. From the moment of this specific attunement, the City comes into being, and it is this attunement which underlies, as something that goes without saying, the entire waking-consciousness of every Culture.

Every springtime of a Culture is *ipso facto* the springtime of a new city-type and civism. The men of the pre-Culture are filled with a deep uneasiness in the presence of these types, with which they cannot get into any inward relation. On the Rhine and the Danube the Germans frequently, as at Strassburg, settled down at the gates of Roman cities that remained uninhabited.[9] In Crete the conquerors built, on the ruins of the burnt-out cities like Gournia and Cnossus—villages. The Orders of the Western pre-Culture, the Benedictines, and particularly the Cluniacs and Premonstratensians, settled like the knights on free land; it was the Franciscans and Dominicans who began to build in the Early Gothic city. There the new soul had just awakened. But even there a tender melancholy still adheres to the architecture, as to Franciscan art as a whole—an almost mystical fear of the individual in presence of the new and bright and conscious, which as yet was only dully accepted by the generality. Man hardly yet dared to cease to be peasant; the first to live with the ripe and considered alertness of genuine megalopolitans are the Jesuits. It is a sign that the countryside is still unconditionally supreme, and does not yet recognize the city, when the ruler shifts his court every spring from palace to palace. In the Egyptian Old Kingdom the thickly populated center of the administration was at the "White Wall' (Memphis), but the residences of the Pharaohs changed incessantly as in Sumerian Babylon and the Carolingian Empire.[10] The Early Chinese rulers of the Chou dynasty had their court as a rule at Lo-Yang (the present Ho-nan-fu) from about 1160, but it was not until 770—corresponding to our sixteenth century —that the locality was promoted to be the permanent royal residence.

Never has the feeling of earth-boundness, of the plantwise-cosmic, expressed itself so powerfully as it did in the architecture of the petty early towns, which consisted of hardly more than a few streets about a market-place or a castle or a place of worship. Here, if anywhere, it is manifest that every grand style is itself plantlike. The Doric column, the Egyptian pyramid, the Gothic cathedral, *grow out of* the ground, earnest big with destiny, Being without waking-consciousness. The Ionic column, the buildings of the Middle Kingdom and those of the Baroque, calmly aware and conscious of themselves, free and sure, *stand on* the ground. There, separated from the power of the land—cut off from it, even, but the pavement underfoot—Being comes more and more languid, sensation and reason more and more powerful. Man becomes intellect, "free" like the nomads, whom he comes to resemble, but narrower and colder than they. "Intellect," "*Geist,*" "*esprit,*" is the specific urban form of the understanding waking-consciousness. All art, all religion

[9] Dehio, *Gesch. d. deutschen Kunst* (1919), pp. 13, *et seq.*
[10] Eduard Meyer, *Gesch. d. Altertums,* I, p. 188.

and science, become slowly intellectualized, alien to the land, incomprehensible to the peasant of the soil. With the Civilization sets in the climacteric. The immemorially old roots of Being are dried up in the stone-masses of its cities. And the free intellect—fateful word!—appears like a flame, mounts splendid into the air, and pitiably dies.

III

The new Soul of the City speaks a new language, which soon comes to be tantamount to the language of the Culture itself. The open land with its village-mankind is wounded; it no longer understands that language, it is nonplussed and dumb. All genuine style-history is played out in the cities. It is exclusively the city's destiny and the life-experience of urban men that speaks to the eye in the logic of visible forms. The very earliest Gothic was still a growth of the soil and laid hold of the farmhouse with its inhabitants and its contents. But the Renaissance style flourished only in the Renaissance *city,* the Baroque only in the Baroque *city*—not to mention the wholly megalopolitan Corinthian column or Rococo. There was perhaps some quiet infiltration from these into the landscape; but the land itself was no longer capable of the smaller creative effort—only of dumb aversion. The peasant and his dwelling remained in all essentials Gothic, and Gothic it is to this day. The Hellenic *countryside* preserved the geometric style, the Egyptian village the cast of the Old Kingdon.

It is, above all, the expression of the city's "visage" that has a history. The play of this facial expression, indeed, is almost the spiritual history of the Culture itself. First we have the little proto-cities of the Gothic and other Early Cultures, which almost efface themselves in the landscape, which are still genuine peasant-houses crowded under the shadow of a stronghold or a sanctuary, and without inward change become town-houses merely in the sense that they have neighbor-houses instead of fields and meadows around them. The peoples of the Early Culture gradually became town-peoples, and accordingly there are not only specifically Chinese, Indian, Apollinian, and Faustian town-forms, but, moreover, Armenian and Syrian, Ionian and Etruscan, German and French and English town physiognomies. There is a city of Phidias, a city of Rembrandt, a city of Luther. These designations, and the mere names of Granada, Venice, and Nürnberg conjure up at once quite definite images, for all that the Culture produces in religion, art, and knowledge has been produced in such cities. While it was still the spirit of knights' castles and rural monasteries that evoked the Crusades, the Reformation is urban and belongs to narrow streets and steep-gabled houses. The great Epic, which speaks and sings of the blood, belongs to *Pfalz* and *Burg*, but the Drama, in which *awakened* life tests itself, is city-poetry, and the great Novel, the survey of all things human by the emancipated intellect, presupposes the world-city. Apart from really genuine folk-song, the only lyrism is of the city. Apart from the "eternal" peasant-art, there is only urban painting and architecture, with a swift and soon-ended history.

And these stone visages that have incorporated in their light-world the humanness of the citizen himself and, like him are all eye and intellect—how distinct the language of form that they talk, how different from the rustic drawl of the landscape! The silhouette of the great city, its roofs and chimneys, the towers and domes on the horizon! What a language is imparted to us through *one* look at Nürnberg or Florence, Damascus or Moscow, Peking or Benares. What do we know of the Classical cities, seeing that we do not know the lines that they presented under the Sourthern noon, under clouds in the morning, in the starry night? The courses of the streets, straight or crooked, broad or narrow; the houses, low or tall, bright or dark, that in all Western cities turn their facades, *their faces,* and in all Eastern cities turn their backs, blank wall and railing, towards the street; the spirit of squares and corners, impasses and prospects, fountains and monuments, churches or temples or mosques, amphitheaters and railway stations, bazaars and town-halls! The suburbs, too, of neat garden-villas or of jumbled blocks of flats, rubbish-heaps and allotments; the fashionable quarter and the slum area, the Suburb of Classical Rome and the Faubourg Saint-Germain of Paris, ancient Baiae and modern Nice, the little town-picture like Bruges and Rothenburg and the sea of houses like Babylon, Tenochtitlán, Rome, and London! All this has history and *is* history. One major political event—and the visage of the town falls into different folds. Napoleon gave to Bourbon Paris, Bismarck gave to worthy little Berlin, a new mien. But the Country stands by, uninfluenced, suspicious, and irritated.

In the earliest time the *landscape-figure alone* dominates man's eyes. It gives form to his soul and vibrates in tune therewith. Feelings and woodland rustlings beat together; the meadows and the copses adapt themselves to its shape, to its course, even to its dress. The village, with its quiet hillocky roofs, its evening smoke, its wells, its hedges, and its beasts, lies completely fused and embedded in the landscape. The country town *confirms* the country, is an intensification of the picture of the country. It is the Late city that first defies the land, contradicts Nature in the lines of its silhouette, *denies* all Nature. It wants to be something different from and higher than Nature. These high-pitched gables, these Baroque cupolas, spires, and pinnacles, neither are, nor desire to be, related with anything in Nature. And then begins the gigantic megalopolis, the *city-as-world*, which suffers nothing beside itself and sets about *annihilating* the country picture. The town that once upon a time humbly accommodated itself to that picture now insists that it shall be the same as itself. *Extra muros*, chausées and woods and pastures become a park, mountains become tourists' view-points; and *intra muros* arises an imitation Nature, fountains in lieu of springs, flower-beds, formal pools, and clipped hedges in lieu of meadows and ponds and bushes. In a village the thatched roof is still hill-like and the street is of the same nature as the baulk of earth between fields. But here the picture is of deep, long gorges between high, stony houses filled with colored dust and strange uproar, and men dwell in these houses, the like of which no nature-being has ever conceived. Costumes, even faces, are adjusted to a background of stone. By day there is a street traffic of strange colors and tones, and by night a new light that outshines the moon. And the yokel stands helpless on the pavement, understanding nothing and understood by nobody, tolerated as a useful type in farce and provider of this world's daily bread.

It follows, however—and this is the most essential point of any— that we cannot comprehend political and economic history at all unless we realize that the city, with its gradual detachment from and final bankrupting of the country, is the determinative form to which the course and sense of higher history generally conforms. *World history is city history.*

An obvious case in point is, of course, the Classical world, in which the Euclidean feeling of existence connected the city-idea with its need of minimizing extension and thus, with ever-increasing emphasis, identified the State with the stone body of the individual Polis. But, quite apart from this instance, we find in every Culture (and very soon) the type of the *capital city*. This, as its name pointedly indicates, is that city whose spirit, with its methods, aims, and decisions of policy and economics, dominates the land. The land with its people is for this controlling spirit a tool and an object. The land does not understand what is going on, and is not even asked. In all countries of all Late Cultures, the great parties, the revolutions, the Caesarisms, the democracies, the parliaments, are the form in which the spirit of the capital tells the country what it is expected to desire and, if called upon, to die for. The Classical forum, the Western press, are, essentially, intellectual engines of the ruling City. Any country-dweller who really understands the meaning of politics in such periods, and feels himself on their level, moves into the City, not perhaps in the body, but certainly in the spirit.[12] The sentiment and public opinion of the peasant's country-side—so far as it can be said to exist—is prescribed and guided by the print and speech of the city. Egypt is Thebes, the *orbis terrarum* is Rome, Islam is Baghdad, France is Paris. The history of every springtime phase is played out in the many small centers of many separate districts. The Egyptian nomes, the Greek peoples of Homer, the Gothic counties and free cities, were the makers of history of old. But gradually Policy gathers itself up into a very few capitals, and everything else retains but a shadow of political existence. Even in the Classical world, the atomizing tendency towards city-states did not hold out against the major movement. As early as the Peloponnesian War it was only Athens and Sparta that were really handling policy, the remaining cities of the Aegean being merely elements within the hegemony of the one or the other; of policies of *their own* there is no longer any question. Finally it is the Forum of the City of Rome alone that is the scene of Classical history. Caesar might campaign in Gaul, his slayers in Macedonia, Antony in Egypt, but, whatever happened in these fields, *it was from their relation to Rome that events acquired meaning.*

IV

All effectual history begins with the primary classes, nobility and priesthood, forming themselves and elevating themselves above the peasantry as such. The opposition of greater and lesser nobility, between king and

---

[12]The phenomenon is perhaps too well known in our days to need exemplification. But it is worthwhile recalling that the usual form of disgrace for a minister or courtier of the seventeenth or eighteenth century was to be commanded to "retire to his estates," and that a student expelled from the univer-

vassal, between worldly and spiritual power, is the basic form of all primitive politics, Homeric, Chinese, or Gothic, until with the coming of the City, the burgher, the *Tiers Etat,* history changes its style. But it is exclusively in these classes as such, in their class-consciousness, that the whole meaning of history inheres. *The peasant is historyless.* The village stands outside world-history, and all evolution from the "Trojan" to the Mithridatic War, from the Saxon emperors to the World War of 1914, passes by these little points on the landscape, occasionally destroying them and wasting their blood, but never in the least toughing their inwardness.

The peasant is the eternal man, independent of every Culture that ensconces itself in the cities. He precedes it, he outlives it, a dumb creature propagating himself from generation to generation, limited to soil-bound callings and aptitudes, a mystical soul, a dry, shrewd understanding that sticks to practical matters, the origin and the ever-flowing sources of the blood that makes world-history in the cities.

Whatever the Culture up there in the city conceives in the way of stateforms, economic customs, articles of faith, implements, knowledge, art, he receives mistrustfully and hesitatingly; though in the end he may accept these things, never is he altered in kind thereby. Thus the West-European peasant outwardly took in all the dogmas of the Councils from the great Lateran to that of Trent, just as he took in the products of mechanical engineering and those of the French Revolution— but he remains what he was, what he already was in Charlemagne's day. The present-day piety of the peasant is older than Christianity; his gods are more ancient than those of any higher religion. Remove from him the pressure of the great cities and he will revert to the state of nature without feeling that he is losing anything. His real ethic, his real metaphysic, which no scholar of the city has yet thought it worth while to discover, lie outside all religious and spiritual history, have in fact no history at all.

The city is intellect. The Megalopolis is "free" intellect. It is in resistance to the "feudal" powers of blood and tradition that the bur-

sities is said to be "rusticated." Since this article was written, a remarkable proof of the reality of this spiritual indrawing by the Megalopolis has been given by the swift spread of radio broadcasting over the West European and American world. For the country-dweller, radio reception means intimate touch with the news, the thought, and the entertainment of the great city, and relieves the *grievance* of "isolation" that the older countryfolk would never have felt as a grievance at all.—Tr.

gherdom or bourgeoisie, the intellectual class, begins to be conscious of its own separate existence. It upsets thrones and limits old rights in the name of reason and above all in the name of "the People," which henceforward means exclusively the people of the city. Democracy is the political form in which the townsman's outlook upon the world is demanded of the peasantry also. The urban intellect reforms the great religion of the springtime and sets up by the side of the old religion of noble and priest, the new religion of the *Tiers Etat, liberal science.* The city assumes the lead and control of economic history in replacing the primitive values of the land, which are forever inseparable from the life and thought of the rustic, by the *absolute idea of money* as distince from goods. The immemorial country word for exchange of goods is "barter"; even when one of the things exchanged is precious metal, the underlying idea of the process is not yet *monetary*—i.e., it does not involve the abstraction of value from things and its fixation in metallic or fictitious quantities intended to *measure* things qua "commodities." Caravan expeditions and Viking voyages in the springtime are made between land-settlements and imply barter or booty, whereas in the Late period they are made between cities and mean "money." This is the distinction between the Normans before and the Hansa and Venetians after the Crusades,[13] and between the seafarers of Mycenaean times and those of the later colonization period in Greece. The City means not only intellect, but also money.

Presently there arrived an epoch when the development of the city had reached such a point of power that it had no longer to defend itself against country and chivalry, but on the contrary had become a despotism against which the land and its basic orders of society were fighting a hopeless defensive battle—in the spiritual domain against nationalism, in the political against democracy, in the economic against money. At this period the number of cities that really counted as historically dominant had already become very small. And with this there arose the profound distinction—which was above all a spiritual distinction—between the great city and the little city or town. The latter, very significantly called the country-town, was a part of the no longer coefficient countryside. It was not that the difference between townsman and rustic had become

[13]In the case of the Venetians the money-outlook was already potent during the earlier Crusades. But the fact that their financial exploitation of the great religious adventure was regarded as scandalous indicates sufficiently that the rural world of the West was not yet fact to face with the money-idea.—*Tr.*

lessened in such towns, but that this difference had become negligible as compared with the new difference between them and the great city. The sly shrewdness of the country and the intelligence of the megalopolis are two forms of waking-consciousness between which reciprocal understanding is scarcely possible. Here again it is evident that what counts is not the number of inhabitants, but the spirit. It is evident, moreover, that in all great cities nooks remained in which relics of an almost rural mankind lived in their byeways much as if they were on the land, and the people on the two sides of the street were almost in the relation of two villages. In fact, a pyramid of mounting civism, of decreasing number and increasing field of view, leads up from such quasi-rural elements, in ever-narrowing layers, to the small number of genuine megalopolitans at the top, who are at home wherever their spiritual postulates are satisfied.

With this the notion of money attains to full abstractness. It no longer merely *serves* for the understanding of economic intercourse, but *subjects* the exchange of goods to *its own* evolution. It values things, no longer as between each other, but *with reference to itself*. Its relation to the soil and to the man of the soil has so completely vanished, that in the economic thought of the leading cities—the "money-markets,"—it is ignored. Money has now become a power, and, moreover, a power that is wholly intellectual and merely figured in the metal it uses, a power the reality of which resides in the waking-consciousness of the upper stratum of an economically active population, a power that makes those concerned with it just as dependent upon itself as the peasant was dependent upon the soil. There is monetary thought, just as there is mathematical or juristic.

But the earth is actual and natural, and money is abstract and artificial, a mere "category"—like "virtue" in the imagination of the Age of Enlightenment. And therefore every primary, pre-civic economy is dependent upon and held in bondage by the cosmic powers, the soil, the climate, the type of man, whereas money, as the pure form of economic intercourse within the waking-consciousness, is no more limited in potential scope by actuality than are the quantities of the mathematical and the logical world. Just as no view of facts hinders us from constructing as many non-Euclidean geometrics as we please, so in the developed megalopolitan economics there is no longer any inherent objection to increasing "money" or to thinking, so to say, in other money-dimensions. This has nothing to do with the availability of gold or with any values in actuality at all. There is no standard and no sort of goods in which the value of the talent in the Persian Wars can be compared with its value in the Egyptian booty of Pompey. Money has become, for man as an economic animal, a form of the activity of waking-consciousness, having no longer any roots in Being. This is the basis of its monstrous power over every beginning Civilization, which is always an unconditional *dictatorship of money*, though taking different forms in different Cultures. But this is the reason, too, for the want of solidarity, which eventually leads to its losing its power and its meaning, so that at the last, as in Diocletian's time, it disappears from the thought of the closing Civilization, and the primary values of the soil return anew to take its place.

Finally, there arises the monstrous symbol and vessel of the completely emancipated intellect, the world-city, the center in which the course of a world-history ends by winding itself up. A handful of gigantic places in each Civilization disfranchises and disvalues the entire motherland of its own Culture under the contemptuous name of "the provinces." The "provinces" are now everything whatsoever—land, town, *and* city—except these two or three points. There are no longer noblesse and bourgeoisie, freemen and slaves, Hellenes and Barbarians, believers and unbelievers, *but only cosmopolitans and provincials.* All others contrasts pale pefore this one, which dominates all events, all habits of life, all views of the world.

The earliest of all world-cities were Babylon and the Thebes of the New Empire—the Minoan world of Crete, for all its splendor, belonged to the Egyptian "provinces." In the Classical the first example is Alexandria, which reduced old Greece at one stroke to the provincial level, and which even Rome, even the resettled Carthage, even Byzantium, could not suppress. In India the giant cities of Ujjaina, Kanauj, and above all Pataliputra were renowned even in China and Java, and everyone knows the fairy-tale reputation of Baghdad and Granada in the West. In the Mexican world, it seems, Uxmal (founded in 950) was the first world-city of the Maya realms, which, however, with the rise of the Toltec world-cities Tezcuco and Tenochtitlán sank to the level of the provinces.

It should not be forgotten that the word "province" first appears as a constitutional designation given by the Romans to Sicily; the subjugation of Sicily, in fact, is the first example of a once preeminent Culture-landscape sinking so far as to be purely and simply an object.

Syracuse, the first real great-city of the Classical world, had flourished when Rome was still an unimportant country town, but thenceforward, *vis-à-vis* Rome, it becomes a provincial city. In just the same way Habsburg Madrid and Papal Rome, leading cities in the Europe of the seventeenth century were from the outset of the eighteenth depressed to the provincial level by the world-cities of Paris and London. And the rise of New York to the position of world-city during the Civil war of 1861–65 may perhaps prove to have been the most pregnant event of the 19th century.

V

The stone Colossus "Cosmopolis" stands at the end of the life's course of every great Culture. The Culture-man whom the land has spiritually formed is seized and possessed by his own creation, the City, and is made into its creature, its executive organ, and finally its victim. This stony mass is the *absolute* city. Its image, as it appears with all its grandiose beauty in the light-world of the human eye, contains the whole noble death-symbolism of the definitive thing-become. The spirit-pervaded stone of Gothic buildings, after a millenium of style-evolution, has become the soulless material of this demonic stone desert.

These final cities are *wholly* intellect. Their houses are no longer, as those of the Ionic and the Baroque were, derivatives of the old peasant's house, whence the Culture took its spring into history. They are, generally speaking, no longer houses in which Vesta and Janus, Lares and Penates, have any sort of footing, but mere premises which have been fashioned, not by blood but by requirements, not be feeling but by the spirit of commercial enterprise. So long as the hearth has a pious meaning as the actual and genuine center of a family, the old relation to the land is not wholly extinct. But when *that*, too, follows the rest into oblivion, and the mass of tenants and bed-occupiers in the sea of houses leads a vagrant existence from shelter to shelter like the hunters and pastors of the "pre-" time, then the intellectual nomad is completely developed. This city is a world, is *the* world. Only as a whole, as a human dwelling-place, has it meaning, the houses being merely the stones of which it is assembled.

Now the old mature cities with their Gothic nucleus of cathedral, town-halls, and high-gabled streets, with their old walls, towers and

gates, ringed about by the Baroque growth of brighter and more elegant patricians' houses, palaces, and hall-churches, begin to overflow
in all directions in formless masses, to eat into the decaying countryside with their multiplied barrack-tenements and utility buildings, and
to destroy the noble aspect of the old time by clearances and rebuildings.
Looking down from one of the old towers upon the sea of houses, we
perceive in this petrification of a historic being the exact epoch that
marks the end of organic growth and the beginning of an inorganic
and therefore unrestrained process of massing without limit. And now,
too, appears that artificial, mathematical, utterly land-alien product of a
pure intellectual satisfaction in the appropriate, the city of the city-
architect. In all Civilizations alike, these cities aim at the chessboard
form, which is the symbol of soullessness. Regular rectangle-blocks
astounded Herodotus in Babylon and Cortez in Tenochtitlán. In the
Classical world the series of "abstract" cities begins with Thurii, which
was "planned" by Hippodamus of Miletus in 441. Priene, whose chessboard scheme entirely ignores the ups and downs of the site, Rhodes,
and Alexandria follow, the become in turn models for innumerable provincial cities of the Imperial Age. The Islamic architects laid out Baghdad from 762, and the giant city of Samarra a century later, according
to plan.[14] In the West-European and American world the layout of
Washington in 1791 is the first big example.[15] There can be no doubt
that the world-cities of the Han period in China and the Maurya dynasty

[14]Samarra exhibits, like the Imperial Fora of Rome and the ruins of Luxor,
truly American proportions. The city stretches for 33 km. (20 mi.) along the
Tigris. The Balkuwara Palace, which the Caliph Mutawakil built for one of his
sons, forms a square of 1250 m. (say, three-quarters of a mile) on each side. One
of the giant mosques measures in plan 260 x 10 m. (858 x 594 ft.). Schwarz, *Die
Abbasidenresidenz Samarra* (1910); Herzfeld, *Ausgrabungen von Samarra* (1912).
Pataliputra, in the days of Chandragupta and Asoka, measured *intra muros*
10 x 2 mi (equal to Manhattan Island or London along the Thames from
Greenwich to Richmond).—*Tr.*

[15]Karlsruhe, with its fan-scheme, and Mannheim, with its rectangles, are earlier than Washington. But both are small places. The one is a sort of extension
of the prince's Rococo park and centered on his *point de vue;* the other, though
its block-numbering, unique in Europe, seems to relate it to the American city,
was really planned as a self-contained military capital, rectangular only within
its oval enceinte, whereas the American rectangles are meant to be added to.
The layout of Petersburg by Peter the Great (which has been adhered to to
this day and is still incompletely filled in in detail) is a much more forcible
example of the arbitrary planning of a megalopolis. Though outside the "European" world, it is of it, for it was the visible symbol of Peter's will to force
Europe upon Russia. It is contemporary with Mannheim and Karlsruhe (early
eighteenth century), but its creator conceived of it as a city *of the future.*—*Tr.*

in India possessed this same geometrical pattern. Even now the world-cities of the Western Civilization are far from having reached the peak of their development. I see, long after A.D. 2000, cities laid out for ten to twenty million inhabitants, spread over enormous areas of countryside, with buildings that will dwarf the biggest of today's and and notions of traffic and communication that we should regard as fantastic to the point of madness.[16]

Even in this final shape of his being, the Classical man's form-ideal remains the corporal point. Whereas the giant cities of our present confess our irrestible tendency towards the infinite—our suburbs and garden cities, invading the wide countryside, our vast and comprehensive network of roads, and within the thickly built areas a controlled fast traffic on, below, and above straight, broad streets—the genuine Classical world-city ever strove, not to expand, but to thicken—the streets narrow and cramped, impossible for fast traffic (although this was fully developed on the great Roman roads), entire unwillingness to live in suburbs or even to make suburbs possible.[17] Even at that stage the city must needs be a body, thick and round, *sōma* in the strictest sense. The synoecism that in the early Classical had gradually drawn the land-folk into the cities, and so created the type of the Polis, repeated itself at the last in absurd form; everyone wanted to live in the middle of the city, in its densest nucleus, for otherwise he could not feel himself to be the urban man that he was. All these cities are only *cités*, inner towns. The new synoecism formed, instead of suburban zones, *the world of the upper floors.* In the year 74 Rome, in spite of its immense population, had the ridiculously small perimeter of nineteen and a half kilometres (twelve miles).[18] Consequently these city bodies extended in general not in breadth, but more and more upward. The block-tenements of Rome such as the famous Insula Feliculae, rose, with a street breadth of only three to five metres (ten to seventeen feet)[19] to heights that have never been seen in Western Europe and are seen

---

[16]In the case of Canada, not merely great regions, but the *whole country* has been picketed out in equal rectangles for future development.—*Tr.*

[17]It has been left to the *Western* Civilization of present-day Rome to build the garden suburbs that the Classical Civilization could have built.—*Tr.*

[18]Friedländer, *Sittengeschichte Roms*, I, p. 5. Compare this with Samarra, which had nothing like this population. The "Late Classical city on Arabian soil was un-Classical in this respect as in others. The garden suburb of Antioch was renowned throughout the East."

[19]The city which the Egyptian "Julian the Apostate," Amenophis IV (Akhenaton) built himself in Tell-el-Amarna had streets up to 45 m. (149 ft.) wide.

in only a few cities in America. Near the Capitol, the roofs already reached to the level of the hill-saddle.[20] But always the splendid mass-cities harbor lamentable poverty and degraded habits, and the attics and mansards, the cellars and back courts are breeding a new type of raw man—in Baghdad and in Babylon, just as in Tenochtitlán and today in London and Berlin. Diodorus tells of a deposed Egyptian king who was reduced to living in one of these wretched upper-floor tenements of Rome.

But no wretchedness, no compulsion, not even a clear vision of the madness of this development, avails to neutralize the attractive force of these demonic creations. The wheel of Destiny rolls on to its end; the birth of the City entails its death. Beginning and end, a peasant cottage and a tenement-block are related to one another as soul and intellect, as blood and stone. But "Time" is no abstract phrase, but a name for the actuality of Irreversibility. Here there is only forward, never back. Long, long ago the country bore the country-town and nourished it with her best blood. Now the giant city sucks the country dry, insatiably and incessantly demanding and devouring fresh streams of men, till it wearies and dies in the midst of an almost uninhabited waste of country. Once the full sinful beauty of this last marvel of all history has captured a victim, it never lets him go. Primitive folk can loose themselves from the soil and wander, but the intellectual nomad never. Homesickness for the great city is keener than any other nostalgia. Home is for him any one of these giant cities, but even the nearest village is alien territory. He would sooner die upon the pavement than go "back" to the land. Even disgust at this pretentiousness, weariness of the thousand-hued glitter, the *taedium vitae* that in the end overcomes many, does not set them free. They take the City with them into the mountains or on the sea. They have lost the country within themselves and will never regain it outside.

What makes the man of the world-cities incapable of living on any but this artificial footing is that the cosmic beat in his being is ever decreasing, while the tensions of his waking-consciousness become more and more dangerous. It must be remembered that in a microcosm the animal, waking side supervenes upon the vegetable side, that of being, and not vice versa. Beat and tension, blood and intellect, Destiny and Causality are to one another as the countryside in bloom is to the city of stone, as something existing *per se* to something existing depen-

[20]Pöhlmann, *Aus Altertum und Gegenwart* (1910), pp. 211, *et seq.*

dently. Tension without cosmic pulsation to animate it is the transition to nothingness. But Civilization is nothing but tension. The head, in all the outstanding men of the Civilizations, is dominated exclusively by an expression of extreme tension. Intelligence is only the capacity for understanding at high tension, and in every Culture these heads are the types of its final men—one has only to compare them with the peasant heads, when such happens to emerge in the swirl of the great city's life. The advance, too, from peasant wisdom—"slimness," mother wit, instinct, based as in other animals upon the sensed beat of life— through the city-spirit to the cosmopolitan intelligence—the very word with its sharp ring betraying the disappearance of the old cosmic foundation—can be described as a steady diminution of the Destiny-feeling and an unrestrained augmentation of needs according to the operation of a casualty. Intelligence is the replacement of unconscious living by exercise in thought, masterly but bloodless and jejune. The intelligent visage is similar in all races—what is recessive in them is, precisely, race. The weaker the feeling for the necessity and self-evidence of Being, the more the habit of "elucidation" grows, the more the fear in the waking-consciousness comes to be stilled by causal methods. Hence the assimilation of knowledge with demonstrability, and the substitution of scientific theory, the causal myth, for the religious. Hence, too, money-in-the-abstract as the pure causality of economic life, in contrast to rustic barter, which is pulsation and not a system of tensions.

Tension, when it has become intellectual, knows no form of recreation but that which is specific to the world-city—namely, *détente*, relaxation, distraction. Genuine play, *joie de vivre*, pleasure, inebriation, are products of the cosmic beat and as such no longer comprehensible in their essence. But the relief of hard, intensive brain-work by its opposite—conscious and practised fooling—of intellectual tension by the bodily tension of sport, of bodily tension by the sensual straining after "pleasure" and the spiritual straining after the "excitements" of betting and competitions, of the pure logic of the day's work by consciously enjoyed mysticism—all this is common to the world-cities of all the Civilizations. Cinema, Expressionism Theosophy, boxing contests, nigger dances, poker, and racing—one can find it all in Rome. Indeed, the connoisseur might extend his researches to the Indian, Chinese, and Arabian world-cities as well. To name but one example, if one reads the Kama-sutram one understands how it was that Buddhism *also* appealed to men's tastes, and then the bullfighting scenes in the Palace of Cnossus will be looked at with quite different eyes. A cult, no doubt, underlay them, but there was a savor over it all, as over Rome's fashionable Isis-cult in the neighborhood of the Circus Maximus.

And then, when Being is sufficiently uprooted and Waking-Being sufficiently strained, there suddenly emerges into the bright light of history a phenomenon that has long been preparing itself underground and now steps forward to make an end of the drama—the *sterility of civilized man*. This is not something that can be grasped as a plain matter of Causality (as modern science naturally enough has tried to grasp it); it is to be understood as an essentially *metaphysical* turn towards death. The last man of the world-city no longer *wants* to live— he may cling to life as an individual, but as a type, as an aggregate, no, for it is a characteristic of this collective existence that it eliminates the terror of death. That which strikes the true peasant with a deep and inexplicable fear, the notion that the family and the name may be extinguished, has now lost its meaning. The continuance of the blood-relation in the visible world is no longer a duty of the blood, and the destiny of being the last of the line is no longer felt as a doom. Children do not happen, not because children have become impossible, but principally because intelligence at the peak of intensity can no longer find any reason for their existence. Let the reader try to merge himself in the soul of the peasant. He has sat on his glebe from primeval times,[21] or has fastened his clutch in it, to adhere to it with his blood. He is rooted in it as the descendant of his forbears and as the forbear of future descendants. *His* house, *his* property, means, here, not the temporary connection of person and thing for a brief span of years, but an enduring and inward union of *eternal* land and *eternal* blood. It is only from this mystical conviction of settlement that the great epochs of the cycle—procreation, birth, and death—derive that metaphysical element of wonder which condenses in the symbolism of custom and religion that all landbound people possess. For the "last men" all this is past and gone. Intelligence and sterility are allied in old families, old peoples, and old Cultures, not merely because in each microcosm the overstrained and fettered animal element is eating up the plant element, but also because the waking-consciousness assumes that Being is normally regulated by causality. That which the man of intelligence, most

[21]Some years ago a French peasant was brought to notice whose family had occupied its glebe since the ninth century.—*Tr.*

significantly and characteristically, labels as "natural impulse" or "life-force," he not only knows, but also values, causally, giving it the place amongst his other needs that his judgment assigns to it. When the ordinary thought of a highly cultivated people begins to regard "having children" as a question of *pro's* and *con's* the great turning-point has come. For Nature knows nothing of *pro* and *con*. Everywhere, wherever life is actual, reigns an inward organic logic, an "it," a drive, that is utterly independent of waking-being, with its causal linkages, and indeed not even observed by it. The abundant proliferation of primitive peoples is a *natural phenomenon*, which is not even thought about, still less judged as to its utility or the reverse. When reasons have to be put forward at all in a question of life, life itself has become questionable. At that point begins prudent limitation of the number of births. In the Classical world the practice was deplored by Polybius as the ruin of Greece, and yet even at his date it had long been established in the great cities; in subsequent Roman times it became appallingly general. At first explained by the economic misery of the times, very soon it ceased to explain itself at all. And at that point, too, in Buddhist India as in Babylon, in Rome as in our own cities, a man's choice of the woman who is to be, not mother of his children as amongst peasants and primitives, but his own "companion for life," becomes a problem of mentalities. The Ibsen marriage appears, the "higher spiritual affinity" in which both parties are "free"—free, that is, as intelligences, free from the plantlike urge of the blood to continue itself, and it becomes possible for a Shaw to say that "unless Woman repudiates her womanliness, her duty to her husband, to her children, to society, to the law, and to everyone but herself, she cannot emancipate herself."[22] The primary woman, the peasant woman, is *mother*. The whole vocation towards which she has yearned from childhood is included in that one word. But now emerges the Ibsen woman, the comrade, the heroine of a whole megalopolitan literature from Northern drama to Parisian novel. Instead of children, she has soul-conflicts; marriage is a craft-art for the achievement of "mutual understanding." It is all the same whether the case against children is the American lady's who would not miss a season for anything, or the Parisienne's who fears that her lover would leave her, or an Ibsen heroine's who "belongs to herself"—they all belong to themselves and they are all unfruitful. The same fact, in conjunction with the same arguments, is to be found

[22]Shaw, *The Quintessence of Ibsen.*

in the Alexandrian, in the Roman, and, as a matter or course, in every other civilized society—and conspicuously in that in which Buddha grew up. And in Hellenism and in the nineteenth century, as in the times of Lao-Tzu and the Charvaka doctrine,[23] there is an ethic for childless intelligences, and a literature about the inner conflicts of Nora and Nana. The "quiverful," which was still an honorable enough spectacle in the days of Werther, becomes something rather provincial. The father of many children is for the great city a subject for caricature; Ibsen did not fail to note it, and presented it in his *Love's Comedy*.

At this level all Civilizations enter upon a stage, which lasts for centuries, of appalling depopulation. The whole pyramid of cultural man vanishes. It crumbles from the summit, first the world-cities, then the provincial forms, and finally the land itself, whose best blood has incontinently poured into the towns, merely to bolster them up awhile. At the last, only the primitive blood remains, alive, but robbed of its strongest and most promising elements. This residue is the *Fellah type*.

If anything has demonstrated the fact that Causality has nothing to do with history, it is the familiar "decline" of the Classical, which accomplished itself long before the irruption of Germanic migrants[24] The Imperium enjoyed the completest peace; it was rich and highly developed; it was well organized; and it possessed in its emperors from Nerva to Marcus Aurelius a series of rulers such as the Caesarism of no other Civilization can show. And yet the population dwindled, quickly and wholesale. The desperate marriage-and-children laws of Augustus— amongst them the *Lex de maritandis ordinibus*, which dismayed Roman society more than the destruction of Varus's legions—the wholesale adoptions, the incessant plantation of soldiers of barbarian origin to fill the depleted countryside, the immense food-charities of Nerva and Trajan for the children of poor parents—nothing availed to check the process. Italy, then North Africa and Gaul, and finally Spain, which under the early Caesars had been one of the densely populated parts of the Empire, become empty and desolate. The famous saying of Pliny— so often and so significantly quoted today in connexion with national economics—"*Latifundia perdidere Italiam jam, vero et provincias,*"[25] inverts the order of the process; the large estates would never have got to

---

[23]An ancient Hindu materialism.—*Tr.*
[24]For what follows see Eduard Meyer, *Kl. Schriften* (1910), pp. 145, *et seq.*
[25]*Hist. Nat.,* XVIII, 7.—*Tr.*

this point if the peasantry had not already been sucked into the towns and, if not openly, at any rate inwardly, surrendered their soil. The terrible truth came out at last in the edict of Pertinaz, A.D. 193, by which anyone in Italy or the provinces was permitted to take possession of untended land, and if he brought it under cultivation, to hold it as his legal property. The historical student has only to turn his attention seriously to other Civilizations to find the same phenomenon everywhere. Depopulation can be distinctly traced in the background of the Egyptian New Empire, especially from the XIX dynasty onwards. Street widths like those of Amenophis IV at Tell-el-Amarna—of fifty yards—would have been unthinkable with the denser population of the old days. The onset of the "Sea-peoples," too, was only barely repulsed—their chances of obtaining possession of the realm were certainly not less promising than those of the Germans of the fourth century *vis-à-vis* the Roman world. And finally the incessant infiltration of Libyans into the Delta culminated when one of their leaders seized the power, in 945 B.C.— precisely as Odoacer seized it in A.D. 476. But the same tendency can be felt in the history of political Buddhism after the Caesar Asoka.[26] If the Maya population literally vanished within a very short time after the Spanish conquest, and their great empty cities were reabsorbed by the jungle, this does not prove merely the brutality of the conqueror— which in this regard would have been helpless before the self-renewing power of a young and fruitful Culture-mankind—but an extinction from within that no doubt had long been in progress. And if we turn to our own civilization, we find that the old families of the French noblesse were not, in the great majority of cases, eradicated in the Revolution, but have died out since 1815, and their sterility has spread to the bourgeoisie and, since 1870, to the peasantry which that very Revolution almost re-created. In England, and still more in the United States— particularly in the East, the very states where the stock is best and oldest—the process of "race suicide" denounced by Roosevelt set in long ago on the largest scale.

Consequently we find everywhere in these Civilizations that the provincial cities at an early stage, and the giant cities in turn at the end of the evolution, stand empty, harboring in their stone masses a small population of fellaheen who shelter in them as the men of the

---

[26]We know of measures to promote increase of population in China in the third century *B.C.*, precisely the Augustan Age of Chinese evolution. See Rosthorn, *Das soziale Leben der Chinesen* (1919), p. 6.

Stone Age sheltered in caves and pile-dwellings.[27] Samarra was abandoned by the tenth century; Pataliputra, Asoka's capital, was an immense and completely uninhabited waste of houses when the Chinese traveller Hiouentsang visited it about A.D. 635, and many of the great Maya cities must have been in that condition even in Cortez's time. In a long series of Classical writers from Polybius onward[28] we read of old, renowned cities in which the streets have become lines of empty, crumbling shells, where the cattle browse in forum and gymnasium, and the amphitheatre is a sown field,[29] dotted with emergent statues and herms. Rome had in the fifth century of our era the population of a village, but its Imperial palaces were still habitable.

This, then, is the conclusion of the city's history; growing from primitive barter-center to Culture-city and at last to world-city, it sacrifices first the blood and soul of its creators to the needs of its majestic evolution, and then the last flower of that growth to the spirit of Civilization—and so, doomed, moves on to final self-destruction.

VI

If the Early period is characterized by the birth of the City out of the country, and the Late by the battle between city and country, the period Civilization is that of the victory of city over country, whereby it frees itself from the grip of the ground, but to its own ultimate ruin. Rootless, dead to the cosmic, irrevocably committed to stone and to intellectualism it develops a form-language that reproduces every trait of its essence—not the language of a becoming and growth, but that of a becomeness and completion, capable of alteration certainly, but not of evolution. Not now Destiny, but Causality, not now living Direction, but Extension, rules. It follows from this that whereas every form-language of a Culture, together with the history of its evolution, adheres to the original spot, civilized forms are at home anywhere and capable, therefore, of unlimited extension as soon as they appear. It is quite

---

[27] The *amphitheaters* of Nimes and Arles were filled up by mean townlets that used the outer wall as their fortifications.—*Tr.*

[28] Strabo, Pausanias, Dio Chrysostom, Avienus, etc. See E. Meyer, *Kl. Schriften*, pp. 164, *et seq.*

[29] The Colosseum of Rome itself in due course fell into this decay and we read in the guide-books that "its flora were once famous"—420 wild species lived in its ruins. If this could happen in Rome, we need not be surprised at the quick, almost catastrophic, conquest of the Maya cities by tropical vegetation.—*Tr.*

true that the Hanse Towns in their north-Russian staples built Goth-
ically, and the Spaniards in South America in the Baroque style, but
that even the smallest chapter of Gothic style-*history* should *evolve* outside the limits of West Europe was impossible, as impossible as that
Attic or English drama, or the art of fugue, or the Lutheran or the
Orphic religion should be propagated, or even inwardly assimilated, by
men of alien Cultures. But the essence of Alexandrinism and of our
Romanticism is something which belongs to all urban men without
distinction. Romanticism marks the beginning of that which Goethe,
with his wide vision, called world-literature—the literature of the leading world-*city*, against which a provincial literature, native to the soil
but negligible, struggles everywhere with difficulty to maintain itself.
The state of Venice, or that of Frederick the Great, or the English
Parliament (as an effective reality), cannot be reproduced, but "modern
constitutions" can be "introduced" into any African of Asiatic state as
Classical Poleis could be set up amongst Numidians and ancient Britons.
In Egypt the writing that came into common use was not the hiero-
glyphic, but the letter-script, which was without doubt a technical discovery of the Civilization Age.[30] And so in general—it is not true Cul-
ture-languages like the Greek of Sophocles or the German of Luther,
but world-languages like the Greek Koine and Arabic and Babylonian
and English, the outcome of daily practical usage in a world-city,
which are capable of being acquired by anybody and everybody. Consequently, in all Civilizations the "modern" cities assume a more and
more uniform type. Go where we may, there are Berlin, London, and
New York for us, just as the Roman traveller would find his columnar
architecture, his fora with their statuary, and his temples in Palmyra
or Trier or Timgad or the Hellenic cities that extended out to the Indus
and the Aral. But that which was thus disseminated was no longer a
style, but a taste, not genuine custom but mannerism, not national
costume but the fashion. This, of course, makes it possible for remote
peoples not only to accept the "permanent" gains of a Civilization, but
even to re-radiate them in an independent form. Such regions of "moon-
light" civilization are south China and especially Japan (which were
first Sinized at the close of the Han period, about A.D. 220); Java as a
relay of the Brahman Civilization; and Carthage, which obtained its
forms from Babylon.

[30]According to the researches of K. Sethe. Cf Robert Eisler, *Die kenitischen
Weihinschriften der Hyksoszeit,* etc. (1919).

All these are forms of a waking-consciousness now acute to excess, mitigated or limited by no cosmic force, purely intellectual and extensive, but on that very account capable of so powerful an output that their last flickering rays reach out and superpose effects over almost the whole earth. Fragments of the forms of Chinese Civilization are probably to be found in Scandinavian wood-architecture, Babylonian measures probably in the South Seas, Classical coins in South Africa, Egyptian and Indian influences probably in the land of the Incas.

But while this process of extension was overpassing all frontiers, the development of inner form of the Civilization was fulfilling itself with impressive consistency. Three stages are clearly to be distinguished —the release from the Culture, the production of the thoroughbred Civilization-form, and the final hardening. For us this development has now set in, and, as I see it, it is Germany that is destined, as the last nation of the West, to crown the mighty edifice. In this stage all questions of the life—the Apollinian, Magian, or Faustian life—have been thought upon the limit, and brought to a final clear condition of knowledge and not-knowledge. For or about ideas men fight no more. The last idea—that of the Civilization itself—is formulated in outline, and technics and economics are, as *problems,* enunciated and prepared for handling. But this is only the beginning of a vast task; the postulates have to be unfolded and these forms applied to the whole existence of the earth. Only when this has been accomplished and the Civilization has become definitely established not only in shape, but in mass, does the hardening of the form set in. Style, in the Cultures, has been the *rhythm of the process of self-implementing.* But the Civilized style (if we may use the word at all) arises as the *expression of the state of completeness.* It attains—in Egypt and China especially—to a splendid perfection, and imparts this perfection to all the utterances of a life that is now inwardly unalterable, to its ceremonial and mien as to the superfine and studied forms of its art-practice. Of history, in the sense of an urge towards a form-ideal, there can now be no question, but there is an unfailing and easy superficial adaptiveness which again and again manages to coax fresh little art-problems and solutions out of the now basically stable language. Of this kind is the whole "history" of Chinese-Japanese painting (as we know it) and of Indian architecture. And just as the real history of the Gothic style differs from this pseudo-history, so the Knight of the Crusades differs from the Chinese Mandarin—*the becoming state from the finished.* The one *is* history;

the other has long ago overcome history. "Long ago," I say; for the history of these Civilizations is merely apparent, like their great cities, which constantly change in face, but never become other than what they are. In these cities there is no Soul. They are land in petrified form.

What is it that perishes here? And what that survives? It is a mere incident the German peoples, under pressure from the Huns take possession of the Roman landscape and so prevent the Classical from prolonging itself in a "Chinese" end-state. The movement of the "Sea-peoples" (similar to the Germanic, even down to the details) which set in against the Egyptian Civilization from 1400 B.C. succeeded only as regards the Cretan island-realm—their mighty expeditions against the Libyan and Phoenician coasts, with the accompaniment of Viking fleets, failed, as those of the Huns failed against China. And thus the Classical is our one example of a Civilization broken off in the moment of full splendour. Yet the Germans only destroyed the upper layer of the forms and replaced it by the life of their own pre-Culture. The "eternal" layer was never reached. It remains, hidden and completely shrouded by a new form-language, in the underground of the whole following history, and to this day in southern France, southern Italy, and northern Spain tangible relics of it endure. In these countries the popular Catholicism is tinged from beneath with a Late Classical coloring, that sets it off quite distinctly from the Church Catholicism of the West-European layer above it. South Italian Church-festivals disclose Classical (and even pre-Classical) cults, and generally in this field there are to be found deities (saints) in whose worship the Classical constitution is visible behind the Catholic names.

Here, however, another element comes into the picture, an element with a significance of its own. We stand before the problem of Race.

THREE

THE CHICAGO SCHOOL

THE CITY: SUGGESTIONS
FOR THE INVESTIGATION
OF HUMAN BEHAVIOR
IN THE URBAN ENVIRONMENT
Robert Park

The city, from the point of view of this paper, is something more than a congeries of individual men and of social conveniences—streets, buildings, electric lights, tramways, and telephones, etc.; something more, also, than a mere constellation of institutions and administrative devices—courts, hospitals, schools, police, and civil functionaries of various sorts. The city is, rather, a state of mine, a body of customs and traditions, and of the organized attitudes and sentiments that inhere in these customs and are transmitted with this tradition. The city is not, in other words, merely a physical mechanism and an artifical construction. It is involved in the vital process of the people who compose it; it is a product of nature, and particularly of human nature.

The city has, as Oswald Spengler has recently pointed out, its own culture: "What his house is to the peasant, the city is to civilized man. As the house has its household gods, so has the city its protecting Deity, its local saint. The city also, like the peasant's hut, has its roots in the soil."[1]

The city has been studied, in recent times, from the point of view of its geography, and still more recently from the point of view of its ecology. There are forces at work within the limits of the urban community—within the limits of any natural area of human habitation, in fact—which tend to bring about an orderly and typical grouping of its population and institutions. The science which seeks to isolate these

Reprinted by permission of the University of Chicago from *The American Journal of Sociology*, Vol. XX. Copyright 1916 by the University of Chicago.

[1] Oswald Spengler, *Der Untergang des Abendlandes*, IV (München, 922), 105.

factors and to describe the typical constellation of persons and institutions which the co-operation of these forces produces, is what we call
human, as distinguished from plant and animal, ecology.

Transportation and communication, tramways and telephones,
newspapers and advertising, steel construction and elevators—all things,
in fact, which tend to bring about at once a greater mobility and a
greater concentration of the urban populations—are primary factors in
the ecological organization of the city.

The city is not, however, merely a geographical and ecological
unit; it is at the same time an economic unit. The economic organization of the city is based on the division of labor. The multiplication
of occupations and professions within the limits of the urban population
is one of the most striking and least understood aspects of modern city
life. From this point of view, we may, if we choose, think of the city,
that is to say, the place and the people, with all the machinery and administrative devices that go with them, as organically related; a kind of
psychophysical mechanism in and through which private and political
interests find not merely a collective but a corporate expression.

Much of what we ordinarily regard as the city—its charters, formal organization, buildings, street railways, and so forth—is, or seems
to be, mere artifact. But these things in themselves are utilities, adventitious devices which become part of the living city only when, and in
so far as, through use and wont they connect themselves, like a tool in
the hand of man, with the vital forces resident in individuals and in
the community.

The city is, finally, the natural habitat of civilized man. It is for
that reason a cultural area characterized by its own peculiar cultural
type:

"It is a quite certain, but never fully recognized, fact," says Spengler, "that all great cultures are city-born. The outstanding man of the
second generation is a city-building animal. This is the actual criterion
of world-history, as distinguished from the history of mankind: world-
history is the history of city men. Nations, governments, politics, and
religions—all rest on the basic phenomenon of human existence, the
city."[2]

Anthropology, the science of man, has been mainly concerned up
to the present with the study of primitive peoples. But civilized man is
quite as interesting an object of investigation, and at the same time

[2]Oswald Spengler, *Untergang des Abendlandes,* IV, 106.

his life is more open to observation and study. Urban life and culture are more varied, subtle, and complicated, but the fundamental motives are in both instances the same. The same patient methods of observation which anthropologists like Boas and Lowie have expended on the study of the life and manners of the North American Indian might be even more fruitfully employed in the investigation of the customs, beliefs, social practices, and general conception of life prevalent in Little Italy on the lower North Side in Chicago, or in recording the more sophisticated folkways of the inhabitants of Greenwich Village and the neighborhood of Washington Square, New York.

We are mainly indebted to writers of fiction for our more intimate knowledge of contemporary urban life. But the life of our cities demands a more searching and disinterested study than even Emile Zola has given us in his "experimental" novels and the annals of the Rougon-Macquart family.

We need such studies, if for no other reason than to enable us to read the newspapers intelligently. The reason that the daily chronicle of the newspaper is so shocking, and at the same time so fascinating, to the average reader is because the average reader knows so little about the life of which the newspaper is the record.

The observations which follow are intended to define a point of view and to indicate a program for the study of urban life: its physical organization, its occupations, and its culture.

I. The City Plan and Local Organization

The city, particularly the modern American city, strikes one at first blush as so little a product of the artless processes of nature and growth, that it is difficult to recognize it as a living entity. The ground plan of most American cities, for example, is a checkerboard. The unit of distance is the block. This geometrical form suggests that the city is a purely artificial construction which might conceivably be taken apart and put together again, like a house of blocks.

The fact is, however, that the city is rooted in the habits and customs of the people who inhabit it. The consequence is that the city possesses a moral as well as a physical organization, and these two mutually interact in characteristic ways to mold and modify one another. It is the structure of the city which first impresses us by its visible vastness and complexity. But this structure has its basis, nevertheless, in human nature, of which it is an expression. On the other hand, this vast organization which has arisen in response to the needs of its inhabitants, one formed, imposes itself upon them as a crude external fact, and form them, in turn, in accordance with the design and interests which it incorporates. Structure and tradition are but different aspects of a single cultural complex which determines what is characteristic and peculiar to city, as distinguished from village, life and the life of the open fields.

The City Plan

It is because the city has a life quite its own that there is a limit to the arbitrary modifications which it is possibe to make (1) in its physical structure and (2) in its moral order.

The city plan, for example, establishes metes and bounds, fixes in a general way the location and character of the city's constructions, and imposes an orderly arrangement, within the city area, upon the buildings which are erected by private initiative as well as by public authority. Within the limitations prescribed, however, the inevitable processes of human nature proceed to give these regions and these buildings a character which it is less easy to control. Under our system of individual ownership, for instance, it is not possible to determine in advance the extent of concentration of population which is likely to occur in any given area. The city cannot fix land values, and we leave to private enterprise, for the most part, the task of determining the city's limits and the location of its residential and industrial districts. Personal tastes and convenience, vocational and economic interests, infallibly tend to segregate and thus to classify the populations of great cities. In this way the city acquires an organization and distribution of population which is neither designed nor controlled.

The Bell Telephone Company is now making, particularly in New York and Chicago, elaborate investigations, the purpose of which is to determine, in advance of its actual changes, the probable growth and distribution of the urban population within the metropolitan areas. The Sage Foundation, in the course of its city-planning studies sought to find mathematical formulae that would enable them to predict future expansion and limits of population in New York City. The recent development of chain stores has made the problem of location a matter of concern to different chain-store corporations. The result has been the rise of a new profession.

There is now a class of experts whose sole occupation is to discover and locate, with something like scientific accuracy, taking account of the changes which present tendencies seem likely to bring about, restaurants, cigar stores, drug-stores, and other smaller retail business units whose success depends largely on location. Real estate men are not infrequently willing to finance a local business of this sort in locations which they believe will be profitable, accepting as their rent a percentage of the profits.

Physical geography, natural advantages and disadvantages, including means of transportation, determine in advance the general outlines of the urban plan. As the city increases in population, the subtler influences of sympathy, rivalry, and economic necessity tend to control the distribution of population. Business and industry seek advantageous locations and draw around them certain portions of the population. There spring up fashionable residence quarters from which the poorer classes are excluded because of the increased value of the land. Then there grow up slums which are inhabited by great numbers of the poorer classes who are unable to defend themselves from association with the derelict and vicious.

In the course of time every section and quarter of the city takes on something of the character and qualities of its inhabitants. Each separate part of the city is inevitably stained with the peculiar sentiments of its population. The effect of this is to convert what was at first a mere geographical expression into a neighborhood, that is to say, a locality with sentiments, traditions, and a history of its own. Within this neighborhood the continuity of the historical processes is somehow maintained. The past imposes itself upon the present, and the life of every locality moves on with a certain momentum of its own, more or less independent of the larger circle of life and interests about it.

The organization of the city, the character of the urban environment and of the discipline which it imposes is finally determined by the size of the population, its concentration and distribution within the city area. For this reason it is important to study the growth of cities, to compare the idiosyncrasies in the distribution of city populations. Some of the first things we want to know about the city, therefore are:

What are the sources of the city's population?

What part of its population growth is normal, i.e., due to excess of births over deaths?

What part is due to migration (*a*) of native stocks? (*b*) foreign stocks?

What are the outstanding "natural" areas, i.e., areas of population segregation?

How is distribution of population within the city area affected by (*a*) economic interest, i.e., land values? (*b*) by sentimental interest, race? vocation, etc.?

Where within the city is the population declining? Where is it expanding?

Where are population growth and the size of families within the different natural areas of the city correlated with births and deaths, with marriages and divorces, with house rents and standards of living?

The Neighborhood

Proximity and neighborly contact are the basis for the simplest and most elementary form of association with which we have to do in the organization of city life. Local interests and associations breed local sentiment, and, under a system which makes residence the basis for participation in the government, the neighborhood becomes the basis of political control. In the social and political organization of the city it is the smallest local unit.

It is surely one of the most remarkable of all social facts that, coming down from untold ages, there should be this instinctive understanding that the man who establishes his home beside yours begins to have a claim upon your sense of comradeship. . . . . The neighborhood is a social unit which, by its clear definition of outline, its inner organic completeness, its hair-trigger reactions, may be fairly considered as functioning like a social mind. . . . . The local boss, however autocratic he may be in the larger sphere of the city with the power he gets from the neighborhood, must always be in and of the people; and he is very careful not to try to deceive the local people so far as their local interests are concerned. It is hard to fool a neighborhood about its own affairs.[3]

The neighborhood exists without formal organization. The local improvement society is a structure erected on the basis of the spontaneous neighborhood organization and exists for the purpose of giving

[3]Robert A. Woods, "The Neighborhood in Social Reconstruction," *Papers and Proceedings of the Eighth Annual Meeting of the American Sociological Society, 1913.*

expression to the local sentiment in regard to matters of local interest.

Under the complex influences of the city life, what may be called the normal neighborhood sentiment has undergone many curious and interesting changes, and produced many unusual types of local communities. More than that, there are nascent neighborhoods and neighborhoods in process of dissolution. Consider, for example, Fifth Avenue, New York, which probably never had an improvement association, and compare with it 135th Street in the Bronx (where the Negro population is probably more concentrated than in any other single spot in the world), which is rapidly becoming a very intimate and highly organized community.

In the history of New York the significance of the name Harlem has changed from Dutch to Irish to Jewish to Negro. Of these changes the last has come most swiftly. Throughout colored America, from Massachusetts to Mississippi and across the continent to Los Angeles and Seattle, its name, which as late as fifteen years ago had scarcely been heard, now stands for the Negro metropolis. Harlem is, indeed, the great Mecca for the sight-seer, the pleasure-seeker, the curious, the adventurous, the enterprising, the ambitious, and the talented of the Negro world; for the lure of it has reached down to every island of the Carib Sea and has penetrated even into Africa.[4]

It is important to know what are the forces which tend to break up the tensions, interests, and sentiments which give neighborhoods their individual character. In general these may be said to be anything and everything that tends to render the population unstable, to divide and concentrate attentions upon widely separated objects of interest.

What part of the population is floating?

Of what elements, i.e., races, classes, etc., is this population composed?

How many people live in hotels, apartments, and tenements?

How many people own their own homes?

What proportion of the population consists of nomads, hobos, gypsies?

On the other hand, certain urban neighborhoods suffer from isolation. Efforts have been made at different times to reconstruct and quicken the life of city neighborhoods and to bring them in touch with the larger interests of the community. Such is, in part, the purpose of the social settlements. These organizations and others which

[4] James Weldon Johnson, "The Making of Harlem," *Survey Graphic*, March 1, 1925.

are attempting to reconstruct city life have developed certain methods
and a technique for stimulating and controlling local communities. We
should study, in connection with the investigation of these agencies,
these methods and this technique, since it is just the method by which
objects are practically controlled that reveals their essential nature,
that is to say, their predictable character (*Gesetzmässigkeit.*)[5]

In many of the European cities, and to some extent in this country, reconstruction of city life has gone to the length of building garden suburbs, or replacing unhealthful and run-down tenements with
model buildings owned and controlled by the municipality.

In American cities the attempt has been made to renovate evil
neighborhoods by the construction of playgrounds and the introduction of supervised sports of various kinds, including municipal dances
in municipal dance halls. These and other devices which are intended
primarily to elevate the moral tone of the segregated populations of
great cities should be studied in connection with the investigation of
the neighborhood in general. They should be studied, in short, not
merely for their own sake, but for what they can reveal to us of human
behavior and human nature generally.

Colonies and Segregated Areas

In the city environment the neighborhood tends to lose much of the
significance which it possessed in simpler and more primitive forms of
society. The easy means of communication and of transportation, which
enable individuals to distribute their attention and to live at the same
time in several different worlds, tend to destroy the permanency and
intimacy of the neighborhood. On the other hand, the isolation of the
immigrant and racial colonies of the so-called ghettos and areas of
population segregation tend to preserve and, where there is racial prejudice, to intensify the intimacies and solidarity of the local and neighborhood groups. Where individuals of the same race or of the same

---

[5]"Wenn wir daher das Wort (Natur) als einen logischen Terminus in der
Wissenschaftslehre gabrauchen wollen, so werden wir sagen dürfen, dass Natur
die Wirklichkeit ist mit Rücksicht auf ihren gesetzmässigen Zusammenhang.
Diese Bedeutung finden wir z. B. in dem Worte Naturgesetz. Dann aber kön-
nen wir die Natur der Dinge auch das nennen was in die Begriffe eingeht,
oder am kürzesten uns dahin ausdrücken: die Natur ist die Wirklichkeit mit
Rücksicht auf das Allgemeine. So gewinnt dann das Wort erst eine logische
Bedeutung" (H. Rickert, *Die Grenzen der naturwissenschaftlichen Begriffs-
bildung,* p. 212).

vocation live together in segregated groups, neighborhood sentiment tends to fuse together with racial antagonisms and class interests.

Physical and sentimental distances reinforce each other, and the influences of local distribution of the population participate with the influences of class and race in the evolution of the social organization. Every great city has its racial colonies, like the Chinatowns of San Francisco and New York, the Little Sicily of Chicago, and various other less pronounced types. In addition to these, most cities have their segregated vice districts, like that which until recently existed in Chicago, their rendezvous for criminals of various sorts. Every large city has its occupational suburbs, like the Stockyards in Chicago, and its residential enclaves, like Brookline in Boston, the so-called "Gold Coast" in Chicago, Greenwich Village in New York, each of which has the size and character of a complete separate town, village, or city, except that its population is a selected one. Undoubtedly the most remarkable of these cities within cities, of which the most interesting characteristic is that they are composed of persons of the same race, or of persons of different races but of the same social class, is East London, with a population of 2,000,000 laborers.

The people of the original East London have now overflowed and crossed the Lea, and spread themselves over the marshes and meadows beyond. This population has created new towns which were formerly rural villages. West Ham, with a population of nearly 300,000; East Ham, with 90,000; Stratford, with its "daughters," 150,000; and other "hamlets" similarly overgrown. Including these new populations, we have an aggregate of nearly two millions of people. The population is greater than that of Berlin or Vienna, or St. Petersburg, or Philadelphia.

It is a city full of churches and places of worship, yet there are no cathedrals, either Anglican or Roman; it has a sufficient supply of elementary schools, but it has no public or high school, and it has no colleges for the higher education and no university; the people all read newspapers, yet there is no East London paper except of the smaller and local kind. . . . In the streets there are never seen any private carriages; there is no fasionable quarter . . . one meets no ladies in the principal thoroughfares. People, shops, houses, conveyances–all together are stamped with the unmistakable seal of the working class.

Perhaps the strangest thing of all is this: in a city of two millions of people there are no hotels! That means, of course, that there are no visitors.[6]

In the older cities of Europe, where the processes of segregation

[6]Walter Besant, *East London*, pp. 7-9.

have gone farther, neighborhood distinctions are likely to be more marked than they are in America. East London is a city of a single class, but within the limits of that city the population is segregated again and again by racial, cultural, and vocational interests. Neighborhood sentiment, deeply rooted in local tradition and in local custom, exercises a decisive selective influence upon the populations of the older European cities and shows itself ultimately in a marked way in the characteristics of the inhabitants.

What we want to know of these neighborhoods, racial communities, and segregated city areas, existing within or on the outer rims of great cities, is what we want to know of all other social groups:

What are the elements of which they are composed?

To what extent are they the product of a selective process?

How do people get in and out of the group thus formed?

What are the relative permanence and stability of their populations?

What about the age, sex, and social condition of the people?

What about the children? How many of them are born, and how many of them remain?

What is the history of the neighborhood? What is there in the subconsciousness—in the forgotten or dimly remembered experiences—of this neighborhood which determines its sentiments and attitudes?

What is there in clear consciousness, i.e., what are its avowed sentiments, doctrines, etc.?

What does it regard as matter of fact? What is news? What is the general run of attention? What models does it imitate and are these within or without the group?

What is the social ritual, i.e., what things must one do in the neighborhood in order to escape being regarded with suspicion or looked upon as peculiar?

Who are the leaders? What interests of the neighborhood do they incorporate in themselves and what is the technique by which they exercise control?

II. Industrial Organization and the Moral Order

The ancient city was primarily a fortress, a place of refuge in time of war. The modern city, on the contrary, is primarily a convenience of commerce, and owes its existence to the market place around which it sprang up. Industrial competition and the division of labor, which have probably done most to develop the latent powers of mankind, are possible only upon condition of the existence of markets, of money, and other devices for the facilitation of trade and commerce.

An old German adage declares that "city air makes men free" (*Stadt Luft macht frei*). This is doubtless a reference to the days when the free cities of Germany enjoyed the patronage of the emperor, and laws made the fugitive serf a free man if he succeeded for a year and a day in breathing city air. Law, of itself, could not, however, have made the craftsman free. An open market in which he might sell the products of his labor was a necessary incident of his freedom, and it was the application of the money economy to the relations of master and man that completed the emancipation of the serf.

Vocational Classes and Vocational Types

The old adage which describes the city as the natural environment of the free man still holds so far as the individual man finds in the chances, the diversity of interests and tasks, and in the vast unconscious co-operation of city life the opportunity to choose his own vocation and develop his peculiar individual talents. The city offers a market for the special talents of individual men. Personal competition tends to select for each special task the individual who is best suited to perform it.

The difference of natural talents in different men is, in reality, much less than we are aware of; and the very different genius which appears to distinguish men of different professions, when grown up to maturity, is not upon many occasions so much the cause, as the effect of the division of labour. The difference between the most dissimilar characters, between a philosopher and a common street porter, for example, seems to arise not so much from nature, as from habit custom, and education. When they came into the world, and for the first six or eight years of their existence, they were perhaps very much alike, and neither their parents nor playfellows could perceive any remarkable difference. About that age, or soon after, they come to be employed in different occupations. The difference of talents comes then to be taken notice of, and widens by degrees, till at last the vanity of the philosopher is willing to acknowledge scarce any resemblance. But without the disposition to truck, barter, and exchange, every man must have procured to himself every necessary and conveniency of life which he wanted. All must have had the same duties to perform, and the same work to do, and there could have been no such difference of employment as could alone give occasion to any great difference of talent. . . .

As it is the power of exchanging that gives occasion to the division of labour, so the extent of this division must always be limited by the extent of that power, or, in other words, by the extent of the market. . . .There are some sorts of industry, even of the lowest kind, which can be carried on nowhere but in a great town.[7]

Success, under conditions of personal competition, depends upon concentration upon some single task, and this concentration stimulates the demand for rational methods, technical devices, and exceptional skill. Exceptional skill, while based on natural talent, requires special preparation, and it has called into existence the trade and professional schools, and finally bureaus for vocational guidance. All of these, either directly or indirectly, serve at once to select and emphasize individual differences.

Every device which facilitates trade and industry prepares the way for a further division of labor and so tends further to specialize the tasks in which men find their vocations.

The outcome of this process is to break down or modify the older social and economic organization of society, which was based on family ties, local associations, on culture, caste, and status, and to substitute for it an organization based on occupation and vocational interests.

In the city every vocation, even that of a beggar, tends to assume the character of a profession and the discipline which success in any vocation imposes, together with the associations that it enforces, emphasizes this tendency—the tendency, namely, not merely to specialize, but to rationalize one's occupation and to develop a specific and conscious technique for carrying it on.

The effect of the vocations and the division of labor is to produce, in the first instance, not social groups, but vocational types: the actor, the plumber, and the lumber-jack. The organizations, like the trade and labor unions which men of the same trade or profession form, are based on common interests. In this respect they differ from forms of association like the neighborhood, which are based on contiguity, personal association, and the common ties of humanity. The different trades and professions seem disposed to group themselves in classes, that is to say, the artisan, business, and professional classes. But in the modern democratic state the classes have as yet attained no effective organization. Socialism, founded or an effort to create an organization based on "class consciousness," has never succeeded, except, perhaps, in Russia, in creating more than a political party.

[7]Adam Smith, *The Wealth of Nations*, pp. 28-29.

The effects of the division of labor as a discipline, i.e., as means of molding character, may therefore be best studied in the vocational types it has produced. Among the types which it would be interesting to study are: the shopgirl, the policeman, the peddler, the cabman, the nightwatchmen, the clairvoyant, the vaudeville performer, the quack doctor, the bartender, the ward boss, the strikebreaker, the labor agitator, the school teacher, the reporter, the stockbroker, the pawnbroker; all of these are characteristic products of the conditions of city life; each, with its special experience, insight, and point of view determines for each vocational group and for the city as a whole its individuality.

To what extent is the grade of intelligence represented in the different trades and professions dependent upon natural ability?

To what extent is intelligence determined by the character of the occupation and the conditions under which it is practiced?

To what extent is success in the occupations dependent upon sound judgment and common-sense; to what extent upon technical ability?

Does native ability or special training determine success in the different vocations?

What prestige and what prejudices attach to different trades and professions and why?

Is the choice of the occupation determined by temperamental, by economic, or by sentimental considerations?

In what occupations do men, in what occupations do women, succeed better, and why?

How far is occupation, rather than association, responsible for the mental attitude and moral predilections? Do men in the same profession or trade, but representing different nationalities and different cultural groups, hold characteristic and identical opinions?

To what extent is the social or political creed, that is, socialism, anarchism, syndicalism, etc., determined by occupation? by temperament?

To what extent have social doctrine and social idealism superseded and taken the place of religious faith in the different occupations, and why?

Do social classes tend to assume the character of cultural groups? That is to say, do the classes tend to acquire the exclusiveness and independence of a caste or nationality; or is each class always dependent upon the existence of a corresponding class?

To what extent do children follow the vocations of their parents and why?

To what extent do indiviuals move from one class to another, and how does this fact modify the character of class relationships?

News and the Mobility of the Social Group

The division of labor, in making individual success dependent upon concentration upon a special task, has had the effect of increasing the interdependence of the different vocations. A social organization is thus created in which the individual becomes increasingly dependent upon the community of which he is an integral part. The effect, under conditions of personal competition, of this increasing interdependence of the parts is to create in the industrial organization as a whole a certain sort of social solidarity, but a solidarity based, not on sentiment and habit, but on community of interests.

In the sense in which the terms are here used, sentiment is the more concrete, interest the more abstract, term. We may cherish a sentiment for a person, a place, or any object whatsoever, It may be a sentiment of aversion, or a sentiment of possession. But to possess or to be possessed by a sentiment for, or in regard to, anything means that we are incapable of acting toward it in a thoroughly rational way. It means that the object of our sentiment corresponds in some special way to some inherited or acquired disposition. Such a disposition is the affection of a mother for her child, which is instinctive. Or even the feeling she may have for the child's empty cradle, which is acquired.

The existence of a sentimental attitude indicates that there are motives for action of which the individual who is moved by them is not wholly conscious; motives over which he has only a partial control. Every sentiment has a history, either in the experience of the individual, or in the experience of the race, but the person who acts on the sentiment may not be aware of the history.

Interests are directed less toward specific objects than toward the ends which this or that particular object at one time or another embodies. Interests imply, therefore, the existence of means and a consciousness of the distinction between means and ends. Our sentiments are related to our prejudices, and prejudices may attach to anything— persons, races, as well as inanimate things. Prejudices are related also to taboos, and so tend to maintain "social distances" and the existing social organization. Sentiment and prejudice are elementary forms of conservatism. Our interests are rational and mobile, and make for change.

Money is the cardinal device by which values have become rationalized and sentiments have been replaced by interests. It is just because we feel no personal and no sentimental attitude toward our money, such as we do toward, for example, our home, that money becomes a valuable means of exchange. We will be interested in acquiring a certain amount of money in order to achieve a certain purpose, but provided that purpose may be achieved in any other way we are likely to be just as well satisfied. It is only the miser who becomes sentimental about money, and in that case he is likely to prefer one sort of money, say gold, to another, irrespective of its value. In this case the value of gold is determined by personal sentiment rather than by reason.

An organization which is composed of competing individuals and of competing groups of individuals is in a state of unstable equilibrium, and this equilibrium can be maintained only by a process of continuous readjustment. This aspect of social life and this type of social organization are best represented in the world of business which is the special object of investigation of political economy.

The extension of industrial organization, which is based on the impersonal relations defined by money, has gone forward hand in hand with an increasing mobility of the population. The laboring man and the artisan fitted to perform a specific task are compelled, under the conditions created by city life, to move from one region to another in search of the particular kind of employment which they are fitted to perform. The tide of immigration which moves back and forth between Europe and America is to some extent a measure of this same mobility.[8]

On the other hand, the tradesman, the manufacturer, the professional man, the specialist in every vocation, seeks his clients as the difficulties of travel and communication decrease over an ever widening area of territory. This is another way in which the mobility of the population may be measured. However, mobility in an individual or in a population is measured, not merely by change of location, but rather by the number and variety of the stimulations to which the individual or the population responds. Mobility depends, not merely upon transportation, but upon communication. Education and the ability to read, the extension of the money economy to an ever increasing number of the interests of life, in so far as it has tended to depersonalize social relations, has at the same time vastly increased the mobility of modern peoples.

The term "mobility," like its correlative, "isolation," covers a wide range of phenomena. It may represent at the same time a character and

[8]Walter Bagehot *The Postulates of Political Economy* (London, 1885), pp. 7-8.

a condition. As isolation may be due to the existence of purely physical barriers to communication, or to a peculiarity of temperament and a lack of education, so mobility may be a consequence of the natural means of communication or of an agreeable manner and college education.

It is now clearly recognized that what we ordinarily call a lack of intelligence in individuals, races, and communities is frequently a result of isolation. On the other hand, the mobility of a population is unquestionably a very large factor in its intellectual development.

There is an intimate connection between the immobility of the primitive man and his so-called inability to use abstract ideas. The knowledge which a peasant ordinarily possesses, from the very nature of his occupation, is concrete and personal. He knows individually and personally every member of the flock he tends. He becomes in the course of years so attached to the land he tills that the mere transposition from the strip of soil on which he has grown up to another with which he is less intimately acquainted is felt by him as a personal loss. For such a man the neighboring valley, or even the strip of land at the other end of the village is in a certain sense alien territory. A large part of the peasant's efficiency as an agricultural laborer depends upon this intimate and personal acquaintance with the idiosyncrasies of a single plot of land to the care of which he has been bred. It is apparent that, under conditions like there, very little of the peasant's practical knowledge will take the abstract form of scientific generalization. He thinks in concrete terms because he knows and needs no other.

On the other hand, the intellectual characteristics of the Jew and his generally recognized interest in abstract and radical ideas are unquestionably connected with the fact that the Jews are, before all else, a city folk. The "Wandering Jew" acquires abstract terms with which to describe the various scenes which he visits. His knowledge of the world is based upon identities and differences, that is to say, on analysis and classification. Reared in intimate association with the bustle and business of the market place, constantly intent on the shrewd and fascinating game of buying and selling, in which he employs that most interesting of abstractions, money, he has neither opportunity nor inclination to cultivate that intimate attachment to places and persons which is characteristic of the immobile person.[8a]

Concentration of populations in cities, the wider markets, the division of labor, the concentration of individuals and groups or special tasks, have continually changed the material conditions of life, and in doing this have made readjustments to novel conditions increasingly

---

[8a]Cf. W. I. Thomas, *Source Book of Social Origins*, p. 169.

necessary. Out of this necessity there have grown up a number of special organizations which exist for the special purpose of facilitating these readjustments. The market which brought the modern city into existence is one of these devices. More interesting however, are the exchanges, particularly the stock exchange and the board of trade, where prices are constantly being made in response to changes, or rather the reports of changes, in economic conditions all over the world.

These reports, so far as they are calculated to cause readjustments, have the character of what we call news. It is the existence of a critical situation which converts what were otherwise mere information into news. Where there is an issue at stake, where, in short, there is crisis, there information which might affect the outcome one way or another becomes "live matter," as the newspaper men say. Live matter is news; dead matter is mere information.

What is the relation of mobility to suggestion, imitation, etc.?

What are the practical devices by which suggestibility and mobility are increased in a community or in an individual?

Are there pathological conditions in communities corresponding to hysteria in individuals? If so, how are they produced and how controlled?

To what extent is fashion an indication of mobility?

What is the difference in the manner in which fashions and customs are transmitted?

What is social unrest, and what are the conditions under which it manifests itself?

What are the characteristics of a progressive, what the characteristics of a static, community in respect to its resistence to novel suggestions?

What mental characteristics of the gypsy, of the hobo, and of the nomad generally can be traced to these nomadic habits?

The Stock Exchanges and the Mob

The exchanges, upon which we may watch the fluctuation of prices in response to the news of economic conditions in different parts of the world, are typical. Similar readjustments are taking place in every department of social life, where, however, the devices for making these readjustments are not so complete and perfect. For example, the professional and trade papers, which keep the profession and the trades informed in regard to new methods, experiences, and devices, serve to keep the members of these trades and professions abreast of the times, which means that they facilitate readjustments to changing conditions.

There is, however, this important distinction to be made: Competition in the exchanges is more intense; changes are more rapid and, as far as the individuals directly concerned, more momentous. In contrast with such a constellation of forces as we find on the exchanges, where competing dealers meet to buy and sell, so mobile a form of social organization as the crowd and the mob exhibits a relative stability.

It is a commonplace that decisive factors in the movements of crowds, as in the fluctuations of markets, are psychologic. This means that among the individuals who make up the crowd, or who compose the public which participates in the movements reflected in the market, a condition of instability exists which corresponds to what has been defined elsewhere as crisis. It is true of the exchanges, as it is of crowds, that the situation they represent is always critical, that is to say, the tensions are such that a slight cause may precipitate an enormous effect. The current euphemism, "the psychological moment," defines such a critical condition.

Psychological moments may arise in any social situation, but they occur more frequently in a society which has acquired a high state of mobility. They occur more frequently in a society where education is general, where railways, telegraph, and the printing press have become an indispensable part of the social economy. They occur more frequently in cities than in smaller communities. In the crowd and the public every moment may be said to be "psychological."

Crisis may be said to be the normal condition on the exchanges. What are called financial crises are merely an extension of this critical condition to the larger business community. Financial panics which sometimes follow upon financial crises are a precipitate of this critical condition.

The fascinating thing about the study of crises, as of crowds, is that in so far as they are in fact due to psychological causes, that is, in so far as they are the result of the mobility of the communities in which they occur, they can be controlled. The evidence for this is the fact that they can be manipulated, and there is abundant evidence of manipulation in the transactions of the stock market. The evidence for the manipulation of crowds is less accessible. Labor organizations have, however, known how to develop a pretty definite technique for the instigation and control of strikes. The Salvation Army has worked out a book of tactics which is very largely devoted to the handling of street crowds; and professional revivalists, like Billy Sunday, have an elaborate technique for conducting their revivals.

Under the title of collective psychology much has been written in recent years in regard to crowds and kindred phenomena of social life. Most that has been written thus far has been based upon general observation and almost no systematic methods exist for the study of this type of social organization. The practical methods which practical men like the political boss, the labor agitator, the stock-exchange speculator, and others have worked out for the control and manipulation of the public and the crowd furnish a body of materials from which it is possible to make a more detailed, a more intimate study of what may be called, in order to distinguish it from that of more highly organized groups, collective behavior.

The city, and particularly the great city, in which more than elsewhere human relations are likely to be impersonal and rational, defined in terms of interest and in terms of cash, is in a very real sense a laboratory for the investigation of collective behavior. Strikes and minor revolutionary movements are endemic in the urban environment. Cities, and particularly the great cities, are in unstable equilibrium. The result is that the vast casual and mobile aggregations which constitute our urban populations are in a state of perpetual agitation, swept by every new wind of doctrine, subect to constant alarms, and in consequence the community is in a chronic condition of crisis.

What has been said suggests first of all the importance of a more detailed and fundamental study of collective behavior. The questions which follow will perhaps suggest lines of investigation that could be followed profitably by students of urban life.

What is the psychology of crisis? What is the cycle of events involved in the evolution of a crisis, political or economic?

To what extent may the parliamentary system, including the electoral system, be regarded as an attempt to regularize revolution and to meet and control crises?

To what extent are mob violence, strikes, and radical political movement the results of the same general conditions that provoke financial panics, real estate booms, and mass movements in the population generally?

To what extent are the existing unstable equilibrium and social ferment due to the extent and speed of economic changes as reflected in the stock exchange?

What are the effects of the extension of communication and of news upon fluctuations in the stock market and economic changes generally?

Does the scale of stocks on the exchanges tend to exaggerate the fluctuations in the market, or to stabilize them?

Do the reports in the newspapers, so far as they represent the facts, and to speed up social changes, or to stabilize a movement already in progress?

What is the effect of propaganda and rumor in cases where the sources of accurate information are cut off?

To what extent can fluctuations of the stock market be controlled by formal regulation?

To what extent can social changes, strikes, and revolutionary movement be controlled by the censorship?

To what extent can the scientific forecasting of economic and social changes exercise a useful control over the trend of prices and of events?

To what extent can the prices recorded by the stock exchange be compared with public opinion as recorded by the newspaper?

To what extent can the city, which responds more quickly and more decisively to changing events, be regarded as a nerve center of the social organism?

III. Secondary Relations and Social Control

Modern methods of urban transportation and communication—the electric railway, the automobile, the telephone, and the radio—have silently and rapidly changed in recent years the social and industrial organization of the modern city. They have been the means of concentrating traffic in the business districts, have changed the whole character of retail trade, multiplying the residence suburbs and making the department store possible. These changes in the industrial organization and in the distribution of the population have been accompanied by corresponding changes in the habits, sentiments, and character of the urban population.

The general nature of these changes is indicated by the fact that the growth of cities has been accompanied by the substitution of indirect, "secondary," for direct, face-to-face, "primary" relations in the association of individuals in the community.

By primary groups I mean those characterized by intimate face-to-face association and co-operation. They are primary in several senses, but chiefly in that they are fundamental in forming the social nature and ideals of the individual. The result of intimate association, psychologically, is a certain fusion of individualities in a common whole, so that one's very self, for many purposes at least, is the common life and purpose of the group. Perhaps the simplest way of describing this wholeness is by saying that it is a "we"; it involves the sort of sympathy and mutual identification of which "we" is the natural expression. One lives in the feeling of the whole and finds the chief aims of his will in that feeling. . . .[9]

Touch and sight, physical contact, are the basis for the first and most elementary human relationships. Mother and child, husband and wife, father and son, master and servant, kinsman and neighbor, minister, physician, and teacher—these are the most intimate and real relationships of life, and in the small community they are practically inclusive.

The interactions which take place among the members of a community so constituted are immediate and unreflecting. Intercourse is carried on largely within the region of instinct and feeling. Social control arises, for the most part spontaneously, in direct response to personal influences and public sentiment. It is the result of a personal accommodation, rather than the formulation of a rational and abstract principle.

The Church, the School, and the Family

In a great city, where the population is unstable, where parents and children are employed out of the house and often in distant parts of the city, where thousands of people live side by side for years without so much as bowing acquaintance, these intimate relationships of the primary group are weakened and the moral order which rested upon them is gradually dissolved.

Under the disintegrating influences of city life most of our traditional institutions, the church, the school, and the family, have been greatly modified. The school, for example, has taken over some of the functions of the family. It is around the public school and its solicitude for the moral and physical welfare of the children that something like a new neighborhood and community spirit tends to get itself organized.

The church, on the other hand, which has lost much of its influence since the printed page has so largely taken the place of the pulpit in the interpretation of life, seems at present to be in process of readjustment to the new conditions.

It is important that the church, the school, and the family should be

[9]Charles Horton Cooley, *Social Organization,* p. 15.

studied from the point of view of this readjustment to the conditions of city life.

What changes have taken place in recent years in the family sentiments? in the attitudes of husbands toward wives? of wives toward husbands? of children toward parents, etc.?

What do the records of the juvenile and morals courts indicate in regard to this matter?

In what regions of social life have the mores on the subject of the family life changed most?

To what extent have these changes taken place in response to the influences of the city environment?

Similarly, investigations might be carried on with reference to the school and the church. Here, too, there is a changed attitude and changed policy in response to a changed environment. This is important because it is, in the last analysis, upon these institutions in which the immediate and vital interests of life find a corporate expression that social organizations ultimately rests.

It is probably the breaking down of local attachments and the weaking of the restraints and inhibitions of the primary group, under the influence of the urban environment, which are largely responsible for the increase of vice and crime in great cities. It would be interesting in this connection to determine by investigation how far the increase in crime keeps pace with the increasing mobility of the population and to what extent this mobility is a function of the growth of population. It is from this point of view that we should seek to interpret all those statistics which register the disintegration of the moral order, for example, the statistics of divorce, of truancy, and of crime.

What is the effect of ownership of property, particularly of the home, on truancy, on divorce, and on crime?

In what regions and classes are certain kinds of crime endemic?

In what classes does divorce occur most frequently? What is the difference in this respect between farmers and, say, actors?

To what extent in any given racial group, for example, the Italians in New York or the Poles in Chicago, do parents and children live in the same world, speak the same language, and share the same ideas, and how far do the conditions found account for juvenile delinquency in that particular group?

How far are the home mores responsible for criminal manifestations of an immigrant group?

Crisis and the Courts

It is characteristic of city life that all sorts of people meet and mingle together who never fully comprehend one another. The anarchist and the club man, the priest and the Levite, the actor and the missionary who touch elbows on the street still live in totally different worlds. So complete is the segregation of vocational classes that it is possible within the limits of the city to live in an isolation almost as complete as that of some remote rural community.

Walter Besant tells the following anecdote of his experience as editor of the *People's Palace Journal:*

In that capacity I endeavored to encourage literary effort, in the hope of lighting upon some unknown and latent genius. The readers of the *Journal* were the members of the various classes connected with the educational side of the place. They were young clerks chiefly—some of them very good fellows. They had a debating society which I attended from time to time. Alas! They carried on their debates in an ignorance the most profound, the most unconscious, and the most satisfied. I endeavored to persuade them that it was desirable at least to master the facts of the case before they spoke. In vain. Then I proposed subjects for essays, and offered prizes for verses. I discovered, to my amazement, that among all the thousands of these young people, lads and girls, there was not discoverable the least rudimentary indication of any literary power whatever. In all other towns there are young people who nourish literary ambitions, with some measure of literary ability. How should there be any in this town, where there were no books, no papers, no journals, and, at that time, no free libraries?[10]

In the immigrant colonies which are now well established in every large city, foreign populations live in an isolation which is different from that of the population of East London, but in some respects more complete.

The difference is that each one of these little colonies has a more or less independent political and social organization of its own, and is the center of a more or less vigorous nationalist propaganda. For example, each one of these groups has one or more papers printed in its own language. In New York City there were, a few years ago, 270 publications, most of them supported by the local population, printed in 23 different languages. In Chicago there were 19 daily papers

[10]Walter Besant, *East London,* p. 13.

published in 7 foreign languages with a combined daily circulation of 368,000 papers.

Under these conditions the social ritual and the moral order which these immigrants brought with them from their native countries have succeeded in maintaining themselves for a considerable time under the influences of the American environment. Social control, based on the home mores, breaks down, however, in the second generation.

We may express the relation of the city to this fact in general terms by saying that the effect of the urban environment is to intensify all effects on crisis.

The term "crisis" is not to be understood in a violent sense. It is involved in any disturbance of habit. There is a crisis in the boy's life when he leaves home. The emancipation of the Negro and the immigration of the European peasant are group crises. Any strain of crisis involves three possible changes: greater fitness, reduced efficiency, or death. In biological terms, "survival" means successful adjustment to crisis, accompanied typically by a modification of structure. In man it means mental stimulation and greater intelligence, or mental depression, in case of failure.[11]

Under the conditions imposed by city life in which individuals and groups of individuals, widely removed in sympathy and understanding, live together under conditions of interdependence, if not of intimacy, the conditions of social control are greatly altered and the difficulties increased.

The problem thus created is usually characterized as one of "assimilation." It is assumed that the reason for rapid increase of crime in our large cities is due to the fact that the foreign element in our population has not succeeded in assimilating American culture and does not conform to the American mores. This would be interesting, if true, but the facts seem to suggest that perhaps the truth must be sought in the opposite direction.

One of the most important facts established by the investigation concerns the American-born children of immigrants—the "second generation." The records of convictions in the New York Court of General Sessions during the period from October 1, 1908, to June 30, 1909, and of all commitments to Massachusetts penal institutions, except those to the state farm, during the year ending September 30, 1909, form the basis of this

[11]William I. Thomas. "Race Psychology: Standpoint and Questionnaire with Particular Reference to the Immigrant and Negro," *American Journal or Sociology*, XVII (May, 1912), 736.

analysis of the criminal tendencies of the second generation.

From these records it appears that a clear tendency exists on the part of the second generation to differ from the first or immigrant generation in the character of its criminality. It also appears that this difference is much more frequently in the direction of the criminality of the American-born of non-immigrant parentage than it is in the opposite direction. This means that the movement of the second-generation crime is away from the crimes peculiar to immigrants and toward those of the American of native parentage. Sometimes this movement has carried second-generation criminality even beyond that of the native-born of native parentage. Of the second-generation groups submitted to this comparison, one maintains a constant adherence to the general rule above referred to, while all the others at some point fail to follow it. This unique group is the Irish second generation.[12]

What we do observe, as a result of the crisis, is that control that was formerly based on mores was replaced by control based on positive law. This change runs parallel to the movement by which secondary relationships have taken the place of primary relationships in the association of individuals in the city environment.

It is characteristic of the United States that great political changes should be effected experimentally under the pressure of agitation or upon the initiative of small but militant minorities. There is probably no other country in the world in which so many "reforms" are in progress as at the present time in the United States. Reform has, in fact, become a kind of popular "indoor sport." The reforms thus effected, almost without exception, involve some sort of restriction or governmental control over activities that were formerly "free" or controlled only by the mores and public opinion.

The effect of this extension of what is called the police power has been to produce a change, not merely in the fundamental policy of the law, but in the character and standing of the courts.

The juvenile and morals courts illustrate a change which is perhaps taking place elsewhere. In these courts the judges have assumed something of the functions of administrative officers, their duties consisting less in the interpretation of law than in prescribing remedies and administering advice intended to restore delinquents brought before them to their normal place in society.

A similar tendency to give judges a wide discretion and to im-

[12]*Reports of the United States Immigration Commission, VI*, 14-16.

pose upon them a further responsibility is manifest in those courts which have to deal with the technical affairs of the business world, and in the growth in popularity of commissions in which judicial and administrative functions are combined, for example, the Interstate Commerce Commission.

In order to interpret in a fundamental way the facts in regard to social control it is important to start with a clear conception of the nature of corporate action.

Corporate action begins when there is some sort of communication between individuals who constitute a group. Communication may take place at different levels; that is, suggestions may be given and responded to on the instinctive, senso-motor, or ideo-motor levels. The mechanism of communication is very subtle, so subtle, in fact, that it is often difficult to conceive how suggestions are conveyed from one mind to another. This does not imply that there is any special form of consciousness, any special sense of kinship or consciousness of kind, necessary to explain corporate action.

In fact, it has recently been shown that in the case of certain highly organized and static societies, like that of the well-known ant, probably nothing that we would call communication takes place.

It is a well-known fact that if an ant be removed from a nest and afterward put back it will not be attacked, while almost invariably an ant belonging to another nest will be attacked. It has been customary to use the words memory, enmity, friendship, in describing this fact. Now Bethe made the following experiment. An ant was placed in the liquids (blood and lymph) squeezed out from the bodies of nest companions and was then put back into its nest; it was not attacked. It was then put in the juice taken from the inmates of a "hostile" nest, and was at once attacked and killed.[13]

A further instance of the manner in which ants communicate will illustrate how simple and automatic communication may become on the instinctive level.

An ant, when taking a new direction from the nest for the first time, always returns by the same path. This shows that some trace must be left behind which serves as a guide back to the nest. If an ant returning by this path bears no spoils, Bethe found that no other ants try this direction. But if it bring back honey or sugar, other ants are sure to try

[13]Jacques Loeb, *Comparative Physiology of the Brain,* pp. 220-21.

the path. Hence something of the substances carried over this path by the ants must remain on the path. These substances must be strong enough to affect the ants chemically.[14]

The important fact is that by means of this comparatively simple device corporate action is made possible.

Individuals not only react upon one another in this reflex way, but they inevitably communicate their sentiments, attitudes, and organic excitements, and in doing so they necessarily react, not merely to what each individual actually does, but to what he intends, desires, or hopes to do. The fact that individuals often betray sentiments and attitudes to others of which they are themselves only dimly conscious makes it possible for individual A, for example, to act upon motives and tensions in B as soon, or even before, B is able to do so. Furthermore, A may act upon the suggestions that emanate from B without himself being clearly conscious of the source from which his motives spring. So subtle and intimate may the reactions be which control individuals who are bound together in a social-psychological process.

It is upon the basis of this sort of instinctive and spontaneous control that every more formal sort of control must be based in order to be effective.

Changes in the form of social control may for the purposes of investigation be grouped under the general heads:

1. The substitution of positive law for custom, and the extension of municipal control to activities that were formerly left to individual intiative and discretion.

2. The disposition of judges in municipal and criminal courts to assume administrative function so that the administration of the criminal law ceases to be a mere application of the social ritual and becomes an application of rational and technical methods, requiring expert knowledge or advice, in order to restore the individual to society and repair the injury that his delinquency has caused.

3. Changes and divergencies in the mores among the different isolated and segregated groups in the city. What are the mores, for example, of the shop-girl? the immigrant? the politician? and the labor agitator?

It should be the aim of these investigations to distinguish not merely the causes of these changes, the direction in which they are moving, but also the forces that are likely to minimize and neutralize them. For example, it is important to know whether the motives which are at present

14*Ibid.*, p. 221.

multiplying the positive restrictions on the individual will necessarily go as far in this country as they have already done in Germany. Will they eventually bring about a condition approaching socialism?

Commercialized Vice and the Liquor Traffic

Social control, under the conditions of city life, can, perhaps, be best studied in its attempts to stamp out vice and control the liquor traffic.

The saloon and the vice establishments have come into existence as a means of exploiting appetites and instincts fundamental to human nature. This makes the efforts that have been made to regulate and suppress these forms of exploitation and traffic interesting and important as subjects of investigation.

Such an investigation should be based upon thorough study: (1) of the human nature upon which the commerce has been erected, (2) of the social conditions which tend to convert normal appetites into social vices, (3) of the practical effects of the efforts to limit, control, and stamp out the vice traffic and to do away with the use and sale of liquor.

Among the things that we should desire to know are:

To what extent is the appetite for alcoholic stimulus a prenatal disposition?

To what extent may such an appetite be transferred from one form of stimulation to another; that is, e.g., from whiskey to cocaine, etc.?

To what extent is it possible to substitute normal and healthful for pathological and vicious stimulations?

What are the social and moral effects of secret drinking?

Where a taboo is established early in life, does it have the effect of idealizing the delights of indulgence? Does it do this in some cases and not in others? If so, what are the contributing circumstances? Do men suddenly lose the taste for liquor and other stimulants? What are the conditions under which this happens?

Many of these questions can be answered only by a study of individual experiences. Vices undoubtedly have their natural history, like certain forms of disease. They may therefore be regarded as independent entities which find their habitat in human environment, are stimulated by certain conditions, inhibited by others, but invariably exhibit through all changes a character that is typical.

In the early days the temperance movement had something of the character of a religious revival, and the effects were highly picturesque. In recent years the leaders have displayed a more delibate strategy, but the struggle against the liquor traffic still has all the characteristics of a big popular movement, a movement which, having first conquered the rural districts, is now seeking to enforce itself in the cities.

On the other hand, the vice crusade started with the cities, where, in fact, commercialized vice is indigenous. The mere discussion of this subject in public has meant an enormous change in the sex mores. The fact that this movement is everywhere coincident with the entrance of women into a greater freedom, into industry, the professions, and party politics, is significant.

There are conditions peculiar to the life of great cities (referred to under the heading "Mobility of the Population of Great Cities") which make the control of vice especially difficult. For example, crusades and religious movements generally do not have the same success in the city environment that they do in the smaller and less heterogeneous communities. What are the conditions which make this true?

Perhaps the facts most worth studying in connection with the movement for suppresison of vice are those which indicate the changes which have taken place in fifty years in sex mores, particularly with reference to what is regarded as modest and immodest in the dress and behavior, and with reference to the freedom with which sexual matters are now discussed by young men and young women.

It seems, in fact, as if we were in the presence of two epoch-making changes, the one which seems destined finally to put intoxicating liquors in the category of poisonous drugs, and the other to lift the taboo which particularly among Anglo-Saxon peoples, has effectually prevented up to the present time the frank discussion of the facts of sex.

Party Politics and Publicity

There is everywhere at present a disposition to increase the power of the executive branch of the government at the expense of the legislative. The influence of state legislatures and of city councils has been diminished in some instances by the introduction of the referendum and the recall. In others they have been largely superseded by the commission form of government. The ostensible reason for these changes is that they offer a means for overthrowing the power of the professional politicians. The real ground seems to me the recognition of the fact that the form of government which had its origin in the town meeting and was well suited to the needs of a small community based on primary relations is not suitable to the government of the changing and heterogeneous populations of cities of three or four millions.

Much, of course, depends upon the character and size of the population. Where it is of American stock, and the number of voting citizens is not too great for thorough and calm discussion, no better school of politics can be imagined nor any method of managing affairs more certain to prevent jobbery and waste, to stimulate vigilance and breed contentment. When, however, the town meeting has grown to exceed seven or eight hundred persons, and, still more, when any considerable section are strangers, such as Irish or French Canadians, who have latterly poured into New England, the institution works less perfectly because the multitude is too large for debate, factions are likely to spring up, and the immigrants, untrained in self-government, become the prey of wire pullers or petty demagogues.[15]

For one thing, the problems of city government have become, with the growth and organization of city life, so complicated that it is no longer desirable to leave them to the control of men whose only qualification for handling them consists in the fact that they have succeeded in gaining office through the ordinary machinery of ward politics.

Another circumstance which has made the selection of city officials by popular vote impractical under the conditions of city life is the fact that, except in special cases, the voter knows little or nothing about the officials he is voting for; knows little or nothing about the functions of the office to which that official is to be elected; and, besides all the rest, is too busy elsewhere to inform himself about conditions and needs of the city as a whole.

At a recent election in Chicago, for example, voters were called upon to select candidates from a ballot containing 250 names, most of them unknown to the voters. Under these circumstances the citizen who wishes to vote intelligently relies on some more or less interested organization or some more or less interested advisor to tell him how to vote.

To meet this emergency, created primarily by conditions imposed by city life, two types of organization have come into existence for controlling those artificial crises that we call elections. One of these

[15]James Bryce, *The American Commonwealth*, I, 566.

is the organization represented by the political boss and the political machine. The other is that represented by the independent voters' leagues, taxpayers' associations, and organizations like the bureaus of municipal research.

It is an indication of the rather primitive conditions in which our political parties were formed that they sought to govern the country on the principle that the remedy for all sorts of administrative evils was to "turn the rascals out," as the popular phrase expressed it, a change of government. The political machine and the political boss have come into existence in the interest of party politics. The parties were necessarily organized to capture elections. The political machine is merely a technical device invented for the purpose of achieving this end. The boss is the expert who runs the machine. He is as necessary to the winning of an election as a professional coach is necessary to success at football.

It is characteristic of the two types of organization which have grown up for the purpose of controlling the popular vote that the first, the political machine, is based, on the whole, on local, personal, that is to say, primary, relationships. The second, the good-government organizations, make their appeal to the public, and the public, as we ordinarily understand that expression, is a group based on secondary relationships. Members of a public are not as a rule personally acquainted.

The political machine is, in fact, an attempt to maintain, inside the formal administrative organization of the city, the control of a primary group. The organizations thus built up, of which Tammany Hall is the classic illustration, appear to be thoroughly feudal in their character. The relations between the boss and his ward captain seem to be precisely that, of personal loyalty on one side and personal protection on the other, which the feudal relation implies. The virtues which such an organization calls out are the old tribal ones of fidelity, loyalty, and devotion to the interests of the chief and the clan. The people within the organization, their friends and supporters, constitute a "we" group, while the rest of the city is merely the outer world, which is not quite alive and not quite human in the sense in which the members of the "we" group are. We have here something approaching the condition of primitive society.

The conception of "primitive society" which we ought to form is that of small groups scattered over a territory. The size of the groups is determined by the conditions of the struggle for existence. The internal organization of each group corresponds to its size. A group of groups may have some relation to each other (kin, neighborhood, alliance, *connubium,* and *commercium*) which draws them together and differentiates them from others. Thus a differentiation arises between ourselves, the we-group or in-group, and everybody else or the others-groups, out-groups. The insiders in a we-group are in a relation of peace, order, law, government, and industry, to each other. Their relation to all outsiders, or others-groups, is one of war and plunder, except so far as agreements have modified it.

The relation of comradeship and peace in the we-group and that of hostility and war toward others-groups are correlative to each other. The exigencies of war with outsiders are what make peace inside, least internal discord should weaken the we-group for war. These exigencies also make government and law in the in-group, in order to prevent quarrels and enforce discipline.[16]

The politics of most great cities offer abundant materials for the study of the type represented by the political boss, as well as the social mechanisms created by and embodied in the political machine. It is necessary, however, that we study them disinterestedly. Some of the questions we should seek to answer are:

What, as a matter of fact, is the political organization at any point within the city? What are the sentiments and attitudes and interests which find expression through it?

What are the practical devices it employs for mobilizing its forces and putting them into action?

What is the character of the party appeal in the different moral regions of which the city is made up?

How much of the interest in politics is practical and how much is mere sport?

What part of the cost of elections is advertising? How much of it can be classed as "educational publicity," and how much is pure graft?

To what extent, under existing conditions, particularly as we find them in great cities, can elections be practically controlled by purely technical devices, card catalogues, torch-light processions, spellbinders—machinery?

What effect will the introduction of the referendum and recall have upon present methods of conducting elections in cities?

[16]Sumner, *Folkways,* p. 12.

Advertising and Social Control

In contrast with the political machine, which has founded its organized action on the local, personal, and immediate interests represented by the different neighborhoods and localities, the good-government organizations, the bureaus of municipal research, and the like have sought to represent the interests of the city as a whole and have appealed to a sentiment and opinion neither local nor personal. These agencies have sought to secure efficiency and good government by the education of the voter, that is to say, by investigating and publishing the facts regarding the government.

In this way publicity has come to be a recognized form of social control, and advertising—"social advertising"—has become a profession with an elaborate technique supported by a body of special knowledge.

It is one of the characteristic phenomena of city life and of society founded on secondary relationships that advertising should have come to occupy so important a place in its economy.

In recent years every individual and organization which has had to deal with the public, that is to say the public outside the smaller and more intimate communities of the village and small town, has come to have its press agent, who is often less an advertising man than a diplomatic man accredited to the newspapers, and through them to the world at large. Institutions like the Russell Sage Foundation and, to a less extent, the General Education Board have sought to influence public opinion directly through the medium of publicity. The Carnegie Report upon Medical Education, the Pittsburgh Survey, the Russell Sage Foundation Report on Comparative Costs of Public-School Education in the several states, are something more than scientific reports. They are rather a high form of journalism, dealing with existing conditions critically, and seeking through the agency of publicity to bring about radical reforms. The work of the Bureau of Municipal Research in New York has had a similar practical purpose. To these must be added the work accomplished by the child-welfare exhibits, by the social surveys undertaken in different parts of the country, and by similar propaganda in favor of public health.

As a source of social control public opinion becomes important in societies founded on secondary relationships, of which great cities are a type. In the city every social group tends to create its own milieu and, as these conditions become fixed, the mores tend to accommodate themselves to the conditions thus created. In secondary groups and in the city fashion tends to take the place of custom, and public opinion, rather than the mores, becomes the dominant force in social control.

In any attempt to understand the nature of public opinion and its relation to social control it is important to investigate first of all the agencies and devices which have come into practical use in the effort to control, enlighten, and exploit it.

The first and the most important of these is the press, that is, the daily newspaper and other forms of current literature, including books classed as current.[17]

After the newspaper, the bureaus of research which are now springing up in all the large cities are the most interesting and the most promising devices for using publicity as a means of control.

The fruits of these investigations do not reach the public directly, but are disseminated through the medium of the press, the pulpit, and other sources of popular enlightenment.

In addition to these there are the educational campaigns in the interest of better health conditions, the child-welfare exhibits, and the numerous "social advertising" devices which are now employed, sometimes upon the initiative of private societies, sometimes upon that of popular magazines or newspapers, in order to educate the public and enlist the masses of the people in the movement for the improvement conditions of community life.

The newspaper is the great medium of communication within the city, and it is on the basis of the information which it supplies that public opinion rests. The first function which a newspaper supplies is that which formerly was performed by the village gossip.

In spite, however, of the industry with which newspapers pursue facts of personal intelligence and human interest, they cannot compete with the village gossips as a means of social control. For one thing, the newspaper maintains some reservations not recognized by gossip, in the matters of personal intelligence. For example, until they run for office or commit some other overt act that brings them before the public conspicuously, the private life of individual men or women is a subject that is, for the newspaper, taboo. It is not so with gossip, partly because in a small community no individual is so obscure that his private affairs escape observation and discussion; partly because the field is smaller. In small communities there is a perfectly amazing

[17]Cf. Bryce, *The American Commonwealth*, p. 267.

amount of personal information afloat among the individuals who compose them.

The absence of this in the city is what, in large part, makes the city what it is.

Some of the questions that arise in regard to the nature and function of the newspaper and of publicity generally are:

What is news?

What are the methods and motives of the newspaper man? Are they those of an artist? a historian? or merely those of a merchant?

To what extent does the newspaper control and to what extent is it controlled by public sentiment?

What is a "fake" and why?

What is yellow journalism and why is it yellow?

What would be the effect of making the newspaper a municipal monopoly?

What is the difference between advertising and news?

IV. Temperament and the Urban Environment

Great cities have always been the melting-pots of races and of cultures. Out of the vivid and subtle interactions of which they have been the centers, there have come the newer breeds and the newer social types. The great cities of the United States, for example, have drawn from the isolation of their native villages great masses of the rural populations of Europe and America. Under the shock of the new contacts the latent energies of these primitive peoples have been released, and the subtler processes of interaction have brought into existence not merely vocational, but temperamental, types.

Mobilization of the Individual Man

Transportation and communication have effected, among many other silent but far-reaching changes, what I have called the "mobilization of the individual man." They have multiplied the opportunities of the individual man for contact and for association with his fellows, but they have made these contacts and associations more transitory and less stable. A very large part of the populations of great cities, including those who make their homes in tenements and apartment houses, live much as people do in some great hotel, meeting but not knowing one another. The effect of this is to substitute fortuitous and casual relationship for the more intimate and permanent associations of the smaller community.

Under these circumstances the individual's status is determined to a considerable degree by conventional signs—by fashion and "front" —and the art of life is largely reduced to skating on thin surfaces and a scrupulous study of style and manners.

Not only transportation and communication, but the segregation of the urban population tends to facilitate the mobility of the individual man. The processes of segregation establish moral distances which make the city a mosaic of little worlds which tough but do not interpenetrate. This makes it possible for individuals to pass quickly and easily from one moral milieu to another, and encourages the fascinating but dangerous experiment of living at the same time in several different contiguous, but otherwise widely separated, worlds. All this tends to give to city life a superficial and adventitious character; it tends to complicate social relationships and to produce new and divergent individual types. It introduces, at the same time, an element of chance and adventure which adds to the stimulus of city life and gives it, for young and fresh nerves, a peculiar attractiveness. The lure of great cities is perhaps a consequence of stimulations which act directly upon the reflexes. As a type of human behavior it may be explained, like the attraction of the flame for the moth, as a sort of tropism.

The attraction of the metropolis is due in part, however, to the fact that in the long run every individual finds somewhere among the varied manifestations of city life the sort of environment in which he expands and feels at ease; finds, in short, the moral climate in which his peculiar nature obtains the stimulations that bring his innate dispositions to full and free expression. It is, I suspect, motives of this kind which have their basis, not in interest nor even in sentiment, but in something more fundamental and primitive which draw many, if not most, of the young men and young women from the security of their homes in the country into the big, booming confusion and excitement of city life. In a small community it is the normal man, the man without eccentricity or genius, who seems most likely to succeed. The small community often tolerates eccentricity. The city, on the contrary, rewards it. Neither the criminal, the defective, nor the genius has the same opportunity to develop his innate disposition in a small town that he invariably finds in a great city.

Fifty years ago every village had one or two eccentric characters who were treated ordinarily with a benevolent toleration, but who were regarded meanwhile as impracticable and queer. These exceptional individuals lived an isolated existence, cut off by their very ecentricities, whether of genius or of defect, from genuinely intimate intercourse with their fellows. If they had the making of criminals, the restraints and inhibitions of the small community rendered them harmless. If they had the stuff of genius in them, they remained sterile for lack of appreciation or opportunity. Mark Twain's story of *Pudd'n Head Wilson* is a description of one such obscure and unappreciated genius. It is not so true as it was when

> Full many a flower is born to blush unseen
> And waste its fragrance on the desert air.

Gray wrote the "Elegy in a Country Churchyard" before the rise of the modern metropolis.

In the city many of these divergent types now find a milieu in which, for good or for ill, their dispositions and talents parturiate and bear fruit.

In the investigation of those exceptional and tempermental types which the city has produced we should seek to distinguish, as far as possible, between those abstract mental qualities upon which technical excellence is based and those more fundamental native characteristics which find expression in temperament. We may therefore ask:

To what extent are the moral qualities of individuals based on native character? To what extent are they conventionalized habits imposed upon by them or taken over by them from the group?

What are the native qualities and characteristics upon which the moral or immoral character accepted and conventionalized by the group are based?

What connection or what divorce appears to exist between mental and moral qualities in the groups and in the individuals composing them?

Are criminals as a rule of a lower order of intelligence than non-criminals? If so, what types of intelligence are associated with different types of crime? For example, do professional burglars and professional confidence men represent different mental types?

What are the effects upon these different types of isolation and of mobility, of stimulus and of repression?

To what extent can playgrounds and other forms of recreation supply the stimulation which is otherwise sought for in vicious pleasures?

To what extent can vocational guidance assist individuals in finding vocations in which they will be able to obtain a free expression of their temperamental qualities?

The Moral Region

It is inevitable that individuals who seek the same forms of excitement, whether that excitement be furnished by a horse race or by grand opera, should find themselves from time to time in the same places. The result of this is that in the organization which city life spontaneously assumes the population tends to segregate itself, not merely in accordance with its interests, but in accordance with its tastes or its temperaments. The resulting distribution of the population is likely to be quite different from that brought about by occupational interests or economic conditions.

Every neighborhood, under the influences which tend to distribute and segregate city populations, may assume the character of a "moral region." Such, for example, are the vice districts, which are found in most cities. A moral region is not necessarily a place of abode. It may be a mere rendezvous, a place of resort.

In order to understand the forces which in every large city tend to develop these detached milieus in which vagrant and suppressed impulses, passions, and ideals emancipate themselves from the dominant moral order, it is necessary to refer to the fact or theory of latent impulses of men.

The fact seems to be that men are brought into the world with all the passions, instincts, and appetites, uncontrolled and undisciplined. Civilization, in the interests of the common welfare, demands the suppression sometimes, and the control always, of the these wild, natural dispositions. In the process of imposing its discipline upon the individual, in making over the individual in accordance with the accepted community model, much is suppressed altogether, and much more finds a vicarious expression in forms that are socially valuable, or at least innocuous. It is at this point that sport, play, and art function. They permit the individual to purge himself by means of symbolic expression of these wild and suppressed impulses. This is the catharsis of which Aristotle wrote in the *Poetic*, and which has been given new and more positive significance by the investigations of Sigmund Freud and the psychoanalysts.

No doubt many other social phenomena such as strikes, wars, popular elections, and religious revivals perform a similar function in releasing the subconscious tensions. But within smaller communities, where social relations are more intimate and inhibitions more imperative, there are many exceptional individuals who find within the limits of the communal activity no normal and healthful expression of their individual aptitudes and temperaments.

The causes which give rise to what are here described as "moral regions" are due in part to the restrictions which urban life imposes; in part to the license which these same conditions offer. We have, until very recently, given much consideration to the temptations of city life, but we have not given the same consideration to the effects of inhibitions and suppressions of natural impulses and instincts under the changed conditions of metropolitan life. For one thing, children, which in the country are counted as an asset, become in the city a liability. Aside from this fact it is very much more difficult to rear a family in the city than on the farm. Marriage takes place later in the city, and sometimes it doesn't take place at all. These facts have consequences the significance of which we are as yet wholly unable to estimate.

Investigation of the problems involved might well begin by a study and comparison of the characteristic types of social organization which exist in the regions referred to.

What are the external facts in regard to the life in Bohemia, the half-world, the red-light district, and other "moral regions" less pronounced in character?

What is the nature of the vocations which connect themselves with the ordinary life of these regions? What are the characteristic mental types which are attracted by the freedom which they offer?

How do individuals find their way into these regions? How do they escape from them?

To what extent are the regions referred to the product of the license; to what extent are they due to the restrictions imposed by city life on the natural man?

Temperament and Social Contagion

What lends special importance to the segregation of the poor, the vicious, the criminal, and exceptional persons generally, which is so characteristic a feature of city life, is the fact that social contagion tends to stimulate in divergent types the common temperamental differences, and to suppress characters which unite them with the normal types about them. Association with others of their own ilk provides also not merely a stimulus, but a moral support for the traits they have in common which they would not find in a less select society. In the great city the poor, the vicious, and the delinquent, crushed together in an unhealthful and contagious intimacy, breed in and in, soul and body, so that it has often occured to me that those long genealogies of the Jukes and the tribes of Ishmael would not show such a persistent and distressing uniformity of vice, crime, and poverty unless they were peculiarly fit for the environment in which they are condemned to exist.

We must then accept these "moral regions" and the more or less eccentric and exceptional people who inhabit them, in a sense, at least, a part of the natural, if not the normal, life of a city.

It is not necessary to understand by the expression "moral region" a place or a society that is either necessarily criminal or abnormal. It is intended rather to apply to regions in which a divergent moral code prevails, because it is a region in which the people who inhabit it are dominated, as people are ordinarily not dominated, by a taste or by a passion or by some interest which has its roots directly in the original nature of the individual. It may be an art, like music, or a sport, like horse-racing. Such a region would differ from other social groups by the fact that its interests are more immediate and more fundamental. For this reason its differences are likely to be due to moral, rather than intellectual, isolation.

Because of the opportunity it offers, particularly to the exceptional and abnormal types of man, a great city tends to spread out and lay bare to the public view in a massive manner all the human characters and traits which are ordinarily obscured and suppressed in smaller communities. The city, in short, shows the good and evil in human nature in excess. It is this fact, perhaps, more than any other, which justifies the view that would make of the city a laboratory or clinic in which human nature and social processes may be conveniently and profitably studied.

Robert Park

HUMAN MIGRATION
AND THE MARGINAL MAN

Abstract

Migrations, with all the incidental collision, conflicts, and fusions of peoples and of cultures which they occasion, have been accounted among the decisive forces in history. Every advance in culture, is has been said, commences with a new period of migration and movement of populations. Present tendencies indicate that while the mobility of individuals has increased, the migration of peoples has relatively decreased. The consequences, however, of migration and mobility seem, on the whole, to be the same. In both cases the "cake of custom" is broken and the individual is freed for new enterprises and for new associations. One of the consequences of migration is to create a situation in which the same individual—who may or may not be a mixed blood—finds himself striving to live in two diverse cultural groups. The effect is to produce an unstable character—a personality type with characteristic forms of behavior. This is the "marginal man." It is in the mind of the marginal man that conflicting cultures meet and fuse. It is, therefore, in the mind of the marginal man that the process of civilization is visibly going on, and it is in the mind of the marginal man that the processs of civilization may best be studied.

Students of the great society, looking at mankind in the long perspective of history, have frequently been disposed to seek an explanation of existing cultural differences among races and peoples in some single dominating cause or condition. One school of thought, represented most conspicuously by Montesquieu, has found that explanation in climate and in the physical environment. Another school, identified with the name of Arthur de Gobineau, author of *The Inequality of Human Races*, has sought an explanation of divergent cultures in the innate qualities of races biologically inherited. These two theories have this in common, namely, that they both conceive civilization and society to be the result of evolutionary processes—processes by which man has acquired new inheritable traits—rather then processes by which new relations have been established between men.

In contrast to both of these, Frederick Teggart has recently restated and amplified what may be called catastrophic theory of civilization, a theory that goes back to Hume in England, and to Turgot in France. From this point of view, climate and innate racial traits, important as they may have been in the evolution of races, have been of only minor influence in creating existing cultural differences. In fact, races and cultures, so far from being in any sense identical—or even the product of similar conditions and forces—are perhaps to be set over against one another as contrast effects, the results of antagonistic tendencies, so that civilization may be said to flourish at the expense of racial differences rather than to be conserved by them. At any rate, if it is true that races are the products of isolation and inbreeding, it is just as certain that civilization, on the other hand, is a consequence of contact and communication. The forces which have been decisive in the history of mankind are those which have brought men together in competition, conflict, and co-operation.

Among the most important of these influences have been—according to what I have called the catastrophic theory of progress—migration and the incidental collisions, conflicts, and fusions of people and cultures which they have occasioned.

"Every advance in culture," says Bücher, in his *Industrial Evolution*, "commences, so to speak, with a new period of wandering," and in support of this thesis he points out that the earlier forms of trade were migratory, that the first industries to free themselves from the household husbandry and become independent occupations were carried on itinerantly. "The great founders of religion, the earliest poets and philosophers, the musicians and actors of past epochs, are all great wanderers. Even today, do not the inventor, the preacher of a new doctrine, and the virtuoso travel from place to place in search of adherents and admirers—notwithstanding the immense recent development in the means of communicating information?"[1]

The influences of migrations have not been limited, of course, by the changes which they have effected in existing cultures. In the long run, they have determined the racial characteristics of historical peoples.

[1]Carl Bücher, *Industrial Evolution*, p. 347.

"The whole teaching of ethnology," as Griffith Taylor remarks, "shows that peoples of mixed race are the rule and not the exception."[2] Every nation, upon examination, turns out to have been a more or less successful melting-pot. To this constant sifting of races and peoples, human geographers have given the title "the historical movement," because, as Miss Semple says in her volume *Influences of Geographic Environment,* "it underlies most written history and constitutes the major part of unwritten history, especially that of savage and nomadic tribes."[3]

Changes in race, it is true, do inevitably follow, at some distance, changes in culture. The movements and mingling of peoples which bring rapid, sudden, and often catastrophic, changes in customs and habits are followed, in the course of time, as a result of interbreeding, by corresponding modifications in temperament and physique. There has probably never been an instance where races have lived together in the intimate contacts which a common economy enforces in which racial contiguity has not produced racial hybrids. However, changes in racial characteristics and in cultural traits proceed at very different rates, and it is notorious that cultural changes are not consolidated and transmitted biologically, or at least to only a very slight extent, if at all. Acquired characteristics are not biologically inherited.

Writers who emphasize the importance of migration as an agency of progress are invariably led to ascribe a similar rôle to war. Thus Waitz, commenting upon the rôle of migration as an agency of civilization, points out that migrations are "rarely of a peaceful nature at first." Of war he says: "The first consequence of war is that fixed relations are established between peoples, which render friendly intercourse possible, an intercourse which becomes more important from the interchange of knowledge and experience than from the mere interchange of commodities."[4] And then he adds:

Whenever we see a people, of whatever degree of civilization, not living in contact and reciprocal action with others, we shall generally find a certain stagnation, a mental inertness, and a want of activity, which render any change of social and political condition next to impossible. These are, in times of peace, transmitted like an everlasting disease, and war appears then, in spite of what the apostles of peace may say, as a saving angel, who rouses the national spirit, and renders all forces more elastic.[5]

[2]Griffith Taylor, *Environment and Race: A Study of the Evolution, Migration, Settlement, and Status of the Races of Men,* p. 336.

[3]Ellen Churchill Semple, *Influences of Geographic Environment,* p. 75.

[4]Theodor Waitz, *Introduction to Anthropology,* p. 347.

[5]*Ibid.,* p. 348.

Among the writers who conceive the historical process in terms of intrusions, either peaceful or hostile, of one people into the domain of another, must be reckoned such sociologists as Gumplowicz and Oppenheim. The former, in an effort to define the social process abstractly, has described it as the interaction of heterogeneous ethnic groups, the resulting subordination and superordination of races constituting the social order—society, in fact.

In much the same way, Oppenheim, in his study of the sociological origin of the state, believes he has shown that in every instance the state has had its historical beginnings in the imposition, by conquest and force, of the authority of a nomadic upon a sedentary and agricultural people. The facts which Oppenheim has gathered to sustain his thesis show, at any rate, that social institutions have actually, in many instances at least, come into existence abruptly by a mutation, rather than by a process of evolutionary selection and the gradual accumulation of relatively slight variations.[6]

It is not at once apparent why a theory which insists upon the importance of catastrophic change in the evolution of civilization should not at the same time take some account of revolution as a factor in progress. If peace and stagnation, as Waitz suggest, tend to assume the form of a social disease; if, as Sumner says, "society needs to have some ferment in it" to break up this stagnation and emancipate the energies of individuals imprisoned within an existing social order; it seems that some "adventurous folly' like the crusades of the middle ages, or some romantic enthusiasm like that which found expression in the French Revolution, or in the more recent Bolshevist adventure in Russia, might serve quite as effectively as either migration or war to interrupt the routine of existing habit and break the cake of custom. Revolutionary doctrines are naturally based upon a conception of catastrophic rather than of evolutionary change. Revolutionary strategy, as it has been worked out and rationalized in Sorel's *Reflections on Violence*, makes the great catastrophe, the general strike, an article of faith. As such it becomes a means of maintaining morale and enforcing discipline in the revolutionary masses.[7]

The first and most obvious difference between revolution and migration is that in migration the breakdown of social order is ini-

---

[6]Franz Oppenheim, *The State: Its History and Development Viewed Sociologically* (1914).

[7]George Sorel, *Reflections on Violence* (New York, 1914).

tiated by the impact of an invading population, and completed by the contact and fusion of native with alien peoples. In the case of the former, revolutionary ferment and the forces which have disrupted society have ordinarily had, or seem to have had, their sources and origins mainly if not wholly within, rather than without, the society affected. It is doubtful whether it can be successfully maintained that every revolution, every *Aufklärung*, every intellectual awakening and renaissance has been and will be provoked by some invading population movement or by the intrusion of some alien cultural agency. At least it seems as if some modification of this view is necessary, since with the growth of commerce and communication there is progressively and relatively more movement and less migration. Commerce, in bringing the ends of the earth together, has made travel relatively secure. Moreover, with the development of machine industry and the growth of cities, it is the commodities rather than men which circulate. The peddler, who carries his stock on his back, gives way to the traveling salesman, and the catalogue of the mail order house now reaches remote regions which even the Yankee peddler rarely if ever penetrated. With the development of a world-ecomony and the interpenetration of peoples, migrations, as Bücher has pointed out, have changed their character:

> The migrations occurring at the opening of the history of European peoples are migrations of whole tribes, a pushing and pressing of collective units from east to west which lasted for centuries. The migrations of the Middle Ages ever affect individual classes along; the knights in the crusades, the merchants, the wage craftsmen, the journeyman hand-workers, the jugglers and minstrels, the villeins seeking protection within the walls of a town. Modern migrations, on the contrary, are generally a matter of private concern, the individuals being led by the most varied motives. They are almost invariably without organization. The process repeating itself daily a thousand times is united only through the one characteristic, that it is everywhere a question of change of locality by persons seeking more favorable conditions of life.[8]

Migration, which was formerly an invasion, followed by the forcible displacement or subjugation of one people by another, has assumed the character of a peaceful penetration. Migration of peoples has, in other words, been transmuted into mobility of individuals, and the wars which these movements so frequently occasioned have assumed the char-

[8] Carl Bücher, *Industrial Evolution*, p. 349.

acter of internecine struggles, of which strikes and revolutions are to be regarded as types.

Furthermore, if one were to attempt to reckon with all the forms in which catastrophic changes take place, it would be necessary to include the changes that are effected by the sudden rise of some new religious movement like Mohammedanism or Christianity, both of which began as schismatic and sectarian movements, and which by extension and internal evolution have become independent religions. Looked at from this point of view, migration assumes a character less unique and exceptional that has hitherto been conceived by the writers whom the problem has most intrigued. It appears as one, merely, of a series of forms in which historic changes may take place. Nevertheless, regarded abstractly as a type of collective action, human migration exhibits everywhere characteristics that are sufficiently typical to make it a subject of independent investigation and study, both in respect to its form and in respect to the effects which it produces.

Migration is not, however, to be identified with mere movement. It involves, at the very least, change of residence and the breaking of home ties. The movements of gypsies and other pariah peoples, because they bring about no important changes in cultural life, are to be regarded rather as a geographical fact than a social phenomenon. Nomadic life is stabilized on the basis of movement, and even through gypsies now travel by automobile, they still maintain, comparatively unchanged, their ancient tribal organization and customs. The result is that their relation to the communities in which they may at anytime be found is to be described as symbiotic rather than social. This tends to be true of any section or class of the population—the hobos, for example, and the hotel dwellers—which is unsettled and mobile.

Migration as a social phenomenon must be studied not merely in its grosser effects, as manifested in changes in custom and in the mores, but it may be envisaged in its subjective aspects as manifested in the changed type of personality which it produces. When the traditional organization of society breaks down, as a result of contact and collision with a new invading culture, the effect is, so to speak, to emancipate the individual man. Energies that were formerly controlled by custom and tradition are released. The individual is free for new adventures, but he is more or less without direction and control. Teggart's statement of the matter is as follows:

As a result of the breakdown of customary modes of artion and of thought, the individual experiences a "release" from the restraints and constraints to which he has been subject, and gives evidence of this "release" in aggressive self-assertion. The overexpression of individuality is one of the marked features of all epochs of change. On the other hand, the study of the psychlogical effects of collision and contact between different groups reveals the fact that the most important aspect of "release" lies not in freeing the soldier, warrior, or berserker from the restraint of conventional modes of action, but in freeing the individual judgement from the inhibitions of conventional modes of thought. It will thus be seen (he adds) that the study of the *modus operandi* of change in time gives a common focus to the efforts of political historians, of the historians of literature and of ideas, of psychologists, and of students of ethics and the theory of education.[9]

Social changes, according to Teggart, have their inception in events which "release" the individuals out of which society is composed. Inevitably, however, this released is followed in the course of time by the reintegration of the individuals so released into a new social order. In the meantime, however, certain changes take place—at any rate they are likely to take place—in the character of the individuals themselves. They become, in the process, not merely emancipated, but enlightened.

The emancipated individual invariably becomes in a certain sense and to a certain degree a cosmopolitan. He learns to look upon the world in which he was born and bred with something of the detachment of a stranger. He acquires, in short, an intellectual bias. Simmel has described the position of the stranger in the community, and his personality, in terms of movement and migration.

"If wandering," he says, "considered as the liberation from every given point in space, is the conceptual opposite of fixation at any point, then surely the sociological form of the stranger presents the union of both of these specifications." The stranger stays, but he is not settled. He is a potential wanderer. That means that he is not bound as others are by the local proprieties and conventions. "He is the freer man, practically and theoretically. He views his relation to others with less prejudice; he submits them to more general, more objective standards, and he is not confined in his action by custom, piety or precedents."

[9]Frederick J. Teggart, *Theory of History*, p. 196.

The effect of mobility and migration is to secularize relations which were formerly sacred. One may describe the process, in its dual aspect, perhaps, as the secularization of society and the individuation of the person. For a brief, vivid, and authentic picture of the way in which migration of the earlier sort, the migration of a people, has, in fact, brought about the destruction of an earlier civilization and liberated the peoples involved for the creation of a later, more secular, and freer society, I suggest Gilbert Murray's introduction to *The Rise of the Greek Epic*, in which he seeks to reproduce the events of the Nordic invasion of the Aegean area.

What ensued, he says, was a period of chaos:

A chaos in which an old civilization is shattered into fragments, its laws set at naught, and that intricate web of normal expectation which forms the very essence of human society torn so often and so utterly by continued disappointment that at last there ceases to be any normal expectation at all. For the fugitive settlers on the shores that were afterwards Ionia, and for parts too of Doris and Aeolis, there were no tribal gods or tribal obligations left, because there were no tribes. There were no old laws, because there was no one to administer or even to remember them; only such compulsions as the strongest power of the moment chose to enforce. Household and family life had disappeared, and all its innumerable ties with it. A man was now not living with a wife of his own race, but with a dangerous strange woman, of alien language and alien gods, a woman whose husband or father he had perhaps murdered—or, at best, whom he had bought as a slave from the murderer. The old Aryan husbandman, as we shall see hereafter, had lived with his herds in a sort of familiar connexion. He slew "his brother the ox" only under special stress or for definite religious reasons, and he expected his women to weep when the slaying was performed. But now he had left his own herds far away. They had been devoured by enemies. And he lived on the beasts of strangers whom he robbed or held in servitude. He had left the graves of his fathers, the kindly ghosts of his own blood, who took food from his hand and loved him. He was surrounded by the graves of alien dead, strange ghosts whose names he knew not, and who were beyond his power to control, whom he tried his best to placate with fear and aversion. One only concrete thing existed for him to make henceforth the centre of his allegiance, to supply the place of his old family hearth, his gods, his tribal customs and sanctities. It was a circuit wall of stones, a *Polis*; the wall which he and his fellows, men of diverse tongues and worships united by tremendous need, had built up to be the one barrier between themselves and a world of enemies.[10]

[10]Gilbert Murray, *The Rise of the Greek Epic*, pp. 78-79.

It was within the walls of the *polis* and in this mixed company that Greek civilization was born. The whole secret of ancient Greek life, its relative freedom from the grosser superstitions and from fear of the gods, is bound up, we are told, with this period of transition and chaos, in which the older primitive world perished and from which the freer, more enlightened social order sprang into existence. Thought is emancipated, philosophy is born, public opinion sets itself up as an authority as over against tradition and custom. As Guyot puts it, "The Greek with his festivals, his songs, his poetry, seems to celebrate, in a perpetual hymn, the liberation of man from the mighty fetters of nature."[11]

What took place in Greece first has since taken place in the rest of Europe and is now going on in America. The movement and migration of peoples, the expansion of trade and commerce, and particularly the growth, in modern times, of these vast meltingpots of races and cultures, the metropolitan cities, has loosened local bonds, destroyed the cultures of tribe and folk, and substituted for the local loyalties the freedom of the cities; for the sacred order of tribal custom, the rational organization which we call civilization.

In these great cities, where all the passions, all the energies of mankind are released, we are in position to investigate the processes of civilization, as it were, under a microscope.

It is in the cities that the old clan and kinship groups are broken up and replaced by social organization based on rational interests and temperamental predilections. It is in the cities, more particularly, that the grand division of labor is effected which permits and more or less compels the individual man to concentrate his energies and his talents on the particular task he is best fitted to perform, and in this way emancipates him and his fellows from the control of nature and circumstance which so thoroughly dominates primitive man.

It happens, however, that the process of acculturation and assimilation and the accompanying amalgamation of racial stocks does not proceed with the same ease and the same speed in all cases. Particularly where peoples who come together are of divergent cultures and widely different racial stocks, assimilation and amalgamation do not take place so rapidly as they do in other cases. All our so-called racial problems grow out of situations in which assimilation and amalgamation do

[11]A. H. Guyot, *Earth and Man* (Boston, 1857), cited by Franklin Thomas, *The Environmental Basis of Society* (New York, 1921), p. 205.

not take place at all, or take place very slowly. As I have said elsewhere, the chief obstacle to the cultural assimilation of races is not their different mental, but rather their divergent physical traits. It is not because of the mentality of the Japanese that they do not so easily assimilate as do the Europeans. It is because

the Japanese bears in his features a distinctive racial hallmark, that he wears, so to speak, a racial uniform which classifies him. He cannot become a mere individual indistinguishable in the cosmopolitan mass of the population, as is true, for example, of the Irish, and, to a lesser extent, of some of the other immigrant races. The Japanese, like the Negro, is condemned to remain among us an abstraction, a symbol—and a symbol not merely of his own race but of the Orient and of that vague, ill-defined menace we sometimes refer to as the "yellow peril."[12]

Under such circumstances peoples of different racial stocks may live side by side in a relation of symbiosis, each playing a rôle in a common economy, but not interbreeding to any great extent; each maintaining, like the gypsy or the pariah peoples of India, a more or less complete tribal organization or society of their own. Such was the situation of the Jew in Europe up to modern times, and a somewhat similar relation exists today between the native white and the Hindu populations in Southeast Africa and in the West Indies.

In the long run, however, peoples and races who live together, sharing in the same economy, inevitably interbreed, and in this way if in no other, the relations which were merely co-operative and economic become social and cultural. When migration leads to conquest, either economic or political, assimilation is inevitable. The conquering peoples impose their culture and their standards upon the conquered, and there follows a period of cultural endosmosis.

Sometimes relations between the conquering and the conquered peoples take the form of slavery; sometimes they assume the form, as in India, of a system of caste. But in either case the dominant and the subject peoples become, in time, integral parts of one society. Slavery and caste are merely forms of accommodation, in which the race problem finds a temporary solution. The case of the Jews was different. Jews never were a subject people, at least not in Europe. They were never reduced to the position of an inferior caste. In their

---

[12]"Racial Assimilation in Secondary Groups," *Publications of the American Sociological Society,* Vol VIII (1914).

ghettos in which they first elected, and then were forced, to live, they perserved their own tribal traditions and their cultural, if not their political, independence. The Jew who left the ghetto did not escape; he deserted and became that execrable object, and apostate. The relation of the ghetto Jew to the larger community in which he lived was, and to some extent still is, symbiotic rather than social.

When, however, the walls of the medieval ghetto were torn down and the Jew was permitted to participate in the cultural life of the peoples among whom he lived, there appeared a new type of personality, namely, a cultural hybrid, a man living and sharing intimately in the cultural life and traditions of two distinct peoples; never quite willing to break, even if he were permitted to do so, with his past and his traditions, and not quite accepted, because of racial prejudice, in the new society in which he now sought to find a place. He was a man on the margin of two cultures and two societies, which never completely interpenetrated and fused. The emancipated Jew was, and is, historically and typically the marginal man, the first cosmopolite and citizen of the world. He is, par excellence, the "stranger," whom Simmel, himself a Jew, has described with such profound insight and understanding in his *Sociologie*. Most if not all the characteristics of the Jew, certainly his pre-eminence as a trader and his keen intellectual interest, his sophistication, his idealism and lack of historic sense, are the characteristics of the city man, the man who ranges widely, lives preferably in a hotel—in short, the cosmopolite. The autobiographies of Jewish immigrants, of which a great number have been published in America in recent years, are all different versions of the same story—the story of the marginal man; the man who, emerging from the ghetto in which he lived in Europe, is seeking to find a place in the freer, more comples and cosmopolitan life of an American city. One may learn from these autobiographies how the process of assimilation actually takes place in the individual immigrant. In the more sensitive minds its effects are as profound and as disturbing as some of the religious conversions of which William James has given us so classical an account in his *Varieties of Religious Experience*. In these immigrant autobiographies the conflict of cultures, as it takes place in the mind of the immigrant, is just the conflict of "the divided self," the old self and the new. And frequently there is no satisfying issue of this conflict, which often terminates in a profound disillusionment, as described, for example, in Lewisohn's autobiography *Up Stream*. But Lewisohn's restless wavering between the warm security of the ghetto, which he has abandoned, and the cold freedom of the outer world, in which he is not yet quite at home, is typical. A century earlier, Heinrich Heine, torn with the same conflicting loyalties, struggling to be at the same time a German and a Jew, enacted a similar rôle. It was, according to his latest biographer, the secret and the tragedy of Heine's life that circumstance condemned him to live in two worlds, in neither of which he ever quite belonged. It was this that embittered his intellectual life and gave to his writings that character of spiritual conflict and instability which, as Browne says, is evidence of "spiritual distress." His mind lacked the integrity which is based on conviction: "His arms were weak"—to continue the quotation—"because his mind was divided; his hands were nerveless because his soul was in turmoil."

Something of the same sense of moral dichotomy and conflict is probably characteristic of every immigrant during the period of transition, when old habits are being discarded and new ones are not yet formed. It is inevitably a period of inner turmoil and intense self-consciousness.

There are no doubt periods of transition and crisis in the lives of most of us that are comparable with those which the immigrant experiences when he leaves home to seek his fortunes in a strange country. But in the case of the marginal man the period of crisis is relatively permanent. The result is that he tends to become a personality type. Ordinarily the marginal man is a mixed blood, like the Mulatto in the United States or the Eurasian in Asia, but that is apparently because the man of mixed blood is one who lives in two worlds, in both of which he is more or less of a stranger. The Christian convert in Asia or in Africa exhibits many if not most of the characteristics of the marginal man—the same spiritual instability, intensified self-consciousness, restlessness, and *malaise*.

It is in the mind of the marginal man that the moral turmoil which new cultural contacts occasion manifests itself in the most obvious forms. It is in the mind of the marginal man—where the changes and fusions of culture are going on—that we can best study the processes of civilization and of progress.

URBANISM AS A WAY OF LIFE
Louis Wirth

The City and Contemporary Civilization

Just as the beginning of Western civilization is marked by the permanent settlement of formerly nomadic peoples in the Mediterranean
basin, so the beginning of what is distinctively modern in our civi-
zation is best signalized by the growth of great cities. Nowhere has
mankind been farther removed from organic nature than under the
conditions of life characteristic of these cities. The contemporary world
no longer presents a picture of small isolated groups of human beings
scattered over a vast territory as Sumner described primitive society.[1]
The distinctive feature of man's mode of living in the modern age is
his concentration into gigantic aggregations around which cluster lesser centers and from which radiate the ideas and practices that we call
civilization.

The degree to which the contemporary world may be said to be
"urban" is not fully or accurately measured by the proportion of the
total population living in cities. The influences which cities exert upon
the social life of man are greater than the ratio of the urban population would indicate; for the city is not only increasingly the dwelling-
place and the workshop of modern man, but it is the initiating and controlling center of economic, political, and cultural life that has drawn
the most remote communities of the world into its orbit and woven
diverse areas, peoples, and activities into a cosmos.

The growth of cities and the urbanization of the world comprise

Reprinted by permission of the University of Chicago from *On Cities and
Social Life*, Albert J. Reiss, Jr., ed. Copyright 1938 by the University of Chicago
Press.

[1]William Graham Sumner, *Folkways* (Boston, 1906), p. 12.

one of the most impressive facts of modern times. Although it is impossible to state precisely what proportion of the estimated total world population of approximately 1,800,000,000 is urban, 69.2 percent of the total population of those countries that do distinguish between urban and rural areas is urban.[2] Because the world's population is very unevenly distributed and because the growth of cities is not very far advanced in some of the countries that have only recently been touched by industrialism, this average understates the extent to which urban concentration has proceeded in those countries where the impact of the industrial revolution has been more forceful and of less recent date. This shift from a rural to a predominantly urban society, which has taken place within the span of a single generation in such industrialized areas as the United States and Japan, has been accompanied by profound changes in virtually every phase of social life. It is these changes and their ramifications that invite the attention of the sociologist to the study of the differences between the rural and the urban mode of living. The pursuit of this interest is an indispensable prerequisite for the comprehension and possible mastery of some of the most crucial contemporary problems of social life since it is likely to furnish one of the most revealing perspectives for the understanding of the ongoing changes in human nature and the social order.[3]

Because the city is the product of growth rather than of instantaneous creation, it is to be expected that the influences which it exerts upon the modes of life should not be able to wipe out completely the previously dominant modes of human association. To a greater or lesser degree, therefore, our social life bears the imprint of an earlier folk society, the characteristic modes of settlement of which were the farm, the manor, and the village. This historic influence is reinforced by the circumstances that the population of the city itself is in large measure recruited from the countryside, where a mode of life reminiscent of this earlier form of existence persists. Hence we should not expect to find abrupt and discontinuous variation between urban and

[2]S. V. Pearson, *The Growth and Distribution of Population* (New York, 1935), p. 211.

[3]Whereas rural life in the United States has for a long time been a subject of considerable interest on the part of governmental bureaus, the most notable case of a comprehensive report being that submitted by the Country Life Commission to President Theodore Roosevelt in 1909, no equally comprehensive official inquiry into urban life was undertaken until the establishment of a Research Committee on Urbanism of the National Resources Committee. (Cf. *Our Cities: Their Role in the National Economy* [Washington: Government Printing Office, 1937].)

rural types of personality. The city and the country may be regarded as two poles in reference to one or the other of which all human settlements tend to arrange themselves. In viewing urban-industrial and rural-folk society as ideal types of communities, we may obtain a perspective for the analysis of the basic models of human association as they appear in contemporary civilization.

A Sociological Definition of the City

Despite the preponderant significance of the city in our civilization, our knowledge of the nature of urbanism and the process of urbanization is meager, notwithstanding many attempts to isolate the distinguishing characteristics of urban life. Geographers, historians, economists, and political scientists have incorporated the points of view of their respective disciplines into diverse definitions of the city. While in no sense intended to supersede these, the formulation of a sociological approach to the city may incidentally serve to call attention to the interrelations between them by emphasizing the peculiar characteristics of the city as a particular form of human association. A sociologically significant definition of the city seeks to select those elements of urbanism which mark it as a distinctive mode of human group life.

The characterization of a community as urban on the basis of size alone is obviously arbitrary. It is difficult to defend the present census definition which designates a community of 2,500 and above as urban and all others as rural. The situation would be the same if the criterion were 4,000, 8,000, 10,000 25,000 or 100,000 population, for although in the latter case we might feel that we were more nearly dealing with an urban aggregate than would be the case in communities of lesser size no definition of urbanism can hope to completely satisfying as long as numbers are regarded as the sole criterion. Moreover, it is not difficult to demonstrate that communities of less than the arbitrarily set number of inhabitants, lying within the range of influence of metropolitan centers, have greater claim to recognition as urban communities than do larger ones leading a more isolated existence in a predominantly rural area. Finally, it should be recognized that census definitions are unduly influenced by the fact that the city, statistically speaking, is always an administrative concept in that the corporate limits play a decisive role in delineating the urban area. Nowhere is this more clearly apparent than in the concentrations on the peripheries of great metropolitan centers of people who cross arbitrary administrative boundaries of city, county, state, and nation.

As long as we identify urbanism with the physical entity of the city viewing it merely as rigidly delimited in space, and proceed as if urban attributes abruptly ceased to be manifested beyond an arbitrary boundary line, we are not likely to arrive at any adequate conception of urbanism as a mode of life. The technological developments in transportation and communication which virtually mark a new epoch in human history have accentuated the role of cities as dominant elements in our civilization and have enormously extended the urban mode of living beyond the confines of the city itself. The dominance of the city, especially of the great city, may be regarded as a consequence of the concentration in cities of industrial, commercial, financial, and administrative facilities and activities, transportation and communication lines, and cultural and recreational equipment such as the press, radio stations, theaters, libraries, museums, concert halls, operas, hospitals, colleges, research and publishing centers, professional organizations, and religious and welfare institutions. Were it not for the attraction and suggestions that the city exerts through these instrumentalities upon the rural population, the differences between the rural and the urban modes of life would be even greater than they are. Urbanization no longer denotes merely the process by which persons are attracted to a place called the city and incorporated into its system of life. It refers also to that cumulative accentuation of the characteristics distinctive of the mode of life which is associated with the growth of cities, and finally to the changes in the direction of modes of life recognized as urban which are apparent among people, wherever they may be, who have come under the spell of the influences which the city exerts by virtue of the power of its institutions and personalities operating through the means of communication and transportation.

The shortcomings which attach to number of inhabitants as a criterion of urbanism apply for the most part to density of population as well. Whether we accept the density of 10,000 persons per square mile as Mark Jefferson[4] proposed, or 1,000, which Willcox[5] preferred to regard as the criterion of urban settlements, it is clear that unless density is

---

[4]"The Anthropogeography of Some Great Cities," *Bulletin of the American Geographical Society*, XLI (1909), 537–66.

[5]Walter F. Willcox, "A Definition of 'City' in Terms of Density," in E. W. Burgess, *The Urban Community* (Chicago, 1926), p. 119.

correlated with significant social characteristics it can furnish only an arbitrary basis for differentiating urban from rural communities. Since our census enumerates the night rather than the day population of an area, the locale of the most intensive urban life—the city center—generally has low population density, and the industrial and commercial areas of the city, which contain the most characteristic economic activities underlying urban society, would scarcely anywhere be truly urban if density were literally interpreted as a mark of urbanism. The fact that the urban community is distinguished by a large aggregation and relatively dense concentration of population can scarcely be left out of account in a definition of the city; nevertheless these criteria must be seen as relative to the general cultural context in which cities arise and exist. They are sociologically relevant only in so far as they operate as conditioning factors in social life.

The same criticisms apply to such criteria as the occupation of the inhabitants, the existence of certain physical facilities, institutions, and forms of political organization. The question is not whether cities in our civilization or in others do exhibit these distinctive traits, but how potent they are in molding the character of social life into its specifically urban form. Nor in formulating a fertile definition can we afford to overlook the great variations between cities. By means of a typology of cities based upon size, location, age, and function, such as we have undertaken to establish in our recent report to the National Resources Committee,[6] we have found it feasible to array and classify urban communities from isolated trading-centers in the midst of agricultural regions to thriving world ports and commercial and industrial conurbations. Such differences as these appear crucial because the social characteristics and influences of these different "cities" vary widely.

A serviceable definition of urbanism should not only denote the essential characteristics which all cities—at least those in our culture— have in common, but should lend itself to the discovery of their variations. An industrial city will differ significantly in social respects from a commercial, mining, fishing, resort, university, or capital city. A one-industry city will present sets of social characteristics different from those of a multi-industry city, as will an industrially balanced from an imbalanced city, a suburb from a satellite, a residential suburb from and industrial suburb, a city within a metropolitan region from one lying outside, an old city from a new one, a southern city from a New

[6]*Op. cit.,* p. 8.

England one, a middle western from a Pacific Coast city, a growing from a stable and from a dying city.

A sociological definition must obviously be inclusive enough to comprise whatever essential characteristics these different types of cities have in common as social entities, but it obviously cannot be so detailed as to take account of all the variations implicit in the manifold classes sketched above. Presumably some of the characteristics of cities are more significant in conditioning the nature of urban life than others, and we may expect the outstanding features of the urban-social scene to vary in accordance with size, density, and differences in the functional type of cities. Moreover, we may infer that rural life will bear the imprint of urbanism in the measure that through contact and communication it comes under the influence of cities. It may contribute to the clarity of subsequent statements to repeat that while the locus of urbanism as a mode of life is, of course, to be found characteristically in places which fulfill the requirements we shall set up as a definition of the city, urbanism is not confined to such localities but is manifest in varying degrees wherever the influences of the city reach.

While urbanism, or that complex of traits which makes up the characteristic mode of life in cities, and urbanization, which denotes the development and extensions of these factors, are thus not exclusively found in settlements which are cities in the physical and demographic sense, they do, nevertheless, find their most pronounced expression in such areas, especially in metropolitan cities. In formulating a definition of the city it is necessary to exercise caution in order to avoid identifying urbanism as a way of life with any specific locally or historically conditioned cultural influences which, though they may significantly affect the specific character of the community, are not the essential determinants of its character as a city.

It is particularly important to call attention to the danger of confusing urbanism with industrialism and modern capitalism. The rise of cities in the modern world is undoubtedly not independent of the emergence of modern power-driven machine technology, mass production, and capitalistic enterprise; but different as the cities of earlier epochs may have been by virtue of their development in a preindustrial and precapitalistic order from the great cities of today, they were also cities.

For sociological purposes a city may be defined as a relatively large, dense, and permanent settlement of socially heterogeneous individuals. On the basis of the postulates which this minimal definition

suggests, a theory of urbanism may be formulated in the light of existing knowledge concerning social groups.

A Theory of Urbanism

In the rich literature on the city we look in vain for a theory systema-
tizing the available knowledge concerning the city as a social entity. We
do indeed have excellent formulations of theories on such special problems as the growth of the city viewed as a historical trend and as a recurrent process,[7] and we have a wealth of literature presenting insights
of social relevance and empirical studies offering detailed information
on a variety of particular aspects of urban life. But despite the multiplication of research and textbooks on the city, we do not as yet have a
comprehensive body of compendent hypotheses which may be derived
from a set of postulates implicitly contained in a sociological definition
of the city. Neither have we abstracted such hypotheses from our general sociological knowledge which may be substantiated through empirical research. The closest approximations to a systematic theory of
urbanism are to be found in a penetrating essay, "Die Stadt," by Max
Weber[8] and in a memorable paper by Robert E. Park on "The City:
Suggestions for the Investigation of Human Behavior in the Urban
Environment."[9] But even these excellent contributions are far from constituting an ordered and coherent framework of theory upon which research might profitably proceed.

Given a limited number of identifying characteristics of the city,
I can better assay the consequences or further characteristics of them
in the light of general sociological theory and empirical research. I
hope in this manner to arrive at the essential propositions comprising
a theory of urbanism. Some of these propositions can be supported by
a considerable body of already available research materials; others may
be accepted as hypotheses for which a certain amount of presumtive
evidence exists, but for which more ample and exact verification would
be required. At least such a procedure will, it is hoped, show what
in the way of systematic knowledge of the city we now have and what

[7]See Robert E. Park, Ernest W. Burgess, *et al., The City* (Chicago, 1925),
esp. chaps, ii and iii: Werner Sombart, "Stadtische Siedlung, Stadt, "*Hand-
wörtenbuch de Soziologie*. ed. Alfred Vierkandt (Stuttgart, 1931).
[8]*Wirtschaft und Gesellschaft* (Tübingen, 1925), Part I, chap. viii, pp. 514–601.
[9]Park, Burgess, *et al., op. cit.,* chap. i.

are the crucial and fruitful hypotheses for future research.

The central problem of the sociologist of the city is to discover the forms of social action and organization that typically emerge in relatively permanent, compact settlements of large numbers of heterogeneous individuals. We must also infer that urbanism will assume its most characteristic and extreme form in the measure in which the conditions with which it is congruent are present. Thus the larger, the more densely populated, and the more heterogeneous a community, the more accentuated the characteristics associated with urbanism will be. It should be recognized, however, that social institutions and practices may be accepted and continued for reasons other than those that originally brought them into existence, and that accordingly the urban mode of life may be perpetuated under conditions quite foreign to those necessary for its origin.

Some justification may be in order for the choice of the principal terms comprising our definition of the city, a definition which ought to be as inclusive and at the same time as denotative as possible without unnecessary assumptions. To say that large numbers are necessary to constitute a city means, of course, large numbers in relation to a restricted area or high density of settlement. There are, nevertheless, good reasons for treating large numbers and density as separate factors, because each may be connected with significantly different social consequences. Similarly the need for adding heterogeneity to numbers of population as a necessary and distinct criterion of urbanism might be questioned, since we should expect the range of differences to increase with number. In defense, it may be said that the city shows a kind and degree of heterogeneity of population which cannot be wholly accounted for by the law of large numbers or adequately represented by means of a normal distribution curve. Because the population of the city does not reproduce itself, it must recruit its migrants from other cities, the countryside, and—in the United States until recently—from other countries. The city has thus historically been the melting-pot of races, peoples, and cultures, and a most favorable breeding-ground of new biological and cultural hybrids. It has not only tolerated but rewarded individual differences. It has brought together people from the ends of the earth *because* they are different and thus useful to one another, rather than because they are homogeneous and like-minded.[10]

[10]The justification for including the term "permanent" in the definition may appear necessary. Our failure to give an extensive justification for this qualifying

A number of sociological propositions concerning the relationship between (a) numbers of population, (b) density of settlement, (c) heterogeneity of inhabitants and group life can be formulated on the basis of observation and research.

Size of the Population Aggregate

Ever since Aristotle's *Politics*,[11] it has been recognized that increasing the number of inhabitants in a settlement beyond a certain limit will affect the relationships between them and the character of the city. Lárge numbers involve, as has been pointed out, a greater range of individual variation. Furthermore, the greater the number of individuals participating in a process of interaction, the greater is the *potential* differentiation between them. The personal traits, the occupations, the cultural life, and the ideas of the members of an urban community may, therefore, be expected to range between more widely separated poles than those of rural inhabitants.

That such variations should give rise to the spatial segregation

---

mark of the urban rests on the obvious fact that unless human settlements take a fairly permanent root in a locality the characteristics or urban life cannot arise, and conversely the living together of large numbers of heterogeneous individuals under dense conditions is not possible without the development of a more or less technological structure.

[11]See esp. vii. 4. 4–14, trans. B. Jowett, from which the following be quoted:

"To the size of states there is a limit, as there is to other things, plants, animals, implements; for none of these retain their natural power when they are too large or too small, but they either wholly lose their nature, or are spoiled. . . . [A] state when composed of too few is not as a state ought to be, self-sufficing; when of too many, though self-sufficing in all mere necessaries, it is a nation and not a state, being almost incapable of constitutional government. For who can be the general of such a vast multitude, or who the herald, unless he have the voice of a Stentor?

"A state then only begins to exist when it has attained a population sufficient for a good life in the political community; it may indeed somewhat exceed this number. But, as I was saying, there must be a limit. What should be the limit will be easily ascertained by experience. For both governors and governed have duties to perform; the special functions of a governor are to command and to judge. But if the citizens of a state are to judge and to distribute offices according to merit, then they must know each other's characters; where they do not possess this knowledge, both the election to offices and the decision of lawsuits will go wrong. When the population is very large they are manifestly settled at haphazard, which clearly ought not to be. Besides, in an overpopulous state foreigners and metics will readily acquire the rights of citizens, for who will find them out? Clearly, then, the best limit of the population of a state is the largest number which suffices for the purposes of life, and can be taken in at single view. Enough concerning the size of a city."

of individuals according to color, ethnic heritage, economic and social status, tastes and preferences, may readily be inferred. The bonds of kinship, of neighborliness, and the sentiments arising out of living together for generations under a common folk tradition are likely to be absent or, at best, relatively weak in an aggregate the members of which have such diverse origins and backgrounds. Under such circumstances competition and formal control mechanisms furnish the substitutes for the bonds of solidarity that are relied upon to hold a folk society together.

Increase in the number of inhabitants of a community beyond a few hundred is bound to limit the possibility of each member of the community knowing all the others personally. Max Weber, in recognizing the social signifiance of this fact, explained that from a sociological point of view large numbers of inhabitants and density of settlement mean a lack of that mutual accquaintanceship which ordinarily inheres between the inhabitants in a neighborhood.[12] The increase in numbers thus involves a changed character of the social relationships. As Georg Simmel points out: "[If] the unceasing external contact of numbers of persons in the city should be met by the same number of inner reactions as in the small town, in which one knows almost every person he meets and to each of whom he has a positive relationship, one would be completely atomized internally and would fall into an unthinkable mental condition."[13] The multiplication of persons in a state of interaction under conditions which make their contact as full personalities impossible produces that segmentalization of human relationships which has sometimes been seized upon by students of the mental life of the cities as an explanation for the "schizoid" character of urban personality. This is not to say that the urban inhabitants have fewer acquaintances than rural inhabitants, for the reverse may actually be true; it means rather that in relation to the number of people whom they see and with whom they rub elbows in the course of daily life, they know a smaller proportion, and of these they have less intensive knowledge.

Characteristically, urbanites meet one another in highly segmental roles. They are, to be sure, dependent upon more people for the satisfactions of their life-needs than are rural people and thus are associated

[12]*Op. cit.,* p. 514.
[13]"Die Grosstädte und das Geistesleben," *Die Grösssstadt,* ed. Thodor Petermann (Dresden, 1903), pp. 187–206.

with a great number of organized groups, but they are less dependent upon particular persons, and their dependence upon others is confined to a highly fractionalized aspect of the other's round of activity. This is essentially what is meant by saying that the city is characterized by secondary rather than primary contacts. The contacts of the city may indeed be face to face, but they are nevertheless impersonal, superficial, transitory, and segmental. The reserve, the indifference, and the blasé outlook which urbanites manifest in their relationships may thus be regarded as devices for immunizing themselves against the personal claims and expectations of others.

The superficiality, the anonymity, and the transitory character of urban social relations make intelligible, also, the sophistication and the rationality generally ascribed to city-dwellers. Our acquaintances tend to stand in a relationship of utility to us in the sense that the role which each one plays in our life is overwhelmingly regarded as a means for the achievement of our own ends. Whereas the individual gains, on the one hand, a certain degree of emancipation or freedom from the personal and emotional controls of intimate groups, he loses, on the other hand, the spontaneous self-expression, the morale, and the sense of participation that comes with living in an integrated society. This constitutes essentially the state of *anomie,* or the social void, to which Durkheim alludes in attempting to account for the various forms of social disorganization in technological society.

The segmental character and utilitarian accent of interpersonal relations in the city find their institutional expression in the proliferation of specialized tasks which we see in their most developed form in the professions. The operations of the pecuniary nexus lead to predatory relationships which tend to obstruct the efficient functioning of the social order unless checked by professional codes and occupational etiquette. The premium put upon utility and efficiency suggests the adaptability of the corporate device for the organization of enterprises in which individuals can engage only in groups. The advantage that the corporation has over the individual entrepreneur and the partnership in the urban-industrial world derives not only from the possibility it affords of centralizing the resources of thousands of individuals or from the legal privilege of limited liability and perpetual succession, but from the fact that the corporation has no soul.

The specialization of individuals, particularly in their occupations, can proceed only, as Adam Smith pointed out, upon the basis of an enlarged market, which in turn accentuates the division of labor. This enlarged market is only in part supplied by the city's hinterland; in large measure it is found among the larger numbers that the city itself contains. The dominance of the city over the surrounding hinterland becomes explicable in terms of the division of labor which urban life occasions and promotes. The extreme degree of interdependence and the unstable equilibrium of urban life are closely associated with the division of labor and the specialization of occupations. This interdependence and this instability are increased by the tendency of each city to specialize in those functions in which it has the greatest advantage.

In a community composed of a larger number of individuals than can know one another intimately and can be assembled in one spot, it becomes necessary to communicate through indirect media and to articulate individual interests by a process of delegation. Typically in the city, interests are made effective through representation. The individual counts for little, but the voice of the representative is heard with a deference roughly proportional to the numbers for whom he speaks.

While this characterization of urbanism, in so far as it derives from large numbers, does not by any means exhaust the sociological inferences that might be drawn from our knowledge of the relationship of the size of a group to the characteristic behavior of the members, for the sake of brevity the assertions made may serve to exemplify the sort of propositions that might be developed.

Density

As in the case of numbers, so in the case of concentration in limited space certain consequences of relevance in sociological analysis of the city emerge. Of these only a few can be indicated.

As Darwin pointed out for flora and fauna and as Durkheim noted in the case of human societies,[14] an increase in numbers when area is held constant (i.e., an increase in density) tends to produce differentiation and specialization, since only in this way can the area support increased numbers. Density thus reinforced the effect of numbers in diversifying men and their activities and in increasing the complexity of the social structure.

On the subjective side, as Simmel has suggested, the close physical contact of numerous individuals necessarily produces a shift in the

[14]É. Durkheim, *De la division du travail social* (Paris, 1932), p. 248.

media through which we orient ourselves to the urban milieu, especially to our fellowmen. Typically, our physical contacts are close but our social contacts are distant. The urban world puts a premium on visual recognition. We see the uniform which denotes the role of the functionaries, and are oblivious to the personal eccentricities hidden behind the uniform. We tend to acquire and develop a sensititivity to a world of artifacts, and become progressively farther removed from the world of nature.

We are exposed to glaring contrasts between splendor and squalor, between riches and poverty, intelligence and ignorance, order and chaos. The competition for space is great, so that each area generally tends to be put to the use which yields the greatest economic return. Place of work tends to become dissociated from place of residence, for the proximity of industrial and commercial establishments makes an area both economically and socially undesirable for residential purposes.

Density, land values, rentals, accessibility, healthfulness, prestige, aesthetic consideration, absence of nuisances such as noise, smoke, and dirt determine the desirability of various areas of the city as places of settlement for different sections of the population. Place and nature of work income, racial and ethnic characteristics, social status, custom, habit, taste, preference, and prejudice are among the significant factors in accordance with which the urban population is selected and distributed into more or less distinct settlements. Diverse population elements inhabiting a compact settlement thus become segregated from one another in the degree in which their requirements and modes of life are incompatible and in the measure in which they are antagonistic. Similarly, persons of homogeneous status and needs unwittingly drift into, consciously select, or are forced by circumstances into the same area. The different parts of the city acquire specialized functions, and the city consequently comes to resemble a mosaic of social worlds in which the transition from one to the other is abrupt. The juxtaposition of divergent personalities and modes of life tends to produce a relativistic perspective and a sense of toleration of differences which may be regarded as prerequisites or rationality and which lead toward the secularization of life.[15]

[15]The extent to which the segregation of the population into distinct ecological and cultural areas and the resulting social attitude of tolerance, rationality, and secular mentality are funtions of density as distinguished from heterogeneity is difficult to determine. Most likely we are dealing here with phenomena which are consequences of the simultaneous operation of both factors.

The close living together and working together of individuals who have no sentimental and emotional ties foster a spirit of competition, aggrandizement, and mutual exploitation. Formal controls are instituted to counteract irresponsibility and potential disorder. Without rigid adherence to predictable routines a large compact society would scarcely be able to maintain itself. The clock and the traffic signal are symbolic of the basis of our social order in the urban world. Frequent close physical contact, coupled with great social distance, accentuates the reserve of unattached individuals toward one another and, unless compensated by other opportunities for response, gives rise to loneliness. The necessary frequent movement of great numbers of individuals in a congested habitat causes friction and irritation. Nervous tensions which derive from such personal frustrations are increased by the rapid tempo and the complicated technology under which life in dense areas must be lived.

Heterogeneity

The social interaction among such a variety of personality types in the urban milieu tends to break down the rigidity of caste lines and to complicate the class structure; it thus induces a more ramified and differentiated frame work of social stratification than is found in more integrated societies. The heightened mobility of the individual, which brings him within the range of stimulation by a great number of diverse individuals and subjects him to fluctuating status in the differentiated social groups that compose the social structure of the city, brings him toward the acceptance of instability and insecurity in the world at large as a norm. This fact helps to account too, for the sophistication and cosmopolitanism of the urbanite. No single group has the undivided allegiance of the individual. The groups with which he is affiliated do not lend themselves readily to a simple hierarchical arrangement. By virtue of his different interests arising out of different aspects of social life, the individual acquires membership in widely divergent groups, each of which functions only with reference to a certain segment of his personality. Nor do these groups easily permit of a concentric arrangement so that the narrower ones fall within the circumference of the more inclusive ones, as is more likely to be the case in the rural community or in primitive societies. Rather the groups with which the person typically is affiliated are tangential to each other or intersect in highly variable fashion.

Partly as a result of the physical footlooseness of the population and partly as a result of their social mobility, the turnover in group membership generally is rapid. Place of residence, place and character of employment, income, and interests fluctuate, and the task of holding organizations together and maintaining and promoting intimate and lasting acquaintanceship between the members is difficult. This applies strikingly to the local areas within the city into which persons become segregated more by virtue of differences in race, language, income, and social status than through choice or positive attraction to people like themselves. Overwhelmingly the city-dweller is not a home-owner, and since a transitory habitat does not generate binding traditions and sentiments, only rarely is he a true neighbor. There is little opportunity for the individual to obtain a conception of the city as a whole or to survey his place in the total scheme. Consequently he finds it difficult to determine what is to his own "best interests" and to decide between the issues and leaders presented to him by the agencies of mass suggestion. Individuals who are thus detached from the organized bodies which integrate society comprise the fluid masses that make collective behavior in the urban community so unpredictable and hence so problematical.

Although the city, through the recruitment of variant types to perform its diverse tasks and the accentuation of their uniqueness through competition and the premium upon eccentricity, novelty, efficient performance, and inventiveness, produces a highly differentiated population, it also exercises a leveling influence. Wherever large numbers of differently constituted individuals congregate, the process of depersonalization also enters. This leveling tendency inheres in part in the economic basis of the city. The development of large cities, at least in the modern age, was largely dependent upon the concentrative force of steam. The rise of the factory made possible mass production for an impersonal market. The fullest exploitation of the possibilities of the division of labor and mass production, however, is possible only with standardization of processes and products. A money economy goes hand in hand with such a system of production. Progressively as cities have developed upon a background of this system of production, the pecuniary nexus which implies the purchasability of services and things has displaced personal relations as the basis of association. Individuality under these circumstances must be replaced by categories. When large numbers have to make common use of facilities and institutions, those facilities and institutions must serve the needs of the average person rather than those of particular individuals. The services of the public utilities, of the recreational, educational, and cultural institutions, must be adjusted to mass requirements. Similarly, the cultural institutions, such as the schools, the movies, the radio, and the newspapers, by virtue of their mass clientele, must necessarily operate as leveling influences. The political process as it appears in urban life could not be understood unless one examined the mass appeals made through modern propaganda techniques. If the individual would participate at all in the social, political, and economic life of the city, he must subordinate some of his individuality to the demands of the larger community and in that measure immerse himself in mass movements.

The Relation between a Theory of Urbanism and Sociological Research

By means of a body of theory such as that illustratively sketched above, the complicated and many-sided phenomena of urbanism may be analyzed in terms of a limited number of basic categories. The sociological approach to the city thus acquires an essential unity and coherence enabling the empirical investigator not merely to focus more distinctly upon the problems and processes that properly fall in his province but also to treat his subject matter in a more integrated and systematic fashion. A few typical findings of empirical research in the field of urbanism, with special reference to the United States, may be indicated to substantiate the theoretical propositions set forth in the preceding pages, and some of the crucial problems for further study may be outlined.

On the basis of the three variables, number, density of settlement, and degree of heterogeneity, of the urban population, it appears possible to explain the characteristics of urban life and to account for the differences between cities of various sizes and types.

Urbanism as a characteristic mode of life may be approached empirically from three interrelated perspectives: (1) as a physical structure comprising a population base, a technology, and and ecological order; (2) as a system of social organization involving a characteristic social structure, a series of social institutions, and a typical pattern of social relationships; and (3) as a set of attitudes and ideas, and a constellation of personalities engaging in typical forms of collective behavior and subject to characteristic mechanisms of social control.

Urbanism in Ecological Perspective

Since in the case of physical structure and ecological process we are able to operate with fairly objective indices, it becomes possible to arrive at quite precise and generally quantitative results. The dominance of the city over its hinterland becomes explicable through the functional characteristics of the city which derive in large measure from the effect of numbers and density. Many of the technical facilities and the skills and organizations to which urban life gives rise can grow and prosper only in cities where the demand is sufficiently great. The nature and scope of the services rendered by these organizations and institutions and the advantage which they enjoy over the less developed facilities of smaller towns enhance the dominance of the city, making ever wider regions dependent upon the central metropolis.

The composition of an urban population shows the operation of selective and differentiating factors. Cities contain a larger proportion of persons in the prime of life than rural areas, which contain more old and very young people. In this, as in so many other respects, the larger the city the more this specific characteristic of urbanism is apparent. With the exception of the largest cities, which have attracted the bulk of the foreign-born males, and a few other special types of cities, women predominate numerically over men. The heterogeneity of the urban population is further indicated along racial and ethnic lines. The foreign-born and their children constitute nearly two-thirds of all the inhabitants of cities of one million and over. Their proportion in the urban population declines as the size of the city decreases, until in the rural areas they comprise only about one-sixth of the total population. The larger cities similarly have attracted more Negroes and other racial groups than have the smaller communities. Considering that age, sex, race, and ethnic origin are associated with other factors such as occupation and interest, one sees that a major characteristic of the urban-dweller is his dissimilarity from his fellows. Never before have such large masses of people of diverse traits as we find in our cities been thrown together into such close physical contact as in the great cities of America. Cities generally, and American cities in particular, comprise a motley of peoples and cultures of highly differentiated modes of life between which there often is only the faintest communication, the greatest indifference, the broadest tolerance, occasionally bitter strife, but always the sharpest contrast.

The failure of the urban population to reproduce itself appears to be a biological consequence of a combination of factors in the complex of urban life, and the decline in the birth rate generally may be regarded as one of the most significant signs of the urbanization of the Western world. Though the proportion of deaths in cities is slightly greater than in the country, the outstanding difference between the failure of the present-day cities to maintain their population and that of cities of the past is that in former times it was due to the exceedingly high death rates in cities, whereas today, since cities have become more livable from a health standpoint, it is due to low birth rates. These biological characteristics of the urban population are significant sociologically, not merely because they reflect the urban mode of existence but also because they condition the growth and future dominance of cities and their basic social organization. Since cities are the consumers rather than the producers of men, the value of human life and the social estimation of the personality will not be unaffected by the balance between births and deaths. The pattern of land use, of land values, rentals, and ownership, the nature and functioning of the physical structures, of housing, of transportation and communication facilities, of public utilities—these and many other phases of the physical mechanism of the city are not isolated phenomena unrelated to the city as a social entity but are affected by and affect the urban mode of life.

Urbanism as a Form of Social Organization

The distinctive features of the urban mode of life have often been described sociologically as consisting of the substitution of secondary for primary contacts, the weakening of bonds of kinship, and the declining social signifiance of the family, the disappearance of the neighborhood, and the undermining of the traditional basis of social solidarity. All these phenomena can be substantially verified through objective indices. Thus, for instance, the low and declining urban-reproduction rates suggest that the city is not conducive to the traditional type of family life, including the rearing of children and the maintenance of the home as the locus of a whole round of vital activities. The transfer of industrial, educational, and recreational activities to specialized institutions outside the home has deprived the family of some of its most characteristic historical functions. In cities mothers are more likely to be employed, lodgers are more frequently part of the household, marriage tends to be postponed, and the proportion of single and unattached people is greater. Families are smaller and more frequently without children than in the country. The family as a unit of social life is emancipated from the larger kinship group characteristic of the country, and the individual members pursue their own diverging interests in their vocational, educational, religious, recreational, and political life.

Such functions as the maintenance of health, the methods of alleviating the hardships associated with personal and social insecurity, the provisions for education, recreation, and cultural advancement have given rise to highly specialized institutions on a community-wide, statewide, or even national basis. The same factors which have brought about greater personal insecurity also underlie the wider contrasts between individuals to be found in the urban world. While the city has broken down the rigid caste lines of preindustrial society, it has sharpened and differentiated income and status groups. Generally, a larger proportion of the adult urban population is gainfully employed than is the case with the adult-rural population. The white-collar class, comprising those employed in trade, in clerical, and in professional work, are proportionately more numerous in large cities and in metropolitan centers and in smaller towns than in the country.

On the whole, the city discourages an economic life in which the individual in time of crisis has a basis of subsistence to fall back upon, and it discourages self-employment. While incomes of city people are on the average higher than those of country people, the cost of living seems to be higher in the larger cities. Home-ownership involves greater burdens and is rarer. Rents are higher and absorb a larger proportion of the income. Although the urban-dweller has the benefit of many communal services, he spends a large proportion of his income for such items as recreation and advancement and a smaller proportion for food. What the communal services do not furnish, the urbanite must purchase, and there is virtually no human need which has remained unexploited by commercialism. Catering to thrills and furnishing means of escape from drudgery, monotony, and routine thus become one of the major functions of urban recreation, which at its best furnishes means for creative self-expression and spontaneous group association,

but which more typically in the urban world results in passive spec-
tatorism, on the one hand, or sensational record-smashing feats, on the
other.

Reduced to a stage of virtual impotence as an individual, the
urbanite is bound to exert himself by joining with others of similar interest into groups organized to obtain his ends. This results in the
enormous multiplication of voluntary organizations directed toward as
great a variety of objectives as there are human needs and interests.
While, on the one hand, the traditional ties of human association are
weakened, urban existence involves a much greater degree of interdependence between man and man and a more complicated, fragile, and
volatile form of mutual interrelations over many phases of which the
individual as such can exert scarcely any control. Frequently there is
only the most tenuous relationship between the economic position or
other basic factors that determine the individual's existence in the urban
world and the voluntary groups with which he is affiliated. In a primitive
and in a rural society it is generally possible to predict on the basis of
a few known factors who will belong to what and who will associate with
whom in almost every relationship of life, but in the city we can only
project the general pattern of group formation and affiliation, and this
pattern will display many incongruities and contradictions.

Urban Personality and Collective Behavior

It is largely through the activities of the voluntary groups, be
their objectives economic, political, educational, religious, recreational,
or cultural, that the urbanite expresses and developes his personality,
acquires status, and is able to carry on the round of activities that
constitutes his life career. It may easily be inferred, however, that the
organizational framework which these highly differentiated functions
call into being does not of itself insure the consistency and integrity
of the personalities whose interests it enlists. Personal disorganization,
mental breakdown, suicide, delinquency, crime, corruption, and disorder might be expected under these circumstances to be more prevalent
in the urban than in the rural community. This has been confirmed
in so far as comparable indexes are available, but the mechanisms
underlying these phenomena require further analysis.

Since for most group purposes it is impossible in the city to appeal individually to the large number of discrete and differentiated

citizens, and since it is only through the organizations to which men belong that their interests and resources can be enlisted for a collective cause, it may be inferred that social control in the city should typically proceed through formally organized groups. It follows, too, that the masses of men in the city are subject to manipulation by symbols and stereotypes managed by individuals working from afar or operating invisibly behind the scenes through their control of the instruments of communication. Self-government either in the economic, or political, or the cultural realm is under these circumstances reduced to a mere figure of speech, or, at best, is subject to the unstable equilibrium of pressure groups. In view of the ineffectiveness of actual kinship ties, we create fictional kinship groups. In the face of the disappearance of the territorial unit as a basis of social solidarity, we create interest units. Meanwhile the city as a community resolves itself into a series of tenuous segmental relationships superimposed upon a territorial base with a definite center but without a definite periphery, and upon a division of labor which far transcends the immediate locality and is world-wide in scope. The larger the number of persons in a state of interaction with another, the lower is the level of communication and the greater is the tendency for communication to proceed on an elementary level, *i.e.,* on the basis of those things which are assumed to be common or to be of interest to all.

It is obviously, therefore, to the emerging trends in the communication system and to the production and distribution technology that has come into existence with modern civilization that we must look for the symptoms which will indicate the probable development of urbanism as a mode of social life. The direction of the ongoing changes in urbanism will for good or ill transform not only the city but the world.

It is only in so far as the sociologist, with a workable theory of urbanism, has a clear conception of the city as a social entity that he can hope to develop a unified body of reliable knowledge—which what passes as "urban sociology" is certainly not at the present time. By taking his point of departure from a theory of urbanism such as that sketched in the foregoing pages, a theory to be elaborated, tested, and revised, in the light of further analysis and empirical research, the sociologist can hope to determine the criteria of relevance and validity of factual data. The miscellaneous assortment of disconnected information which has hitherto found its way into sociological treatises on the city may thus be sifted and incorporated into a coherent body of knowledge. Incidentally, only by means of some such theory will the sociologist escape the futile practice of voicing in the name of sociological science a variety of often unsupportable judgments about poverty, housing, city-planning, sanitation, municipal administration, policing, marketing, transportation, and other technical issues. Though the sociologist cannot solve any of these practical problems—at least not by himself—he may, if he discovers his proper function, have an important contribution to make to their comprehension and solution. The prospects for doing this are brightest through a general, theoretical, rather than through an *ad hoc* approach.

Louis Wirth

RURAL-URBAN DIFFERENCES

The separate development of rural and urban sociology in the United States is a regettable historical accident. It was due in some degree to the availablility of relatively large funds to agricultural experiment stations and to the absence in our government of a department concerned with cities and urban life, corresponding roughly to the functions of the Department of Agriculture in the case of rural life. The urban studies of the National Resources Committee marked the first public recognition of this fact.

Because of the administrative separation between rural and urban sociological research, methodical analysis of rural and urban likenesses and differences is lacking today.

The recent profound changes in the technology of living, especially in the United States and to some extent all over the world, have made such notions as we have about rural and urban likenesses and differences obsolete. The city has spilled over into the countryside. City ways of life have in some respects taken on a rural cast, particularly in the suburbs. On the other hand, industry, which hitherto was characteristic of cities, has gone into the countryside. Transportation has made the city accessible to rural people. The radio and, more lately, television promise to produce a virtual revolution. The time has come for a reexamination of the meaning of the concepts "urban" and "rural".

The difficulties that stand in the way of a rigorous comparison of rural and urban modes of life and problems are many, nowhere more numerous than in the United States and the countries of the Western

Reprinted by permission of the University of Chicago from *On Cities and Social Life*, Albert J. Reiss, Jr., ed. Copyright © 1956 by the University of Chicago Press.

world where the fusion of the two is becoming an inescapable fact. Urbanism is no longer synonymous with industrialism, and ruralism is no longer identified with unmechanized labor. Since social contact is no longer intimately dependent upon personal relations, size of community and location are of less significance for the mode of life. The standardization of ways of living tends to make rural life as we have known it look archaic in many respects; we look upon it more and more as a survival from an earlier era.

In "Urbanism as a Way of Life" I attempted to describe the city as a particular form of human association. The assumption obviously was that at the other pole of the city stood the country. I indicated then that "for sociological purposes a city may be defined as a relatively large, dense, and permanent settlement of socially heterogeneous individuals" and attempted to develop a series of interrelated propositions which I thought could be distilled from the existing knowledge of the city based upon the postulates which this minimal definition of the city as a social fact suggests.

Whatever we might discover about the city in this manner would manifestly have to be checked against what we know or could find out about human settlements which are not cities, i.e., against the country. Only after such a comparison was made would we be able to say that we had selected the significant aspects of urban life which made the city a distinctive form of human association. But just as cities differ, so do rural settlements differ from one another. In respect to each of my criteria of urban life—numbers, density, permanence, and heterogeneity—cities represent a vast continuum shading into non-urban settlements. The same is true of rural settlements be they rural non-farm settlements, villages, or scattered open farm areas. To lump the great variety of cities and rural settlements respectively together obscures more than it reveals the distinctive characteristics of each.

To set up ideal-typical polar concepts such as I have done, and many others before me have done, does not prove that city and country are fundamentally and necessarily different. It does not justify mistaking the hypothetical characteristics attributed to the urban and the rural modes of life for established facts, as has so often been done. Rather it suggests certain hypotheses to be tested in the light of empirical evidence which we must assiduously gather. Unfortunately this evidence has not been accumulated in such a fashion as to test critically any major hypothesis that has been proposed.

I do not wish this remark to be misconstrued as an indictment of the rich body of concrete materials that has been accumulated on what are called cities and what are called rural communities. My criticism is directed rather against the mechanical and relatively unsophisticated manner in which we have identified city and country. Here as in so many other fields students of social life have relied heavily upon the data gathered by others; since in our case so large a part of the date has its source in the various governmental censuses which for purposes of classification must necessarily use arbitrary definitions preferably based upon quantitative criteria, we have fallen into the trap of regarding these arbitrary definitions as actual entities, corresponding to something existing in social reality.

What is even more regrettable is the fact that having taken this arbitrary dichotomy as a base—it should be pointed out that technically it is a trichotomy: urban, rural non-farm, and rural farm—we have built our own data upon the same foundation and thus compounded the error. I might add parenthetically that even in respect to this system of classification the reliable knowledge that we have is far from adequate. One looks in vain in the textbooks about urban or rural sociology for a careful, detailed, and reliable comparison of city and country on the basis of: size of family, mortality, marital status, education, ethnic and racial origin, occupation, wealth, income, housing, religion, politics, recreation, stratification, mobility, contacts, associational membership and participation, consumption, savings, illness, physical defects, mental disorder, delinquency and crime, family organization, marriage practices, sex life, rearing of children and many other facts on which continuous time series would seem to be indispensable. This, however, is a deficiency that with patience and diligence might, in the course of a few years, be overcome.

The development of such series for the United States and the rest of the world, while devoutly to be wished, will not cure the fundamental difficulty I mentioned earlier. What we look forward to is not the piling up of a vast body of reliable, continuous information if this labor is to be largely wasted on a basic system of classification such as we have used up to now. The factor-by-factor analysis of any problem in terms of which rural and urban settlements have shown significant differences—whether it be vitality rates, crime rates, family expenditures, political affiliation and participation, or any one of a great number of aspects of human behavior—leads to sterile results. From a sampling of a number of studies, including my own, of the ways in which rural and urban people are supposed to differ, I have found that if we allow for each of these functional factors, virtually all of the differences between rural and urban behavior are accounted for without our resorting to the alleged urban and rural natural dissimilarity. If this should prove to be the experience of students generally, a new approach seems to be called for. What we wish to know is not so much how a settlement of 2,500 differs from one of 2,499 inhabitants, nor even how one kind of human settlement as a settlement differs from another, but rather how one mode of human association which may be closely related to a type of human settlement conditions behavior and problems. This general question for purpose of analysis should lead us to ask how numbers, density, and heterogeneity affect the relations between men. For such a purpose we might have to ignore the statistically defined categories of urban and rural and deal rather with degrees of a continuum.

Population in large numbers suggests individual variability, relative absence of intimate personal acquaintanceship, segmentalization of human relations and their anonymous, superficial, impersonal, transitory, and utilitarian character. Density may be expected to bring about and accentuate diversification and specialization and, given larger numbers of heterogeneous people, to bring about that unique condition of the coincidence of close physical contact with great social distances, glaring contrasts in mode of life and status, complex patterns of segregation, and the predominance of formal controls. Other associated phenomena should also, if our view of human nature in different social settings is correct, be found in accentuated form in the urban settlement: intensified mobility both physical and social, instability of life, flexibility of social structures and institutions, and differential participation of individuals in a great variety of conflicting, competing, and intersecting groups with a high rate of turnover, through which individuals find expression for their interests and meet some of their major life needs.

It is to these and similar *social* characteristics that students of urban and rural life must turn for a realistic understanding of the manner in which type of settlement is associated with mode of life and state of mine. It is important to note that the urban and rural modes of life are not necessarily confined to urban and rural settlements, respectively, for the reasons mentioned earlier, The same man who is the farm laborer from April to September is also the city hobo from October to March. The large-scale agricultural organizations may be no less impersonal than large-scale labor unions or manufacturers' organizations. I have seen forests of television antennae in rural areas of Pennsylvania and noted the absence of such antennae in large blocks of the slums of Chicago. Is the Negro tenant or sharecropper in Mississippi any more closely associated with the farm owner than a similar employee of a steel company in Pittsburgh with the plant manager?

Rather than taking our conjectured rural-urban types for granted, we might turn to what we actually find under specified conditions of life associated with what we call urban and rural communities.

Louis Wirth

HUMAN ECOLOGY

Human ecology as an academically recognized intellectual discipline is considerable younger than our century. It borrowed its conceptual framework and much of its method from plant and animal ecology, which are themselves but recent arrivals in the scientific world. When Ernst Haeckel coined the name for the new brance of biological science in 1869, he sought to call attention to the fact that the structure and behavior of organisms are significantly affected by their living together with other organisms of the same and other species and by their habitat.

Whatever else men are, they are also animals, and as such they exhibit the effects of physical aggregation and of their habitat. Much of what subsequently became human ecology had already been studied in a less systematic and scientific manner by geographers, historians, and philosophers under the general theme of "environmentalism." New impetus was given to the study of human ecology by the interest aroused in the relationship between population and the means of subsistence through the writings of Malthus and by the new understanding of the web of life, including the survival and development of species as postulated by Darwin and the theorists of evolution.

Developments in demography during the nineteenth century and the more accurate description of human settlements as furnished by the human geographers, together with the beginnings of social surveys of specific communities, particularly in England, set the stage for the systematic formulation of problems and the perfection of methods out of which have grown the ecological studies of the last generation.

Sociologists, both rural and urban, were at work studying the

Reprinted by permission of the University of Chicago from *On Cities and Social Life*, Albert J. Reiss, Jr., ed. Copyright 1945 by the University of Chicago Press.

human community by methods which subsequently have been called ecological long before human ecology was recognized as a distinctive field of scientific activity. A series of significant maps of the spatial distribution of vital and social phenomena in England had appeared in Henry Mayhew's *London Labour and the London Poor*. Booth's *Survey of the Life and Labour of the People in London* had furnished a notable example of the importance of a real study of the great metropolis. Von Thünen's *Der isolierte Staat* had given a theoretical framework for the understanding of successive concentric zones of land use of a region. The device of graphically presenting population composition by means of pyramids had already been used by pioneers in the United States Census. There had been studies of urban land use, of housing, and of the incidence of poverty, disease, and crime; and there had also been systematic interpretations of these phenomena on high theoretical levels, of which Henry George's *Progress and Poverty* is perhaps the outstanding example. Studies of the physical aspects of the human community had even found their way into sociological textbooks, exemplified by Albion W. Small and George Vincent's *An Introduction to the Study of Society*. C. J. Galpin, in his surveys of rural communities, notably in his *The Social Anatomy of an Agricultural Community*, had indicated the methods for depicting objectively the interrelations between the trade center and the hinterland. In addition, there had been numerous monographs of a more or less scientific nature on specific communities, towns, and cities in various parts of the country showing their growth, their social characteristics, their physical structure, and the incidence of problems such as housing and social disorganization.

It was not, however, until 1915, when Robert E. Park published his provocative paper on "The City: Suggestions for the Investigation of Human Behavior in City Environment" in the *American Journal of Sociology*, that what subsequently became recognized as the ecological study of the human community was systematically formulated. Park's suggestions stimulated a series of investigations which, in the course of a few years, led not merely to the accumulation of a rich body of objective data but also to an appreciation of the significance of the study of the community as a physical fact for the understanding of it as a social phenomenon and as a state of mind, and eventually to the recognition of the role that human ecology might play in the study of social life generally.

Human ecology, as Park conceived it, was not a brance of sociology but rather a perspective, a method, and a body of knowledge essential for the scientific study of social life, and hence, like social psychology, a general discipline basic to all the social sciences. He recognized its kinship to, and derivation from, geography and biology. But he emphasized that, unlike the former, human ecology was less concerned with the relationship between man and his habitat than with the relationship between man and man as affected, among other factors, by his habitat. In distinguishing it from plant and animal ecology, he stressed the unique characteristics of man and the human community. He noted that, unlike plants and animals, human beings in large measure make their own environment; they have relatively great powers of locomotion and thus are less attached to the immediate habitat in which by nature they are placed; they are conditioned by their capacity for symbolic communication, by rational behavior, and by the possession of an elaborate technology and culture. Moreover, in human aggregations we find the life of the individuals regulated by conscious controls, by rules, norms, and laws, and by formal organizations and institutions. These factors introduce into the study of human ecology complications unknown in the plant and animal world.

The focus of attention of ecological studies has been on localized or territorially delimited social structures and social phenomena. This has given to the community a central position in the conceptual framework of human ecology. Unfortunately this common-sense term, like all other common-sense terms when used in scientific discourse, has had the disadvantage of ambiguity. The early literature of human ecology was much concerned with the distinction between the community and the society. The former stressed the symbiotic relations, spatial and temporal dimensions, physical structure, competition, and the division of labor; the later stressed communication, consensus, common norms, values, conscious social control, and collective action. Unfortunately these two ideal-typical aspects of human social life have frequently been confused with concrete realities. Thus there has been a failure to see that all communities are also societies and all human societies bear at least some of the characteristics of communities. Competition, for instance, among human beings never takes the form of a blind struggle for life and survival. Rather, it manifests itself as a more or less regulated and controlled struggle for a living and for status. Whereas in the plant and the animal world the mechanisms of collective behavior, such as there are, are built into the structure of the organisms and can truly be described in terms of reflexes and instincts, the behavior of the human world can be understood only in the light of habit, custom, institutions, morals, ethics, and laws.

Aside from the considerable theoretical literature that has developed in the field of human ecology, the contributions of the discipline have become increasingly manifest as aspects of specific studies of communities and regions. As the ecological interest and techniques developed, almost all American community studies have given increasing evidence of the use of ecological methods and knowledge. This is as true of the studies of rural and urban communities as it is of those of wider regions. It is not merely because the ecological aspect of human social life yields a degree of objective knowledge, in the sense of non-controversial description of physical facts and offers possibilities for a high degree of mensuration and precision, but also because the relevance of the physical base of human social life is increasingly appreciated for the understanding of sociocultural phenomena that human ecology has found an increasingly important place in community studies and, for the matter, in all studies which have an areal dimension.

The emergence of human ecology as a scientific discipline and its recent development have already been adequately reviewed by others.[1] It is necessary in this review to sketch merely the newly developing interests, problems, procedures, and findings of the discipline. As might be expected, the most important developments and achievements of human ecology are not to be found in studies which pass under that label but are associated with empirical studies of rural and urban communities and of regions undertaken by sociologists, by other social scientists, and by specialists in other practical fields such as market analysis, administration, and planning.

Considerable progress has been made in the methods of delimiting the territorial bounds of social phenomena and relationships. This has called into being the concept of the natural area as distinguished from the administrative area. It has been found that the settlement of human beings, the patterning of social institutions, the incidence of social problems, and the intricate network of social interrelationships does not, except by accident, conform to arbitrarily delimited areas and

[1] See R. D. McKenzie, "The Field and Problems of Demography, Human Geography, and Human Ecology," chap. iv in *The Fields and Methods of Sociology*, ed. L. L. Bernard (New York: Long & Smith, Inc., 1934), pp. 52–66; and James A. Quinn, "Topical Summary of Current Literature on Human Ecology, *"American Journal of Sociology*, XLVI, No. 2 (September, 1940), 191–226.

that hence administrative areas only rarely coincide with the ecological or natural areas. In the study of urban life, for instance, the types of land use and the types of residential areas to be found in the city do not conform to the neat lines of precincts, wards, and other political and administrative boundaries. Neither do crime, disease, family disorganization, and, for that matter, political alignments fit themselves into the static patterns of formally adopted area units. They have patterns of their own, and they shift in accordance with the total conditions of life. Ecologists of humanity have developed the techniques of base maps, spot maps, and rate maps for the more accurate exploration and delineation of the actual incidence and distribution of these phenomena. Burgess' ideal concept of the growth of the city[2] and the many studies of delinquency, family disorganization, racial and economic distribution, housing, incomes, and standards of living in rural, as well as urban, areas have shown that students of social life cannot accept without considerable modification the presentation and analyses of data offered them by official agencies which must use arbitrary administrative areal units. The development of census tracts in cities, for instance, by the United States Bureau of the Census represents a recognition of the need for reducing large arbitrary areal units to the smallest possible units for the purpose of scientific investigation.

Particularly in the study of urban areas and metropolitan regions has it become necessary to discover the actual extent of the influence exerted by the center upon the periphery. This applies as much to social institutions as it does to technology and to population aggregates. A metropolis, through its intricate network of interrelationships, extends its range of influence upon a territory usually far beyond the orbit of the immediately surrounding urbanized fringe. Because the census gives us a picture of human settlements in accordance with where people sleep rather than where they work, we are likely to gain a false impression of the economic and social entity constituting the metropolis and tend to conceive of it primarily as a political unit.

The recognition of the factors which underlie the distribution of people and which account for the differentiation of types of human settlements has important implications for social control, especially government. For instance, whereas the criminal is free to move about, irrespective of political boundaries, the police are hedged in by rigid

[2]Robert E. Park, E. W. Burgess, *et al.*, *The City* (Chicago: University of Chicago Press, 1925), chap. ii.

lines of areal jurisdiction; and whereas disease germs are no respecters of administrative barriers, health officials are often limited to a district. The no-man's-land on the margin of two or more jurisdictions, so frequently the favorite location for contraband activities, is the result of the discrepancy between natural and administrative areas. The lack of coincidence between natural areas (which are defined by the range of actual functions and which are constantly in flux) and administrative areas (which are defined by law and are relatively static) is of particular concern to community organization and planning. Unless the area of community organization and planning is approximately coextensive with the area over which the phenomena to be organized or planned extend, there is bound to be confusion and ineffectiveness.

To the research in human ecology belongs much of the credit for the more realistic conception of the community and the region. The Fifteenth Census of the United States (1930), in its special monograph on *Metropolitan District*,[3] took explicit account of the regional scope of at least our larger urban centers. McKenzie's study of the metropolitan community[4] traced "some of the basic changes that have taken place in American cities since the advent of motor transportation" and "the more important structural changes that are taking place in American settlement" as a result of new technological developments. By taking account of newspaper circulation as one of the factors determining the scope of the metropolitan region and the area of influence of urban institutions, this study suggested a series of subsequent investigations into the ecological aspects of social psychological phenomena which had hitherto been neglected or were not thought to be subject to objective analysis. The numerous studies which followed on radio-listening areas and on the area of influence of urban institutions, such as the stock exchange, the professional organization, and the health, welfare, educational, governmental, and cultural agencies and institutions, gave ample evidence of the theoretical as well as practical usefulness of this approach.

Nowhere has the new conception of the metropolis found greater recognition than in the field of planning. *The Regional Survey of New York and Its Environs*,[5] the National Resources Committee's *Regional*

[3]Washington: Government Printing Office, 1932.
[4]*The Metropolitan Community* (New York: McGraw-Hill Book Co., Inc., 1933).
[5]New York, 1927–31.

Factors in National Planning and Development,[6] and its *Our Cities: Their Role in the National Economy,*[7] together with supplementary reports, and such technical planning manuals as *Action for Cities: A Guide for Community Planning,*[8] show the extent to which the ecological point of view, concepts, methods, and findings have penetrated into the art and science of planning. What is true of urban studies is equally true of rural and wider regional analyses and planning enterprises.[9]

Even when planning was primarily physical planning, it offered great hospitality to the methods and findings of human ecology; but since planning has developed to include the economic and social designing or redesigning of the community, human ecology has found an even more important place in it. Planning aims at the optimum use of resources and the rational integration of community life. Such knowledge as the human ecologist has been able to obtain about the location of industry, the distribution, segregation, and succession of population, the areas of influence of social institutions, and the interrelationship between the physical, the technological, the economic, the political, and the cultural aspects of community life has proved itself indispensable.

It should be noted, however, that human ecology has not been merely the handmaiden either of the other social sciences, on the one hand, or of such practical arts as planning, on the other. It has, in recent years, developed a substantial body of scientific knowledge in its own right and has also drawn upon other branches of social science for its data and hypotheses. For instance, studies of communication, public opinion, markets, and voting have contributed immensely to the formulation of the problems of human ecology, the data with which the discipline works, and the explanations and interpretations toward which it strives.

It should also be noted that, although the most intensive studies of human ecology have been concerned with urban and rural communities, human ecology has also been applied to larger areas and to world-wide phenomena. Thus the patterns of urbanization, the trends of migration, the interrelations between national states, the functions

[6]Washington: Government Printing Office, 1935.

[7]*Ibid.,* 1937.

[8]Published under the sponsorship of the American Municipal Association, the American Society of Planning Officials, and the International City Managers' Association (Chicago: Public Administration Service, 1943).

[9]Cf. Rupert B. Vance, "Rural Life Studies" prepared by the U.S. Department of Agriculture, Bureau of Agricultural Economics.

of frontiers, and the problems of minorities, among others, have been studies at least in a preliminary way by the methods of human ecology; and there is every reason to believe that in the future the knowledge gained from local small-scale research will be applied to the world as a whole.

The accumulation of vast bodies of precise, descriptive material and its graphic presentation by means of maps and diagrams has unfortunately led some investigators to assume that the facts are either self-explanatory or that one set of ecological facts can be adequately interpreted in terms of other ecological data. In the ecological studies of delinquency, insanity, family disorganization, religious life, political behavior, and social institutions it has sometimes been naïvely assumed that, once the spatial distribution of people, institutions, functions, and problems has been traced and their concentration and dispersion noted, there remains nothing for the ecologist to do but to relate these phenomena to other ecological data to arrive at valid explanations. This view overlooks the fact that social life is a complex interdependent whole. Material conditions of existence are, of course, important factors in the determination of social structure and personal characteristics and behavior. Subsistence, competition, the division of labor, spatial and temporal arrangements, and distributions are important aspects of the material conditions of existence and, in turn, of social life. But they are not the whole of social life, On the contrary, as has been adequately demonstrated through numerous investigation, types of attitudes, personalities, cultural forms, and social organizations and institutions may have as significant an effect in shaping ecological patterns and processes as the latter have in conditioning social and social-psychological phenomena. Indeed, in view of our present-day knowledge concerning social causation, we might well be predisposed to follow the general principle that physical factors, while by no means negligible in their influence upon social life and psychological phenomena, are at best conditioning factors offering the possibilities and setting the limits for social and psychological existence and development. In other words, they set the stage for man, the actor. We are not yet far enough advanced to say with confidence what importance shall be ascribed to any one factor operating in the complex sphere of the social and the psychological, much less to evaluate the relative importance of physical as distinguished from social and psychological factors.

This does not, of course, mean that ecological studies are irrelevant to sociology and to the social sciences. They furnish the indispensable framework of knowledge upon which social and psychic existence rests. They often aid us in defining and localizing our problems. They aid us in uncovering interrelationships of which otherwise we might not be fully aware, and they suggest the selection of criteria for controlled study. It is as yet questionable to what extent ecological facts may serve as indexes of social and psychological facts. For instance, the use of income, occupation, area of residence, home-ownership, rental, and duration of settlement may well be justified in the analysis of social status; but if social status is not to be thought of as identical with economic status and if, as we might well suspect, economic status itself is the resultant of factors among which those cited are only a few, then the use of such an index as rental for economic status, not to speak of social status, is likely to be misleading. Used judiciously, however, such an index may prove itself useful for scientific analysis, especially when its correlation with other facts of the same order has been established.

The studies showing significant differences in such phenomena as delinquency and mental disorders between different areas of the city are of the utmost importance for the advance of scientific knowledge. The establishment of gradients for rates of personal and social disorganization passing from the center of the city out toward its periphery is a scientific achievement which carries us far beyond the common-sense knowledge we have had hitherto. But it would be absurd to say that there is something in the inlying areas themselves or in the fact that they are close to the center of the city that produces these high rates of delinquency or other forms of social disorganizations. It is rather to the relative concentration and segregation of certain population groups living under certain conditions and in a certain culture that we must look for an explanation of these facts. Human ecology thus provides us with one of the hitherto neglected aspects of the matrix within which social events take place and hence with a conceptual framework and a battery of techniques through which these social phenomena can be more fully and adequately understood.

It would be vain, however, to expect human ecology to give us more than a segmental view of the group life of man which sociology seeks to depict and to understand. Working in cooperation with students of social organization and social psychology, human ecologists can furnish a more comprehensive and a more realistic analysis of society than would otherwise be possible. They can introduce into the study of social phenomena objective referents which will anchor the generalizations concerning society, for which all sociologists strive, more firmly in time, in space, and material reality. Human ecology is not a substitute for, but a supplement to, the other frames of reference and methods of social investigation. By introducing some of the spirit and much of the substance and methods appropriate to the natural sciences into the study of social phenomena, human ecology has called attention to the wide areas where social life can properly be studied as if the observer were not an integral part of the observed. This beneficent influence would be negated, however, if the human ecologists were to proceed as if they, together with the demographers and the statisticians, were the only true scientists among the sociologists, or as if they, unaided by others using different approaches, alone could comprehend and explain the complicated and elusive realities in the realm of the social.

THE FOLK SOCIETY
Robert Redfield

Abstract

Understanding of society may be gained through construction of an ideal type of primitive or folk society as contrasted with modern urbanized society. Such a society is small, isolated, nonliterate, and homogeneous, with a strong sense of group solidarity. The ways of living are conventionalized into that coherent system which we call "a culture." Behavior is traditional, spontaneous, uncritical, and personal; there is no legislation or habit of experiment and reflection for intellectual ends. Kinship, its relationships and institutions, are the type categories of experience and the familial group is the unit of action. The sacred prevails over the secular; the economy is one of status rather than of the market. These and related characterizations may be restated in terms of "folk mentality." In studying societies comparatively, or one society in the course of change, with the aid of these conceptions, problems arise and are, in part, solved as to the necessary or probable interrelations of some of the elements of the ideal folk society with others. One such relationship is that between disorganization of culture and secularization.

I

Understanding of society in general and of our own modern urbanized society in particular can be gained through consideration of the societies least like our own: the primitive, or folk, societies.[1] All societies are alike in some respects, and each differs from others in other respects;

Reprinted by permission of the University of Chicago from *The American Journal of Sociology*, Vol. LII. Copyright 1947 by the University of Chicago.

[1] Neither the term "primitive" nor any other is denotative, and none has sufficient generally accepted precise meaning to allow us to know in just what

the further assumption made here is that folk societies have certain features in common which enable us to think of them as a type—a type which contrasts with the society of the modern city.[2]

This type is ideal, a mental construction. No known society precisely corresponds with it, but the societies which have been the chief interest of the anthropologist most closely approximate it. The construction of the type depends, indeed, upon special knowledge of tribal and peasant groups. The ideal folk society could be defined through assembling, in the imagination, the characters which are logically opposite those which are to be found in the modern city, only if we had first some knowledge of nonurban peoples to permit us to determine what, indeed, are the characteristic features of modern city living. The complete procedure requires us to gain acquaintance with many folk societies in many parts of the world and to set down in words general enough to describe most of them those characteristics which they have in common with each other and which the modern city does not have.

In short, we move from folk society to folk society, asking ourselves what it is about them that makes them like each other and different from the modern city. So we assemble the elements of the ideal type. The more elements we add, the less will any one real society correspond to it. As

characters of a society to discover the degree to which it is or is not "primitive," "simple," or whatever. The words "nonliterate" or "preliterate" do call attention to a particular character, literacy, but understanding is still required as to when a society is "literate" and as to what form or degree of literacy has significance. There are head-hunting tribes, in other respects as primitive as were the Pawnee Indians in the seventeenth century, that have knowledge of writing. In certain Mexican villages most children and many adults have formal knowledge of the arts of reading and writing, but in most other respects these village societies are much more like tribal societies than they are like our western cities.

The word "folk," which will be used in this paper, is no more precise than any other. It is used here because, better than others, it suggests the inclusion in our comparisons of peasant and rustic people who are not wholly independent of cities and because in its compounds. "folklore" and "folk song," it points, in a rough way, to the presence of folklore and folk songs, as recognized by the collector of such materials, as a sign of a society to be examined in making up the characterization of the ideal type with which we are here concerned. But the question of the word to be used is of small importance.

[2]The reader may compare the conception developed in this paper with the ideal "sacred society" characterized by Howard Becker in "Ionia and Athens" (PhD. dissertation, University of Chicago, 1930), pp. 1–16; with similar conceptions developed in chapter i of *Social Thought from Lore to Science* by Harry Elmer Barnes and Howard Becker (Boston, New York: D. C. Health & Co., 1938); and with the application of the conception in *The Sociology of the Renaissance* by Alfred von Martion (London: Kegan Paul, Trench, Truburn & Co., Ltd., 1945).

the type is constructed, real societies may be arranged in an order of degree of resemblance to it. The conception develops that any one real society is more or less "folk." But the more elements we add, the less possible it becomes to arrange real societies in a single order of degree of resemblance to the type, because one of two societies will be found to resemble the idea type strongly in one character and weakly in another, while in the next society strong resemblance will lie in the latter character and not in the former. This situation, however, is an advantage, for it enables us to ask and perhaps answer questions, first, as to whether certain characters tend to be found together in most societies, and then, if certain of them do, why.

Anyone attempting to describe the ideal folk society must take account of and in large degree include certain characterizations which have been made of many students, each of whom has been attentive to some but not to all aspects of the contrast between folk and modern society. Certain students have derived the characterization from examination of a number of folk societies and have generalized upon them in the light of contrast provided by modern urban society; the procedure defined above and followed by the writer. This is illustrated by Goldenweiser's characterization of five primitive societies. He says that they are small, isolated, nonliterate; that they exhibit local cultures; that they are relatively homogeneous with regard to the distribution of knowledge, attitudes, and functions among the population; that the individual does not figure as a conspicuous unit; and that knowledge is not explicitly systematized.[3]

In other cases the students have compared the state of certain societies at an early time with the same, or historical descendant of the same, society at a later time. In this way Maine arrived at his influential contrasts between society based on kinship and society based on territory, and between a society of status and one of contract.[4] In the case of this procedure, as in the case of the next, broad and illuminating conceptions are offered us to apply to folk societies as we contrast them with modern urban society. We are to find out if one of the contrasting terms is properly applicable to folk society and the other term to modern urban society.

In the work of still other students there is apparent no detailed com-

[3]A. A. Goldenweiser, *Early Civilization* (New York: Alfred A. Knopf, 1922), pp. 117–18.
[4]Henry Maine, *Ancient Law* (London: J. Murray, 1861).

parison of folk with urbanized societies or of early society with later; rather, by inspection of our own society or of society in general, contrasting aspects of all society are recognized and named. This procedure is perhaps never followed in the unqualified manner just described, for in the instances about to be mentioned there is evidence that folk or ancient society has been compared with modern urbanized society. Nevertheless, the emphasis placed by men of this group is upon characteristics which, contrasting logically, in real fact coexist in every society and help to make it up. Here belongs Tönnies' contrast between *Gemeinschaft* and *Gesellschaft*, or that aspect of society which appears in the relations that develop without the deliberate intention of anyone out of the mere fact that men live together, as contrasted with that aspect of society which appears in the relations entered into deliberately by independent individuals through agreement to achieve certain recognized ends.[5] Comparable is Durkheim's distinction between that social solidarity which results from the sharing of common attitudes and sentiments and that which results from the complementary functional usefullnesses of the members of the group. In the "social segment"—the form of society existing in terms of "mechanical solidarity"—the law is "repressive"; in the "social organ"—the form of society existing in terms of "organic solidarity"—the law is "restitutive."[6]

It may be asked how closely the constructed type arrived at by any one investigator who follows the procedure sketched above will resemble that reached by another doing the same. It may be supposed that to the extent to which the real societies examined by the one investigator constitute a sample of the range and variety of societies similar to the sample constituted by the societies examined by the other, and the extent that the general conceptions tentatively held by the one are similar to those held by the other, the results will be (except as modified by other factors) the same. For the purposes of understanding which are served by the method of the constructed type, however, it is not necessary to consider the question. The type is an imagined entity,

[5]Ferdinand Tönnies, *Gemeinschaft und Gesellschaft* (1st ed., 1887), trans. and ed. Charles P. Loomis as *Fundamental Concepts of Sociology* (New York, Cincinnati, etc.: American Book Co., 1940).

[6]*Émile Durkheim on the Division of Labor in Society*, a translation by George Simpson of *De la division du travail social* (New York: Macmillan Co., 1933); Howard Becker, "Constructive Typology in the Social Sciences," *American Sociological Review*, V, No. 1 (February, 1940), 40–55; reprinted in Harry Elmer Barnes, Howard Becker, and Frances Bennett Becker (eds.), *Contemporary Social Theory* (New York: D. Appleton-Century Co., 1940), Part I.

created only because through it we may hope to understand reality. Its
function is to suggest aspects of real societies which deserve study, and
especially to suggest hypotheses as to what, under certain defined conditions, may be generally true about society. Any ideal type will do,
although it is safe to assert that ideal construction has most heuristic
value which depends on close and considered knowledge of real folk
societies and which is guided by an effective scientific imagination—
whatever that may be.

II

"The conception of a 'primitive society which we ought to form,"
wrote Sumner, "is that of small groups scattered over a territory."[7]
The folk society is a small society. There are no more people in it than
can come to know each other well, and they remain in long association
with each other. Among the Western Shoshone the individual parental
family was the group which went about, apart from other families, col-
lecting food; a group of families would assemble and so remain for a
few weeks, from time to time, to hunt together; during the winter
months such a group of families would form a single camp.[8] Such a
temporary village included perhaps a hundred people. The hunting or
food-collecting bands considered by Steward, representing many parts
of the world, contained, in most cases, only a few score people.[9] A
Southwestern pueblo contained no more than a few thousand persons.

The folk society is an isolated society. Probably there is no real
society whose members are in complete ignorance of the existence of
people other than themselves; the Andamanese, although their islands
were avoided by navigators for centuries, knew of outsiders and occasionally came in contact with Malay or Chinese visitors.[10] Nevertheless,
the folk societies we know are made up of people who have little communication with outsiders, and we may conceive of the ideal folk society

[7] W. G. Sumner, *Folkways* (Boston: Ginn & Co., 1907), p. 12.
[8] Julian Steward, *Basin-Plateau Aboriginal Sociopolitical Groups* (Smith-
soian Institution, Bureau of American Ethnology, Bull. 120 (Washington: Government Printing Office, 1938), pp. 230–34.
[9] Julian Steward, "Economic and Social Basis of Primitive Bands,' *Essays
in Anthropology Presented to A. L. Kroeber* (Berkeley: University of California
Press, 1936), pp. 341–42.
[10] A. R. Radcliffe-Brown, *The Andaman Islanders* (Cambridge: At the University Press, 1933), pp. 6–9.

as composed of persons having communication with no outsider.

This isolation is one half of a whole of which the other half is intimate communication among the members of the society. A group of recent castaways is a small and isolated society, but it is not a folk society; and if the castaways have come from different ships and different societies, there will have been no previous intimate communication among them, and the society will not be composed of people who are much alike.

May the isolation of the folk society be identified with the physical immobility of its members? In building this ideal type, we may conceive of the members of the society as remaining always within the small territory they occupy. There are some primitive peoples who have dwelt from time immemorial in the same small valley, and who rarely leave it.[11] Certain of the pueblos of the American Southwest have been occupied by the same people or their descendants for many generations. On the other hand, some of the food-collecting peoples, such as the Shoshone Indians and certain aborigines of Australia, move about within a territory of very considerable extent; and there are Asiatic folk groups that make regular seasonal migrations hundreds of miles in extent.

It is possible to conceive of the members of such a society as moving about physically without communicating with members of other groups than their own. Each of the Indian villages of the midwest highlands of Guatemala is a folk society distinguishable by its customs and even by the physical type of its members from neighboring villages, yet the people are great travelers, and in the case of one of the most distinct communities, Chichicastenango, most of the men travel far and much of their time away from home.[12] This does not result, however, in much intimate communication between those traveling villagers and other peoples. The gypsies have moved about among the various peoples of the earth for generations, and yet they retain many of the characteristics of a folk society.

Through books the civilized people communicate with the minds of other people and other times, and as aspect of the isolation of the folk society is the absence of books. The folk communicate only by word of

---

[11]A. L. Kroeber, *Handbook of Indians of California* (Smithsonian Institution, Bureau of American Ethnology, Bull. 78 (Washington: Government Printing Office, 1925), p. 13.

[12]Robert Redfield, "Primitive Merchants of Guatemala," *Quarterly Journal of Inter-American Relations,* I, No. 4, 42-56.

mouth; therefore the communication upon which understanding is built is only that which takes place among neighbors, within the little society itself. The folk has no access to the thought and experience of the past, whether of other peoples or of their own ancestors, such as books provide. Therefore, oral tradition has no check or competitor. Knowledge of what has gone before reaches no further back than memory and speech between old and young can make it go; behind "the time of our grandfathers" all is legendary and vague. With no form of belief established by written record, there can be no historical sense such as civilized people have, no theology, and no basis for science in recorded experiment. The only form of accumulation of experience, except the tools and other enduring articles of manufacture, is the increase of wisdom which comes as the individual lives longer; therefore the old, knowing more than the young can know until they too have lived that long, have prestige and authority.

The people who make up a folk society are much alike. Having lived in long intimacy with one another, and with no others, they have come to form a single biological type. The somatic homogeneity of local, inbred populations has been noted and studied. Since the people communicate with one another and with no others, one man's learned ways of doing and thinking are the same as another's. Another way of putting this is to say that in the ideal folk society, what one man knows and believes is the same as what all men know and believe. Habits are the same as customs. In real fact, of course, the differences among individuals in a primitive group and the different chances of experience prevent this ideal state of things from coming about. Nevertheless, it is near enough to the truth for the student of a real folk society to report it fairly well by learning what goes on in the minds of a few of its members, and a primitive group has been presented, although sketchily, as learned about from a single member. The similarity among the members is found also as one generation is compared with its successor. Old people find young people doing, as they grow up, what the old people did at the same age, and what they have come to think right and proper. This is another way of saying that in such a society there is little change.

The members of the folk society have a strong sense of belonging together. The group which an outsider might recognize as composed of similar persons different from members of other groups is also the group of people who see their own resemblances and feel correspondingly united. Communicating intimately with each other, each has a strong claim on the sympathies of the others. Moreover, against such knowledge as they have of societies other than their own, they emphasize their own mutual likeness and value themselves as compared with others. They say of themselves "we" as against all others, who are "they."[13]

Thus we may characterize the folk society as small, isolated, non-literate, and homogeneous, with a strong sense of group solidarity. Are we not soon to acknowledge the simplicity of the technology of the ideal folk society? Something should certainly be said about the tools and tool-making of this generalized primitive group, but it is not easy to assign a meaning to "simple," in connection with technology which will do justice to the facts as known from the real folk societies. The preciseness with which each tool, in a large number of such tools, meets its needs in the case of the Eskimo, for example, makes one hesitate to use the word "simple." Some negative statements appear to be safe: compared with primary tools; there is no making of artifacts by multiple, rapid, machine manufacture; there is little or no use of natural power.

There is not much division of labor in the folk society: what one person does is what another does. In the ideal folk society all the tools and ways of production are shared by everybody. The "everybody" must mean "every adult man" or "every adult woman," for the obvious exception to the homogeneity of the folk society lies in the differences between what men do and know and what women do and know. These differences are clear and unexceptional (as compared with our modern urban society where they are less so). "Within the local group there is no such thing as a division of labor save as between the sexes," writes Radcliffe-Brown about the Andaman Islanders." . . . Every man is expected to be able to hunt pig, to harpoon turtle and to catch fish, and also to cut a canoe, to make bows and arrows and all the other objects that are made by men."[14] So all men share the same interests and have, in general, the same experience of life.

We may conceive, also, of the ideal folk society as a group economically independent of all others: the people produce what they consume and consume what they produce. Few, if any, real societies are completely in this situation; some Eskimo groups perhaps most closely approach it. Although each little Andamanese band could get along with-

---

[13]Sumner, *op. cit.*, pp. 13–15.
[14]Radcliffe-Brown, *op. cit.*, p. 43.

out getting anything from any other, exchange of goods occured between bands by a sort of periodic gift-giving.

The foregoing characterizations amount, roughly, to saying that the folk society is a little world off by itself, a world in which the recurrent problems of life are met by all its members in much the same way. This statement, while correct enough, fails to emphasize an important, perhaps the important, aspect of the folk society. The ways in which the members of the society meet the recurrent problems of life are conventionalized ways; they are the results of long intercommunication within the group in the face of these problems; and these conventionalized ways have become interrelated within one another so that they constitute a coherent and self-consistent system. Such a system is what we mean in saying that the folk society is characterized by "a culture." A culture is an organization or integration of conventional understandings. It is, as well, the acts and the objects, in so far as they represent the type characteristic of that society, which express and maintain these understandings. In the folk society this integrated whole, this system, provides for all the recurrent needs of the individual from birth to death and of the society through the seasons and the years. The society is to be described, and distinguished from others, largely by presenting this system.

This is not the same as saying, as was said early in this paper, that in the folk society what one man does is the same as what another man does. What one man does in a mob is the same as what another man does, but a mob is not a folk society. It is, so far as culture is concerned, its very antithesis.[15] The members of a mob (which is a kind of "mass") each do the same thing, it is true, but it is a very immediate and particular thing, and it is done without much reference to tradition. It does not depend upon and express a great many conventional understandings related to one another. A mob is an aggregation of people doing the same simple thing simultaneously. A folk society is an organization of people doing many different things successively as well as simultaneously. The members of a mob act with reference to the same object of attention. The members of a folk society are guided in acting by previously established comprehensive and interdependent conventional understandings; at any one time they do many different things, which are complexly related to one another to express collective

[15]Herbert Blumer, Mass Behavior and the Motion Picture," *Publications of the American Sociological Society,* XXIX, No. 3 (August, 1935), 115–27.

sentiments and conceptions. When the turn comes for the boy to do what a man does, he does what a man does; thus, though in the end the experiences of all individuals of the same sex are alike, the activities of the society, seen at a moment of time, are diverse, while interdependent and consistent.

The Papago Indians, a few hundred of them, constituted a folk society in southern Arizona. Among these Indians a war party was not so simple a thing as a number of men going out together to kill the enemy. It was a complex activity involving everybody in the society both before, during, and after the expedition and dramatizing the religious and moral ideas fundamental to Papago life.[16] Preparation for the expedition involved many practical or ritual acts on the part of the immediate participants, their wives and children, previously success- ful warriors, and many others. While the party was away, the various relatives of the warriors had many things to do or not to do—prayer, fasting, preparation of ritual paraphernalia, etc. These were specialized activities, each appropriate to just that kind of relative or other cate- gory of person. So the war was waged by everybody. These activities, different and special as they were, interlocked, so to speak, with each other to make a large whole, the society-during-a-war-expedition. And all these specialized activities obeyed fundamental principles, understood by all and expressed and reaffirmed in the very forms of the acts—the gestures of the rituals, the words of songs, the implied or expressed explanations and admonitions of the elders to the younger people. All understood that the end in view was the acquistion by the group of the supernatural power of the slain enemy. This power, potentially of great positive value, was dangerous, and the practices and rituals had as their purposes first the success of the war party and then the draining- off of the supernatural power acquired by the slaying into a safe and "usable" form.

We may say, then, that in the folk society conventional behavior is strongly patterned; it tends to conform to a type or a norm. These patterns are interrelated in thought and in action with one another, so that one tends to evoke others and to be consistent with the others. Every customary act among the Papago when the successful warriors return is consistent with and is a special form of the general conceptions held as to supernatural power. We may still further say that the patterns

[16]Ruth Underhill, *The Autobiography of a Papago Woman* ("American An- thropoligical Association, Memoirs," No. 46 [1936]).

of what people think should be done are closely consistent with what they believe is done, and that there is one way, or a very few conventional ways, in which everybody has some understanding and some share, of meeting each need that arises.[17] The culture of a folk society is, therefore, one of those wholes which is greater than its parts. Gaining a livelihood takes support from religion, and the relations of men to men are justified in the conceptions held of the supernatural world or in some other aspect of the culture. Life, for the member of the folk society, is not one activity and then another and different one; it is one large activity out of which one part may not be separated without affecting the rest.

A related characteristic of the folk society was implied when it was declared that the specialized activities incident to the Papogo war party obeyed fundamental principles understood by all. These "principles" had to do with the ends of living, as conceived by the Papago. A near-ultimate good for the Papago was the acquisition of supernatural power. This end was not questioned; it was a sort of axiom in terms of which many lesser activities were understood. This suggests that we may say of the folk society that its ends are taken as given. The activities incident to the war party may be regarded as merely complementarily useful acts, aspects of the division of labor. They may also, and more significantly, be seen as expressions of unquestioned common ends. The folk society exists not so much in the exchange of useful functions as in common understanding as to the ends given. The ends are not stated as matters of doctrine, but are implied by the many acts which make up the living that goes on in the society. Therefore, the morale of a folk society—its power to act consistently over periods of time and to meet crises effectively is not dependent upon discipline exerted by force or upon devotion to some single principle of action but to the concurrence and consistency of many or all of the actions and conceptions which make up the whole round life. In the trite phrase, the folk society is a "design for living."

What is done in the ideal folk society is done not because somebody or some people decided, at once, that it should be done, but because it seems "necessarily" to flow from the very nature of things. There is, moreover, no disposition to reflect upon traditional acts and consider them objectively and critically. In short, behavior in the folk society

[17]Ralph Linton, *The Study of Man* (New York: D. Appleton-Century Co., 1936), chap. xvi, esp. p. 283.

is traditional, spontaneous, and uncritical. In any real folk society, of course, many things are done as a result of decision as to that particular action, but as to that class of actions tradition is the sufficient authority. The Indians decide now to go on a hunt; but it is not a matter of debate whether or not one should, from time to time, hunt.

The folkways are the ways that grow up out of long and intimate association of men with each other; in the society of our conception all the ways are folkways. Men act with reference to each other by understandings which are tacit and traditional. There are no formal contracts or other agreements. The rights and obligations of the individual come about not by special arrangement; they are, chiefly, aspects of the position of the individual as a person of one sex or the other, one age-group or another, one occupational group or another, and as one occupying just that position in a system of relationships which are traditional in the society. The individual's status is thus in large part fixed at birth; it changes as he lives, but it changes in ways which were "foreordained" by the nature of his particular society. The institutions of the folk society are of the sort which has been called "crescive"; they are not of the sort that is created deliberately for special purposes, as was the juvenile court. So, too, law is made up of the traditional conceptions of rights and obligations and the customary procedures whereby these rights and obligations are assured; legislation has no part in it.

If legislation has no part in the law of the ideal folk society, neither has codification, still less jurisprudence. Radin has collected material suggesting the limited extent to which real primitive people do question custom and do systematize their knowledge.[18] In the known folk societies they do these things only to a limited extent. In the ideal folk society there is no objectivity and no systematization of knowledge as guided by what seems to be its "internal" order. The member of this mentally constructed society does not stand off from his customary conduct and subject it to scrutiny apart from its meaning for him as that meaning is defined in culture. Nor is there any habitual exercise of classification, experiment, and abstraction for its own sake, least of all for the sake of intellectual ends. There is common practical knowledge, but there is no science.

Behavior in the folk society is highly conventional, custom fixes the rights and duties of individuals, and knowledge is not critically

---

[18]Paul Radin, *Primitive Man as Philosopher* (New York: D. Appleton-Century Co., 1927).

examined or objectively and systematically formulated; but it must not
be supposed that primitive man is a sort of automaton in which custom
is the mainspring. It would be as mistaken to think of primitive man as
strongly aware that he is constrained by custom. Within the limits set
by custom there is invitation to excel in performance. There is lively
competition, a sense of opportunity, and a feeling that what the culture
moves one to do is well worth doing. "There is no drabness in such a
life. It has about it all the allurements of personal experience, very
much one's own, of competitive skill, of things well done."[19] The interrelations and high degree of consistency among the elements of custom
which are presented to the individual declare to him the importance of
making his endeavors in the directions indicated by tradition. The
culture sets goals which stimulate action by giving great meaning to it.[20]

It has been said that the folk society is small and that its members
have lived in long and intimate association with one another. It has
also been said that in such societies there is little critical or abstract
thinking. These characteristics are related to yet another characteristic
of the folk society: behavior is personal, not impersonal. A "person"
may be defined as that social object which I feel to respond to situations as I do, with all the sentiments and interests which I feel to be
my own; a person is myself in another form, his qualities and values are
inherent within him, and his significance for me is not merely one
of utility. A "thing," on the other hand, is a social object which has no
claim upon my sympathies, which responds to me, as I conceive it,
mechanically; its value for me exists in so far as it serves my end. In
the folk society all human beings admitted to the society are treated
as persons; one does not deal impersonally ("thing-fashion") with any
other participant in the little world of that society. Moreover, in the folk
society much besides human beings is treated personally. The pattern
of behavior which is first suggested by the inner experience of the individual—his wishes, fears, sensitivenesses, and interests of all sorts—
is projected into all objects with which he comes into contact. Thus
nature, too, is treated personally: the elements, the features of the
landscape, the animals, and especially anything in the environment
which by its appearance or behavior suggests that it has the attributes of

[19]A. A. Goldenweiser, "Individual, Pattern and Involution," *Essays in Hon-
or of A. L. Kroeber* (Berkeley: University of California Press, 1936), p. 102.
[20]Ruth Benedict, *Patterns of Culture* (Boston and New York: Houghton
Mifflin Co., 1934).

mankind—to all these are attributed qualities of the human person.[21]

In short, the personal and intimate life of the child in the family is extended, in the folk society, into the social world of the adult and even too into inanimate objects. It is not merely that relations in such a society are personal; it is also that they are familial. The first contacts made as the infant becomes a person are with other persons; moreover, each of these first persons, he comes to learn, has a particular kind of relation to him which is associated with that one's genealogical position. The individual finds himself fixed withing a constellation of familial relationships. The kinship connections provide a pattern in terms of which, in the ideal folk society, all personal relations are conventionalized and categorized. All relations are personal. But relations are not, in content of specific behavior, the same for everyone. As a mother is different from a father, and a grandson from a nephew, so are these classes of personal relationship, originating in genealogical connection, extended outward into all relationships whatever. In this sense, the folk society is a familial society. Lowie[22] has demonstrated the qualification that is to be introduced into the statement of Maine[23] that the primitive society is organized in terms of kinship rather than territory. It is true that the fact that men are neighbors contributes to their sense of belonging together. But the point to be emphasized in understanding the folk society is that whether mere contiguity or relationship as brother or son is the circumstance uniting men into the society, the result is a group of people among whom prevail the personal and categorized relationships that characterize families as we know them, and in which the patterns of kinship tend to be extended outward from the group of genealogically connected individuals into the whole society. The kin are the type persons for all experience.

This general conception may be resolved into component or related conceptions. In the folk society family relationships are clearly distinguished from one another. Very special sorts of behavior may be expected by a mother's brother of his sister's son, and this behavior will be different from that expected by a father's brother of his brother's son. Among certain Australian tribes animals killed by a hunter must be divided so that nine or ten certain parts must be given to nine or

[21]Ruth Benedict, "Animism," *Encyclopaedia of the Social Sciences.*

[22]Robert H. Lowie, *The Origin of the State* (New York: Harcourt, Brace & Co., 1927), pp. 51–73.

[23]Maine, *Op. cit.*

ten corresponding relatives of the successful hunter—the right ribs to the father's brother, a piece of the flank to the mother's brother, and so on.[24] The tendency to extend kinship outward takes many special forms. In many primitive societies kinship terms and kinship behavior (in reduced degree) are extended to persons not known to be genealogically related at all, but who are nevertheless regarded as kin. Among the central Australians, terms of relationship are extended "so as to embrace all persons who come into social contact with one another. . . . In this way the whole society forms a body of relatives."[25] In the folk society groupings which do not arise out of genealogical connection are few, and those that do exist tend to take on the attributes of kinship. Ritual kinship is common in primitive and peasant societies in the forms of blood brotherhood, godparental relationships, and other ceremonial sponsorships.[26] These multiply kinship connections; in these cases the particular individuals to be united depend upon choice. Furthermore, there is frequently a recognizedly fictitious or metaphorical use of kinship terms to designate more casual relationships, as between host and guest or between worshipper and deity.[27]

The real primitive and peasant societies differ very greatly as to the forms assumed by kinship. Nevertheless, it is possible to recognize two main types. In one of these the connection between husband and wife is emphasized, while neither one of the lineages, matrilineal or patrilineal, is singled out as contrasted with the other. In such a folk society the individual parental family is the social unit, and connections with relatives outside this family are of secondary importance. Such family organization is common where the population is small, the means of livelihood are by precarious collection of wild food, and larger units cannot permanently remain together because the natural resources will not allow it. But where a somewhat larger population remains together, either in a village or in a migratory band, there often, although by no means always, is found an emphasis upon one one of consanguine connection rather than the other with subordination of the conjugal con-

[24]A. W. Howitt, *The Native Tribes of Southeastern Australia* (New York: Macmillan Co, 1904), p. 759.

[25]A. R. Radcliffe-Brown, "Three Tribes of Western Australia, *"Journal of the Royal Anthropological Institute*. XLIII, 150–51.

[26]Benjamin Paul, "Ritual Kinship: With Special Reference to Godparenthood in Middle America" (PhD. Thesis, University of Chicago, 1942).

[27]E. C. Parsons, *Notes on Zuni*, Part II ("American Anthropological Association Memoirs," Vol. IV, No. 4 [1917]).

nection.[28] There results a segmentation of the society into equivalent kinship units. These may take the form of extended domestic groups or joint families (as in China) or may include many households of persons related in part through recognized genealogical connection and in part through the sharing of the same name or other symbolic designation, in the latter case we speak of the groups as clans. Even in societies where the individual parental family is an independent economic unit, as in the case of the eastern Eskimo, husband and wife never become a new social and economic unit with the completeness that is characteristic of our own society. When a marriage in primitive society comes to an end, the kinsmen of the dead spouse assert upon his property a claim they have never given up.[29] On the whole, we may think the family among folk peoples as made up of persons consanguinely connected. Marriage is, in comparison with what we in our society directly experience, an incident in the life of the individual who is born, brought up, and dies with his blood kinsmen. In such a society romantic love can hardly be elevated to a major principle.

In so far as the consanguine lines are well defined (and in some cases both lines may be of importance to the individual)[30] the folk society may be thought of as composed of families rather than of individuals. It is the familial groups that act and are acted upon. There is strong solidarity within the kinship group, and the individual is responsible to all his kin as they are responsible to him. "The clan is a natural mutual aid society. . . . A member belongs to the clan, he is not his own; if he is wrong, they will right him; if he does wrong, the responsibility is shared by them."[31] Thus, in folk societies wherein the tendency to maintain consanguine connection has resulted in joint families of clans, it is usual to find that injuries done by an individual are regarded as injuries against his kinship groups, and the group takes the steps to right the wrong. The step may be revenge regulated by custom or a property settlement. A considerable part of primitive law exists in the regulation of claims by one body of kin against another. The fact that the folk society is an organization of families rather than an ag-

[28]Ralph Linton, *The Study of Society* (New York: Century Co.), p. 159.
[29]Ruth Benedict, "Marital Property Rights in Bilateral Societies," *American Anthropologist*, XXXVIII, No. 3 (July-September, 1936), 368–73.
[30]Peter Murdock, "Double Descent, *"American Anthropologist*, XLII (new ser.), No. 4, Part I (October-December, 1940), 555–61.
[31]Edwin W. Smith and Andrew Murray Dale, *The Ila-Speaking Peoples of Northern Rhodesia* (London: Macmillan & Co. Ltd., 1920, I, 296.

gregation of individuals is further expressed in many of those forms of marriage in which a certain kind of relative is the approved spouse. The customs by which in many primitive societies a man is expected to marry his deceased brother's widow or a women to marry her deceased sister's husband express the view of marriage as an undertaking between kinship groups. One of the spouses having failed by death, the undertaking is to be carried on by some other representative of the family group. Indeed, in the arrangements for marriage—the selection of spouses by their relatives, in bride price, dowry, and in many forms of familial negotions leading to a marriage—the nature of marriage as a connubial form of social relations between kindreds finds expression.

It has been said in the foregoing paragraphs that behavior in the folk society is traditional, spontaneous, and uncritical, that what one man does is much the same as what another man does, and that the patterns of conduct are clear and remain constant throughout the generations. It has also been suggested that the congruence of all parts of conventional behavior and social institutions with each other contributes to the sense of rightness which the member of the folk society feels to inhere in his traditional ways of action. In the well-known language of Sumner, the ways of life are folkways, furthermore, the folkways tend to be also mores—ways of doing or thinking to which attach notions of moral worth. The value of every traditional act or object or institution is, thus, something which the members of the society are not disposed to call into question; and should the value be called into question, the doing so is resented. This characteristic of the folk society may be briefly referred to by saying that it is a sacred society. In the folk society one may not, without calling into effect negative social sanctions, challenge as valueless what has come to be traditional in that society.

Presumably, the sacredness of social objects has its source, in part, at least, in the mere fact of habituation; probably the individual organism becomes early adjusted to certain habits, motor and mental, and to certain associations between one activity and another or between certain sense experiences and certain activities, and it is almost physiologically uncomfortable to change or even to entertain the idea of change. There arises "a feeling of impropriety of certain forms, of a particular social or religious value, or a superstitious fear of change."[32] Probably the sacredness of social objects in the folk society is related also to the fact that in such well-organized cultures acts and objects

[32]Franz Boas, *Primitive Art* (Oslo, 1927), p. 150.

suggest the traditions, beliefs and conceptions which all share. There is reason to suppose that when what is traditionally done becomes less meaningful because people no longer know what the acts stand for, life becomes more secular.[33] In the repetitious character of conventional action (aside from technical action) we have ritual; in its expressive character we have ceremony; in the folk society ritual tends also to be ceremonious, and ritual-ceremony tends to be sacred, not secular.

The sacredness of social objects is apparent in the ways in which, in the folk society, such an object is hedged around with restraints and protections that keep it away from the commonplace and the matter-of-fact.[34] In the sacred there is alternatively, or in combination, holiness and dangerousness. When the Papago Indian returned from a successful war expedition, bringing the scalp of a slain Apache, the head-hairs of the enemy were treated as loaded with a tremendous "charge" of supernatural power; only old men, already successful warriors and purified through religious ritual, could touch the object and make it safe for incorporation into the home of the slayer. Made into the doll-like form of an Apache Indian, it was, at last, after much ceremonial preparation, held for an instant by the members of the slayer's family, addressed in respect and awe by kinship terms, and placed in the house, there to give off protective power.[35] The Indians of San Pedro de la Laguna, Guatemala, recognize an officer, serving for life, whose function it is to keep custody of ten or a dozen Latin breviaries printed in the eighteenth century and to read prayers from one or another of these books on certain occasions. No one but this custodian may handle the books, yet the books are not gods—they are objects of sacredness.[36]

In the folk society this disposition to regard objects as sacred extends, characteristically, even into the subsistence activities and into the foodstuffs of the people. Often the foodstuffs are personified as well as sacred. 'My granduncle used to say to me,' explained a Navajo Indian, 'if you are walking along a trail and see a kernel of corn, pick it up. It is like a child lost and starving. According to the legends corn is just the same as a human being, only it is holier. . . . When a man goes into a cornfield he feels that he is in a holy place, that he is

[33]Robert Redfield, *The Folk Culture of Yucatán* (Chicago: University of Chicago Press, 1941), p. 364.

[34]Emile Durkheim, *The Elementary Forms of the Religious Life* (London: Allen & Unwin, 1926).

[35]Underhill, *op. cit.,* p. 18.

[36]Benjamin Paul, Unpublished MS.

walking among Holy People. . . . Agriculture is a holy occupation.
Even before you plant you sing songs. You continue this during the
whole time your crops are growing. You cannot help but feel that you
are in a holy place when you go through your fields and they are
doing well.' "[37] In the folk society, ideally conceived, nothing is solely
a means to an immediate practical end. All activities, even the means
of production, are ends in themselves, activities expressive of the ultimate values of the society.

III

This characterization of the ideal folk society could be greatly
extended. Various of the elements that make up the conception could
be differently combined with one another, and this point or that could
be developed or further emphasized and its relations shown to other
aspects of the conception. For example, it might be pointed out that
where there is little or no systematic and reflective thinking, the customary solutions to problems of practical action only imperfectly take the
form of really effective and understood control of the means appropriate
to accomplish the desired end, and that, instead, they tend to express
the states of mind of the individuals who want the end brought about
and fear that it may not be. We say this briefly in declaring that the
folk society is characterized by much magic, for we may understand
"magic" to refer to action with regard to an end—to instrumental
action—but only to such instrumental action as does not effectively
bring about that end, or is not really understood in so far as it does,
and which is expressive of the way the doer thinks and feels rather than
adapted to accomplishing the end. "Magic is based on specific experience
of emotional states . . . in which the truth is revealed not by reason
but by the play of emotions upon the human organism . . . magic is
founded on the belief that hope cannot fail nor desire deceive."[38]
In the folk society effective technical action is much mixed with magical
activity. What is done tends to take the form of a little drama; it is a
picture of what is desired.

[37]W. W. Hill, *The Agricultural and Hunting Methods of the Navaho Indians*
("Yale University Publications in Anthropology," No. 18 [New Haven: Yale
University Press, 1938]). p. 53.
[38]Bronislaw Malinowski, "Magic, Science and Religion, in *Science, Religion
and Reality*, ed., Joseph Needham (New York: Macmillan Co., 1925). p. 80.

The nature of the folk society could, indeed, be restated in the form of a description of the folk mind. This description would be largely a repetition of what has been written in foregoing pages, except that now the emphasis would be upon the characteristic mental activity of members of the folk society, rather than upon customs and institutions. The man of the folk society tends to make mental associations which are personal and emotional, rather than abstractly categoric or defined in terms of cause and effect." Primitive man views every action not only as adapted to its main object, every thought related to its main end, as we should perceive them but . . . he associates them with other ideas, often of a religious or at least a symbolic nature. Thus he gives to them a higher significance than they seem to us to deserve."[39] A very similar statement of this kind of thinking has been expressed in connection with the thinking of medieval man; the description would apply as well to man in the folk society:

From the causal point of view, symbolism appears as a sort of short-cut of thought. Instead of looking for the relation between two things by following the hidden detours of their causal connections, thought makes a leap and discovers their relation, not in a connection of cause or effects, but in a connection of signification or finality. Such a connection will at once appear convincing, provided only that the two things have an essential quality in common which can be referred to a general value. . . . Symbolic assimilation founded on common properties presupposed the idea that these properties are essential to things. The vision of white and red roses blooming among thorns at once calls up a symbolic association in the medieval mind: for example, that of virgins and martyrs, shining with glory, in the midst of their persecutors. The assimilation is produced because the attributes are the same: the beauty, the tenderness, the purity, the colours of the roses are also those of the virgins, their red color that of the blood of the martyrs. But this similarity will only have a mystic meaning if the middle-term connecting the two terms of the symbolic concept expresses an essentiality common to both; in other words, if redness and whiteness are something more than names for physical differences based on quantity, if they are conceived of as realities. The mind of the savage, of the child, and of the poet never sees them otherwise.[40]

[39]Franz Boas, *The Mind of Primitive Man* (New York: Macmillan Co., 1938, p. 226.
[40]J. Huizenga, *The Waning of the Middle Ages* (London: Arnold & Co., 1924), pp. 184–85. This "symbolic" kind of thinking is related to what Levy-Bruhl called "participation" (see L. Levy-Bruhl, *How Natives Think* [New York: Alfred A. Knopf, 1925], esp. chap. ii.).

The tendency to treat nature personally has recognition in the literature as the "animistic" or "anthropomorphic" quality of primitive thinking, and the contrast between the means-ends pattern of thought more characteristic of modern urban man and the personal thought of primitive man has been specially investigated.[41]

In the foregoing account no mention has been made of the absence of economic behavior characteristic of the market in the folk society. Within the ideal folk society members are bound by religious and kinship ties, and there is no place for the motive of commercial gain. There is no money and nothing is measured by any such common denominator of value. The distribution of goods and services tends to be an aspect of the conventional and personal relationships of status which make up the structure of the society; goods are exchanged as expressions of good will and, in large part, as incidents of ceremonial and ritual activities. "On the whole, then, the compulsion to work, to save, and to expend is given not so much by a rational appreciation of the [material] benefits to be received as by the desire for social recognition, through such behavior."[42]

The conception sketched here takes on meaning if the folk society is seen in contrast to the modern city. The vast, complicated, and rapidly changing world in which the urbanite and even the urbanized country-dweller live today is enormously different from the small, inward-facing folk society, with its well-integrated and little-changing moral and religious conceptions. At one time all men lived in these little folk societies. For many thousands of years men must have lived so; urbanized life began only very recently, as the long history of man on earth is considered, and the extreme development of a secularized and swift-changing world society is only a few generations old.

The tribal groups that still remain around the edges of expanding civilization are the small remainders of this primary state of living. Considering them one by one, and in comparison with the literate or semiliterate societies, the industrialized and the semi-industrialized societies, we may discover how each has developed forms of social life

[41]Hans Kelsen, "Causality and Retribution," *Philosophy of Science,* VIII, No. 4 (October, 1941), pp. 533–56; and Kelsen, *Society and Nature* (Chicago: University of Chicago Press, 1944).

[42]Raymond Firth, *Primitive Economics of the New Zealand Maori* (New York: E. P. Dutton & Co., 1929), p. 484. See also, Frith, *Primitive Polynesian Economy* (London: George Routledge & Sons, 1939), esp. chap. x, "Characteristics of a Primitive Economy."

in accordance with its own special circumstances. Among the polar Eskimos, where each small family had to shift for itself in the rigors of the artic environment, although the ties of kinship were of great importance, no clans or other large unilateral kinship groups came into existence. The sedentary Haida of the Queen Charlotte Islands were divided into two exogamous kinship groups, each composed of clans, with intense pride of decent and healthy rivalry between them. Among the warring and nomadic Comanche initiative and resourcefulness of the ir dividual were looked on more favorably than among the sedentary and closely interdependent Zuni. In West Africa great native states arose, with chiefs and courts and markets, yet the kinship organization remained strong; and in China we have an example of slow growth of a great society, with a literate elite, inclosing within it a multitude of village communities of the folk type. Where cities have arisen, the country people dependent on those cities have developed economic and political relationships, as well as relationships of status, with the city people, and so have become that special kind of rural folk we call peasantry.[43] And even in the newer parts of the world, as in the United States, many a village or small towm has, perhaps, as many points of resemblance with the folk society as with urban life.

Thus the societies of the world do not range themselves in the same order with regard to the degree to which they realize all of the characteristics of the ideal folk society. On the other hand, there is so marked a tendency for some of these characteristics to occur together with others that the interrelations among them must be in no small part that of interdependent variables. Indeed, some of the interrelations are so obvious that we feel no sense of problem. The smallness of the folk society and the long association together of the same inindviduals certainly is related to the prevailingly personal character of relationships. The fewness of secondary and tertiary tools and the absence of machine manufacture are circumstance obviously unfavorable to a very complex division of labor. Many problems present themselves, however, as to the conditions in which certain of these characteristics do not occur in association, and as the circumstances under which certain of them may be expected to change in the direction of their opposites, with or without influencing others to change also.

A study of the local differences in the festival of the patron village

[43]Robert Redfield, "Introduction," in Horace Miner, *St. Denis: A French-Canadian Parish* (Chicago: University of Chicago Press, 1940).

saint in certain communities of Yucatán indicates that some interrelationship exists in that case.[44] In all four communities, differing as to their degrees of isolation from urban centers of modifying influence, the festival expresses a relationship between the village and its patron saint (or cross) which is annually renewed. In it a ritual and worship are combined with a considerable amount of play. The chief activities of the festival are a novena, a folk dance, and a rustic bullfight. In all four communities there is an organization of men and women who for that year undertake the leadership of the festival, handing over the responsibility to a corresponding group of successors at its culmination. So far the institution is the same in all the communities studied. The differences appear when the details of the ritual and play and of the festal organization are compared, and when the essential meanings of these acts and organizations are inquired into. Then it appears that from being an intensely sacred act, made by the village as a collectivity composed of familially defined component groups, with close relationship to the system of religious and moral understandings of the people, the festival becomes, in the more urbanized communities, chiefly an opportunity for recreation for some and of financial profit for others, with little reference to moral and religious conceptions.

In the most isolated and otherwise most folklike of the communities studied the organization of the festival is closely integrated with the whole social structure of the community. The hierarchy of leaders of the community, whose duties are both civil and religious, carry on the festival: it is the chiefs, the men who decide disputes and lead in warfare, who also take principal places in the religious processions and in the conduct of the ceremonies. The community, including several neighboring settlements, is divided into five groups, membership in which descends in the male line. The responsibility for leading the prayers and preparing the festal foods rests in turn on four men chosen from each of the five groups. The festival is held at the head village, at the shrine housing the cross patron of the entire community. The festival consists chiefly of solemnly religious acts: masses, rosaries, procession of images, kneeling of worshipers. The ritual offerings are presented by a special officer, in all solemnity, to the patron cross; certain symbols of divinity are brought from the temple and exposed to the kneeling people as the offerings are made. The transfer of the

[44] Redfield, *The Folk Culture of Yucatán.*

responsibility to lead the festival is attended by ceremony in an atmosphere of sanctity: certain ritual paraphernalia are first-placed on the altar and then, after recitation of prayers and performance of a religious dance, are handed over, in view of all, from the custodians of the sacred charge for that year to their successors.

In the villages that are less isolated the festival is similar in form, but it is less well integrated with the social organization of the community, is less sacred, and allows for more individual enterprise and responsibility. These changes continue in the other communities studied, as one gets nearer to the city of Mérida. In certain seacoast villages the festival of the patron saint is a money-getting enterprise of a few secular-minded townspeople. The novena is in the hands of a few women who receive no help of the municipal authorities; the bullfight is a commercial entertainment, professional bullfighters being hired for the occasion and admission charged; the folk dance is little attended. The festival is enjoyed by young people who come to dance modern dances and to witness the bullfight, and it is an opportunity to the merchants to make a profit. What was an institution of folk culture has become a business enterprise in which individuals, as such, take part for secular ends.

The principal conclusion is that the less isolated and more heterogeneous communities of the peninsula of Yucatán are the more secular and individualistic and the more characterized by disorganization of culture. It further appeared probable that there was, in the changes taking place in Yucatán, a relation of interdependence among these changing characteristics, especially between the disorganization of culture and secularization. "People cease to believe because they cease to understand, and they cease to understand because they cease to do the things that express the understandings."[45] New jobs and other changes in the division of labor bring it about that people cannot participate in the old rituals; and, ceasing to participate, they cease to share the values for which the rituals stood. This is, admittedly, however, only a part of the explanation.

The conception of the folk society has stimulated one small group of field workers to consider the interdependence of independence of these characteristics of society. In Yucatán isolation, homogenity, a personal and "symbolic" view of nature, importance of familial relationships, a high degree of organization of culture, and sacredness of sanctions

[45]*Ibid.*, p. 364.

and institutions were all found in regular association with each other. It was then reported that in certain Indian communities on or near Lake Atitlán in Guatemala this association of characteristics is not repeated.[46] As it appeared that these Guatemalan communities were not in rapid change, but were persisting in their essential nature, the conclusion was reached that "a stable society can be small, unsophisticated, homogeneous in beliefs and practices," have a local, well-organized culture, and still be one "with relationships impersonal, with formal institutions dictating the acts of individuals, and with family organization weak, with life secularized, and with individuals acting more from economic or other personal advantage than from any deep conviction or thought of the social good." It was further pointed out that in these Guatemalan societies a "primitive world view," that is, a disposition to treat nature personally, to regard attributes as entities, and to make "symbolic" rather than causal connections, coexists with a tendency for relations between man and man to be impersonal, commercial, and secular, as they tend to be in the urban society.[47]

These observations lead, in turn, to reconsideration of the circumstances tending to bring about one kind of society or one aspect of society rather than another. The breakdown of familial institutions in recent times in Western society is often ascribed to the development of the city and of modern industry. If, as has been reported, familial institutions are also weak in these Guatemalan villages, there must be alternative causes for the breakdown of the family to the rise of industry and the growth of the city, for these Guatemalan Indians live on or near their farms, practice a domestic handicraft manufacture, and have little or nothing to do with cities. It has been suggested that in the cases of the Guatemalan societies the development, partly before the Conquest and partly afterward, or a pecuniary economy with a peddler's commerce, based on great regional division of labor, together with a system of regulations imposed by an elite with the use of force, may be the circumstances that have brought about reduction in the importance of familial institutions and individual independence, especially in matters of livelihood.[48]

The secular character of life in these highland villages of the Lake

[46]Sol Tax, "Culture and Civilization in Guatemalan Societies," *Scientific Monthly*, XLVIII (May, 1939), 467.

[47]Sol Tax, "World View and Social Relations in Guatemala," *American Anthropologist*, XLIII, No. i (new ser.) (January-March, 1941), 28–42.

[48]Redfield, *The Folk Culture of Yucatán*, pp. 365–67.

Atitlán region is not so well established as in the individuated character of life, but if life is indeed secular there, it is a secularity that has developed without the influence of high personal mobility, of the machine, and of science. In a well-known essay Max Weber showed how capitalistic commercialism could and did get along with piety in the case of the Puritans.[49] Do it may appear that under certain conditions a literate and, indeed, at least partly urbanized society may be both highly commercial and sacred—as witness, also, the Jews—while under certain other conditions an otherwise folklike people may become individualistic, commercial, and perhaps secular. It is, of course, the determination of the limiting conditions that is important.

[49]Max Weber, "Protestant Ethics and the Spirit of Capitalism," cited in Kemper Fullerton, "Calvinism and Capitalism," *Harvard Theological Review,* XXI, 163–95.

Robert Redfield
Milton Singer

THE CULTURAL ROLE OF CITIES

This paper has as its purpose to set forth a framework of ideas that
may prove useful in research on the part played by cities in the development, decline, or transformation of culture. "Culture" is used as in
anthropology. The paper contains no report of research done. It offers
a scheme of constructs; it does not describe observed conditions or
processes; references to particular cities or civilizations are illustrative
and tentative.

Time Perspectives

The cultural role of cities may be considered from at least three different time perspectives. In the long-run perspective of human history as a
single career,[1] the first appearance of cities marks a revolutionary
change: the beginnings of civilization. Within this perspective cities
remain the symbols and carriers of civilization wherever they appear.
In fact the story of civilization may then be told as the story of cities—
from those of the Ancient Near East through those of ancient Greece
and Rome, medieval and modern Europe; and from Europe overseas
to North and South America, Australia, the Far East, and back again

Reprinted by permission of the University of Chicago from *Economic
Development and Cultural Change,* Vol. III. Copyright 1954 by the University
of Chicago.
    [1]Robert Redfield, *The Primitive World and its Transformations,* Ithaca,
New York, 1953, ix-xiii; W. N. Brown and others. "The Beginnings of Civilization," *Journal of the American Oriental Society,* Supplement No. 4, December,
1939, pp. 3-61.

to the modern Near East. In the short-run perspective we may study the cultural role of particular cities in relation to their local hinterlands of towns and villages.[2] The time span here is the several-year period of the field research or, at most, the lifespan of the particular cities that are studied. Between the long- and short-run perspectives, there is a middle-run perspective delimited by the life-history of the different civilizations within which cities have developed.[3] This is the perspective adopted when we consider the cultural bearings of urbanization within Mexican civilization,[4] or Chinese civilization or Indian civilization or Western civilization. It is a perspective usually of several thousand years and embraces within its orbit not just a particular city and its hinterland, but the whole pattern and sequence of urban development characteristic of a particular civilization and its cultural epochs.

While these three perspectives are clearly interrelated, research and analysis may concentrate primarily on one of them. Empirical ethnographic, sociological and geographical research on cities begins in the nature of the case with the short-run perspective, but the significance of such research increases as it becomes linked with ideas and hypotheses drawn from the other perspectives. One begins, say, with an

---

[2]Robert Redfield, *The Folk Culture of Yucatan*, Chicago: University of Chicago Press, 1941. This study, short-run in description, also aims to test some general ideas. Mandelbaum, David G. (ed.) "Integrated Social Science Research for India," *Planning Memo.*, University of California, 1949.

[3]Kroeber has recently discussed the problems of delimiting civilizations in his article, "The Delimitation of Civilizations, "*Journal of the History of Ideas*, Vol. XIV (1953); Mark Jefferson, "Distribution of the world's city folk: a study in comparative civilization," *Geographia*, 1931.

[4]Paul Kirchoff, in "Four, Hundred Years After: General Discussion of Acculturation, Social Change, and the Historical Provenience of Culture Elements," *Heritage of Conquest* by Sol Tax and others (Glencoe, Ill.: The Free Press, 1952), p. 254: It seems to me that the fundamental characteristic of Mesoamerica was that it was a stratified society, one like ours or that of China, based on the axis of city and countryside. There was a native ruling class, with a class ideology and organization, which disappeared entirely; there were great cultural centers which, just as in our life, are so essential if you described the U. S. without New York, Chicago, etc., it would be absurd. The same thing happens when you describe these centers in ancient Mexico. . . . It's not only the arts, crafts and sciences which constitute the great changes, but the basic form of the culture changing from a city structure to the most isolated form, which is, in my opinion, the most total and radical change anywhere in history. . . . When the city is cut off what is left over is attached as a subordinate to the new city-centered culture. . . ."

empirical study of the origins, morphology, functions, and influence of an Asiatic city.[5] Then one may go on to look at this city as a link in the interaction of two distinct civilizations, and see the problem of urbanization of Asia generally as a problem in Westernization,[6] or the problem of Spanish-Indian acculturation of Mexico after the Conquest as a problem of de-urbanization and re-urbanization.[7] Finally, the canvas may be further enlarged to show both Western and Eastern cities as variants of a single and continuing cultural and historical process.[8] In this paper we propose to concentrate on the middle-run perspective, i.e., we shall analyze the role cities play in the formation, maintenance, spread, decline, and transformation of civilizations. We think that links with the long- and short-run perspectives will also emerge in the course of the analysis.

In the many useful studies of cities by urban geographers, sociologists, and ecologists we find frequent reference to "cultural functions" and "cultural centers."[9] Under these rubrics they generally include the religious, educational, artistic centers and activities, and distinguish them from administrative, military, economic centers and functions. This usage of "cultural" is too narrow for the purpose of a comparative analysis of the role cities play in the transformations of the more or less integrated traditional life of a community. Economic and political centers and activities may obviously play as great a role in these processes as the narrowly "cultural" ones. Moreover, these different kinds of centers and activities are variously combined and separated and it is these varying patterns that are significant. In ancient civilizations the urban centers were usually political-religious or political-intellectual; in

[5]Ghosh, S., "The urban pattern of Calcutta," *Economic Geography,* 1950; Weulersse, J., "Antioche, un type de cité de l'Islam." *Congr. int. de Géographie,* Warsaw, 1934, III; D. R. Gadgil, *Poona, A Socio-Economic Survey,* Poona, 1945, 1952.

[6]"Urbanization is part of the Europeanization that is spreading throughout the world," Mark Jefferson in reference (3) above. Kingsley Davis, *The Population of India and Pakistan,* Princeton, 1951, pp. 148–49; M. Zinkin, Asia and the West, London, 1951, Ch. 1, "Eastern Village and Western City."

[7]Kirchhoff, *op. cit.*

[8]See for this approach the books of V. Gordon Childe, and his article in *Town Planning Review,* XXI (1950) on "The Urban Revolution."

[9]Grace M. Kneedler, "Functional types of cities." reprinted in *Reader in Urban Sociology,* edited by Paul K. Hatt and Albert J. Reiss, Jr., The Free Press, Glencoe, Illinois, 1951; R. E. Dickinson, *The West European City,* London: Routledge & Paul, 1951, pp. 253–54; Chauncey Harris, "A functional classification of cities in the United States," *Geogr. Review,* New York, 1943.

the modern world they are economic.[10] The mosque, the temple, the cathedral, the royal palace, the fortress, are the symbolic "centers" of the pre-industrial cities. The "central business district" has become symbolic of the modern urban center. In fact a cross-cultural history of cities might be written from the changing meanings of the words for city. "Civitas" in the Roman Empire meant an administrative or ecclesiastical district. Later, "city" was applied to the ecclesiastical center of a town—usually the cathedral. This usage still survives in names like "Ile de la Cité" for one of the first centers of Paris. With the development of the "free cities," "city" came to mean the independent commercial towns with their down laws.[11] Today, "the city" of London is a financial center, and when Americans speak of "going to town" or "going downtown" they mean they are going to the "central business district." They usually think of any large city as a business and manufacturing center, whereas a Frenchman is more likely to regard his cities—certainly Paris—as "cultural centers."[12]

This symbolism is not of course a completely accurate designation of what goes on in the city for which it stands. The ecclesiastical centers were also in many cases centers of trade and of craftsmen, and the modern "central business district" is very apt to contain libraries, schools, art museums, government offices and churches, in addition to merchandising establishments and business offices. But allowing for this factual distortion, this symbolism does help us to separate two quite distinct cultural roles of cities, and provides a basis for classifying cities that is relevant to their cultural role. As a "central business district," the city is obviously a market-place, a place to buy and sell, "to do business"—to truck, barter and exchange with people who may be complete strangers and of different races, religions and creeds. The city here functions to work out largely impersonal relations among diverse cultural groups. As a religious or intellectual center, on the other hand, the city is a beacon for the faithful, a center for the learn-

[10]Gadgil, *The Industrial Revolution of India in Recent Times,* Oxford, 1944, pp. 6–12; Spate and E. Ahmad, "Five cities of the Gangetic Plain. A cross-section of Indian culture history." *Geog. Rev.,* 1950; P. George, *La Ville,* Paris, 1952; B. Rowland, *The Art and Architecture of India,* Penguin, Baltimore, 1953. Map showing ancient and historic art and religious centers, p. xvii; Fei Hsiao-Tung, *China's Gentry, Essays in Rural-Urban Relations,* Chicago, University of Chicago Press, 1953, pp. 91–117.

[11]R. E. Dickinson, *op. cit.* (note 7), pp. 251–52; H. Pirenne, *Medieval Cities.*

[12]See article on "Urbanization" by W. M. Stewart in 14th edition of Encyclopaedia Britannica for some cultural variables in the definition of "city."

ing, authority and perhaps doctrine that transforms the implicit "little traditions" of the local non urban cultures into an explicit and systematic "great tradition." The varying cultural roles of cities, so separated and grouped into two contrasting kinds of roles with reference to the local tradition of the non-urban peoples, point to a distinction to which we shall soon return and to which we shall then give names.

Types of Cities

In the studies of economic historians (Pirenne, Dopsch) and in the studies of the currently sighificant factors for economic development (Hoselitz),[13] the functions of cities are considered as they effect change; but the change chiefly in view is economic change. Our attention now turns to the roles of cities in effecting change in the content and integration of ideas, interests and ideals.

The distinction Hoselitz takes from Pirenne between political-intellectual urban centers on the one hand and economic centers on the other, points in the direction of the distinction necessary to us in taking up the new topic. But the distinction we need does not fully emerge until we refine the classification by (1) separating the political function from the intellectual and (2) giving new content to the term "intellectual." Delhi, Quito and Peiping are to be contrasted, as Hoselitz says, with Bombay, Guayaquil and Shanghai because the former three cities are "political-intellectual centers" and the later three are "economic centers." (The contrast of Rio to Sào Paolo is less clear.) Let us now add that there are cities with political functions and without significant intellectual functions: New Delhi (if it be fair to separate it from old Delhi), Washington, D. C. and Canberra (the new uinversity there may require a qualification). Further, the intellectual functions of Delhi, Quito and Peiping (and Kyoto, Lhasa, Cuzco, Mecca, medieval Liège and Uaxactun) are to develop, carry forward, elaborate a long-established cultural tradition local to the community in which those cities stand. These are the cities of the literati: clerics, astronomers, theologians, imams and priests. New Delhi and Washington, D. C. do not have, significantly, literati; in spite of its schools and universities. Washington is not a city of great intellectual leadership; these are cities without major intellectual functions. In respect to this lack, New Delhi and Washington, D. C., belong with cities with predominatly economic

[13]B. Hoselitz, "The role of cities in the economic growth of underdeveloped countries," *The Journal of Political Economy,* vol. lxi (1953), esp. 198–99.

functions. On the other hand, not a few old cities with economic functions have also the functions associated with the literati (Florence,
medieval Timbuktoo; Thebes).

We have taken into consideration, in this expanded grouping, both
cities of the modern era and cities of the time before the development of
a world economy. It may be useful now to separate the two historic
periods, retaining the distinction between cities of the literati, cities of
entrepreneurs, and cities of the bureaucracy. The following grouping
results:

BEFORE THE UNIVERSAL OEKUMENE (pre-industrial revolution, pre-Western expansion)

    1. Administrative-cultural cities
       (cities of the literati and the indigenous bureaucracy)

              Peiping
              Lhasa
              Uaxactun
              Kyoto
              Liège
              Allahabad (?)

    2. Cities of native commerce
       (cities of the entrepreneur)

              Bruges
              Marseilles
              Lübeck
              Market towns of native West Africa
              Early Canton

AFTER THE UNIVERSAL OEKUMENE (post-industrial revolution, and post-Western expansion)

    3. Metropolis-cities of the world-wide managerial and entre-
       preneureal class (Park's "cities of the main street of the
       world")

              London
              New York
              Osaka
              Yokahama
              Shanghai
              Singapore
              Bombay

Lesser cities and towns, also carrying on the world's business, may be added here.

4. Cities of modern administration
(cities of the new bureaucracies)
Washington, D. C.
New Delhi
Canberra

A thousand administrative towns, county seats, seats of British and French African colonial administration, etc.

What is the relationship of such a grouping to our topic: the role of cities in processes of cultural change?

The role of cities of Group 1 has already been stated. It is to carry forward, develop, elaborate a long-established local culture or civilization. These are cities that convert the folk culture into its civilized dimension.

But the cities of groups 2, 3, and 4 do not have, or do not have conspicuously and as their central effect, this role in the cultural process. They affect the cultural process in other ways. How? they are cities in which one or both of the following things are true: (1) the prevailing relationships of people and the prevailing common understandings have to do with the technical not the moral order,[14] with administrative regulation, business and technical convenience; (2) these cities are populated by people of diverse cultural orgins removed from the indigenous seats of their cultures.

They are cities in which new states of mind, following from these characteristics, are developed and become prominent. The new states of mind are indifferent to or inconsistent with, or supersede, or overcome, states of mind associated with local cultures and ancient civilizations. The intellectuals of these three groups of cities, if any, are intelligentsia rather than literati.[15]

The distinction that is then basic to consideration of the cultural role of cities is the distinction between the *carrying forward into systematic and reflective dimensions an old culture* and the *creating of original modes of thought that have authority beyond or in conflict with old cultures and civilizations.* We might speak of the orthogenetic cultural role of cities as contrasted with the heterogenetic cultural role.

In both these roles the city is a place in which cultural change takes place. The roles differ as to the character of the change. Insofar as the city has an orthogenetic role, it is not to maintain culture as it

---

[14]Robert Redfield, *The Primitive World and Its Transformations*, Ch. 3.
[15]*Ibid*, Ch. 3.

was; the orthogenetic city is not static; it is the place where religious, philosophical and literary specialists reflect, synthesize and create out of the traditional material new arrangements and developments that are felt by the people to be outgrowths of the old. What is changed is a further statement of what was there before. Insofar as the city has a heterogenetic role, it is a place of conflict of differing traditions, a center of heresy, heterodoxy and dissent, of interruption and destruction of ancient tradition, of rootlessness and anomie. Cities are both these things, and the same events may appear to particular people or groups to be representative of what we here call orthogenesis or representative of heterogenesis. The predominating trend may be in one of the two directions, and so allow us to characterize the city, or that phase of the history of the city as the one or the other. The lists just given suggest that the differences in the degree to which in the city orthogenesis or heterogenesis prevails are in cases strongly marked.

The presence of the market is not of itself a fact of heterogenetic change. Regulated by tradition, maintained by such customs and routines as develop over long periods of time, the market may flourish without heterogenetic change. In the medieval Muslim town we see an orthogenetic city; the market and the keeper of the market submitted economic activities to explicit cultural and religious definition of the norms. In Western Guatemala the people who come to market hardly communicate except with regard to buying and selling, and the market has little heterogenetic role. On the other hand the market in many instances provides occasions when men of diverse traditions may come to communicate and to differ; and also in the market occurs that exchange on the basis of universal standards of utility which is neutral to particular moral orders and in some sense hostile to all of them. The cities of Group 2, therefore, are cities unfavorable to orthogenetic change but not necessarily productive of heterogenetic change.

The City and the Folk Society[16]

The folk society may be conceived as that imagined combination of societal elements which would characterize a long-established, homogeneous, isolated and non-literate integral (self-contained) community;

[16]Robert Redfield, "The Natural History of the Folk Society," *Social Forces*, Vol. 31 (1953). pp. 224–28.

the folk culture is that society seen as a system of common understandings. Such a society can be approximately realized in a tribal band or village; it cannot be approximately realized in a city. What are characteristics of the city that may be conceived as a contrast to those of the folk society?

The city may be imagined as that community in which orthogenetic and heterogenetic transformations of the folk society have most fully occurred. The former has brought about the Great Tradition and its special intellectual class, administrative officers and rules closely derived from the moral and religious life of the local culture, and advanced economic institutions, also obedient to these local cultural controls. The heterogenetic transformations have accomplished the freeing of the intellectual, esthetic, economic and political life from the local moral norms, and have developed on the one hand an individuated expediential motivation, and on the other a revolutionary, nativistic, humanistic or ecumenical viewpoint, now directed toward reform, progress and designed change.

As these two aspects of the effects of the city on culture may be in part incongruent with each other, and as in fact we know them to occur in different degrees and arrangements in particular cities, we may now review the classification of cities offered above so as to recognize at least two types of cities conceived from this point of view.

A. *The city of orthogenetic transformation: the city of the moral order;* the city of culture carried forward. In the early civilizations the first cities were of this kind and usually combined this developmental cultural function with political power and administrative control. But it is to be emphasized that this combination occurred because the local moral and religious norms prevailed and found intellectual development in the literati and exercise of control of the community in the ruler and the laws. Some of these early cities combined these two "functions" with commerce and economic production; others had little of these. It is as cities of predominating orthogenetic civilization that we are to view Peiping, Lhasa, Uaxactun, fourteenth-century Liège.

B. *The city of heterogenetic transformation: the city of the technical order;* the city where local cultures are disintegrated and new integrations of mind and society are developed of the kinds described above ("The heterogenetic role of cities"). In cities of this kind men are concerned with the market, with "rational" organization of production of goods, with expediential relations between buyer and seller, ruler and ruled, and native and foreigner. In this kind of city the predominant social types are businessmen, administrators alien to those they administer, and rebels, reformers, planners and plotters of many varieties. It is in cities of this kind that priority comes to be given to economic growth and the expansion of power among the goods of life. The modern metropolis exhibits very much of this aspect of the city; the town built in the tropics by the United Fruit Company and the city built around the Russian uranium mine must have much that represents it; the towns of the colonial administration in Africa must show many of its features. Indeed, in one way or another, all the cities of groups 2, 3 and 4 (*supra*) are cities of the technical order, and are cities favorable to heterogenetic transformation of the moral order.[17]

This type of city may be subdivided into the administrative city, city of the bureaucracy (Washington, D. C., Canberra), and the city of the entrepreneur (Hamburg, Shanghai). Of course many cities exhibit both characteristics.

"In every tribal settlement there is civilization; in every city is the folk-society." We may look at any city and see within it the folk society insofar as ethnic communities that make it up preserve folklike characteristics, and we may see in a town in ancient Mesopotamia or in aboriginal West Africa a halfway station between folk society and orthogenetic civilization. We may also see in every city its double urban characteristics: we may identify the institutions and mental habits there prevailing with the one or the other of the two lines of transformation of folk life which the city brings about. The heterogentic transformations have grown with the course of history, and the development of modern industrial world-wide economy, together with the great movements of peoples and especially those incident to the expansion of the West, have increased and accelerated this aspect of urbanization. The later cities are predominantly cities of the technical order. We see almost side by side persisting cities of the moral order and those of the technical order: Peiping and Shanghai, Cuzco and Guayaquil, a

---

[17]In the heterogenetic transformation the city and its hinterland become mutually involved: the conservative or reactionary prophet in the country inveighs against the innovations or backslidings of the city; and the reformer with the radically progressive message moves back from Medina against Mecca, or enters Jerusalem.

native town in Nigeria and an administrative post and railway center hard by.

The ancient city, predominantly orthogenetic, was not (as remarked by W. Eberhard) in particular cases the simple outgrowth of a single pre-civilized culture, but was rather (as in the case of Loyang) a city in which conquered and conqueror lived together, the conqueror extending his tradition over the conquered, or accepting the later's culture. What makes the orthogenetic aspect of a city is the integration and uniform interpretation of preceding culture, whether its origins be one or several. Salt Lake City and early Philadelphia, cities with much orthogenetic character, were established by purposive acts of founders. Salt Lake City created its own hinterland on the frontier (as pointed out by C. Harris). Other variations on the simple pattern of origin and development of a city from an established folk people can no doubt be adduced.

Transformation of Folk Societies: Primary Urbanization and Secondary Urbanization

The preceding account of different types of cities is perhaps satisfactory as a preliminary, but their cultural roles in the civilizations which they represent cannot be fully understood except in relation to the entire pattern of urbanization within that civilization, i.e., the number, size, composition, distribution, duration, sequence, morphology, function rates of growth and decline, and the relation to the countryside and to each other of the cities within a civilization. Such information is rare for any civilization. In the present state of our knowledge it may be useful to guide further inquiry by assuming two hypothetical patterns of urbanization: primary and secondary.[18] In the primary phase a precivilized folk society is transformed by urbanization into a peasant society and correlated urban center. It is primary in the sense that the peoples making up the precivilized folk more or less share a common culture which remains the matrix too for the peasant and urban cultures which develop from it in the course of urbanization. Such a development, occuring slowly in communities not radically distrubed, tends to

[18]This distinction is an extension of the distinction between the primary and secondary phases of folk transformations in Redfield, *The Primitive World and Its Transformations*, p. 41.

produce a "sacred culture" which is gradually transmuted by the *literati* of the cities into a "Great Tradition." Primary urbanization thus takes place almost entirely within the framework of a core culture that develops, as the local cultures become urbanized and transformed, into an indigenous civilization. This core culture dominates the civilization despite occasional intrusions of foreign peoples and cultures. When the encounter with other peoples and civilizations is too rapid and intense in indigenous civilization may be destroyed by de-urbanization or be variously mixed with other civilizations.[19]

This leads to the secondary pattern of urbanization: the case in which a folk society, precivilized, peasant, or partly urbanized, is further urbanized by contact with peoples of widely different cultures from that of its own members. This comes about through expansion of a local culture, now partly urbanized, to regions inhabited by peoples of different cultures, or by the invasion of a culture-civilization by alien colonists or conquerors. This secondary pattern produces not only a new form of urban life in some part in conflict with local folk cultures but also new social types in both city and country. In the city appear "marginal" and cosmopolitan" men and an "intelligentsia"; in the country various types of marginal folk: enclaved-, minority-, imperialized, transplanted-, remade-, quasi-folk, etc., depending on the kind of relation to the urban center.

This discussion takes up a story of the contact of peoples at the appearance of cities. But, here parenthetically, it is necessary to note that even before the appearance of cities the relations between small and primitive communities may be seen as on the one hand characterized by common culture and on the other by mutual usefulness with awareness of cultural difference. The "primary phase of urbanization" is a continuation of the extension of common culture from a small primitive settlement to a town and its hinterland, as no doubt could be shown for parts of West Africa. The "secondary phase of urbanization" is begun, before cities, in the institutions of travel and trade among local communities with different cultures. In Western Guatemala today simple Indian villagers live also in a wider trade-community of pluralistic cultures;[20] we do not know to what extent either the pre-Columbian semi-urban centers or the cities of the Spanish-modern conquerors and

[19]Kirchhoff, *op. cit.*

[20]R. Redfield, "Primitive Merchants of Guatemala," *Quarterly Journal of Inter-American Relations*, Vol. 1, No. 4, 1939, pp. 48–49.

rulers, have shaped this social system; it may be that these people were already on the way to secondary urbanization before any native religious and political center rose to prominence.

While we do not know universal sequences within primary or secondary urbanization, it is likely that the degree to which any civilization is characterized by patterns of primary or secondary urbanization depends on the rate of technical development and the scope and intensity of contact with other cultures. If technical development is slow and the civilization is relatively isolated, we may expect to find a pattern of primary urbanization prevailing. If, on the other hand, technical development is rapid and contacts multiple and intense, secondary urbanization will prevail.

It may be that in the history of every civilization there is, of necessity, secondary urbanization. In modern Western civilization conditions are such as to make secondary urbanization the rule. But even in older civilizations it is not easy to find clear-cut examples of primary urbanization—because of multiple interactions, violent fluctuations in economic and military fortunes, conflicts and competition among cities and dynasties, and the raids of nomads. The Maya before the Spanish Conquest are perhaps a good example of primary urbanization.[21] The cases of the Roman, Greek, Hindu, Egyptian and Mesopotamian civilizations, although characterized by distinctive indigenous civilizations, are nevertheless complex because little is known about the degree of cultural homogeneity of the peoples who formed the core cultures and because as these civilizations became imperial they sought to assimilate more and more diverse peoples. Alternatively the irritant "seed" of a city may have been sown in some of them by the conquering raid of an outside empire, the desire to copy another empire in having a capital, or simple theft from another people—with the *subsequent* development around this seed of the "pearl" of a relatively indigenous, primary urban growth, sending out its own imperial secondary strands in due time. Thus while Rome, Athens, Chang-An and Loyang in early China and Peiping in later, Pataliputra and Benares, Memphis and Thebes, Nippur and Ur, may have been for a time at least symbolic vehicles for loyalty to the respective empires and indigenous civilizations, it was not these relatively "orthogenetic" cities but the mixed cities on the

<hr>

[21]Redfield, *The Primitive World and Its Transformations*, pp. 58–73. See also Morley, *The Ancient Maya*, and Thomas Gann and J. Eric Thompson, *The History of the Maya*, New York, 1931.

periphery of an empire–the "colonial cities" which carried the core culture to other peoples. And in such cities, usually quite mixed in character, the imperial great tradition was not only bound to be very dilute but would also have to meet the challenge of conflicting local traditions. At the imperial peripheries, primary urbanization turns into secondary urbanization.[22]

Similar trends can be perceived in modern times: Russian cities in Southern Europe and Asia appear to be very mixed,[23] non-Arabic Muslim cities have developed in Africa and South Asia, and the colonial cities of the European powers admit native employees daily at the doors of their skyscraper banks. Possibly the nuclear cultures are homogeneous and create indigenous civilizations but as they expand into new areas far afield from the home cultures they have no choice but to build "heterogenetic" cities.

Modern "colonial" cities (e.g., Jakarta, Manila, Saigon, Bangkok, Singapore, Calcutta) raise the interesting question whether they can reverse from the "heterogenetic" to the "orthogenetic" role. For the last one hundred or more years they have developed as the outposts of imperial civilizations, but as the countries in which they are located achieve political independence, will the cities change their cultural roles and contribute more to the formation of a civilization indigenous to their areas? Many obstacles lie in the path of such a course. These cities have large, culturally diverse populations, not necessarily European, for example, the Chinese in Southeast Asia, Muslims and Hindu refugees from faraway provinces, in India; they often have segregated ethnic quarters, and their established administrative, military and economic functions are not easily changed. Many new problems have been created by a sudden influx of postwar refugee populations, and the cities' changing positions in national and global political and economic systems. While many of these colonial cities have been centers of na-

---

[22]The case of China is particularly striking, since the evidence for a dominant core culture is unmistakable but its relation to local cultures which may have been its basis is unknown. See Chi Li, *The Formation of the Chinese People*, Cambridge, Harvard University Press, 1928, and Wolfram Eberhard, *Early Chinese Cultures and their Development*, Smithsonian Institution Annual Report, 1937, Washington, 1938. For a good study of imperial "spread" and "dilution," see A. H. M. Jones, *The Greek City from Alexander to Justinian*, Oxford, 1940.

[23]Chauncy Harris, "Ethnic groups in cities of the Soviet Union," *Geog. Rev.*, 1945.

tionalism and of movements for revival of the local cultures, they are not likely to live down their "heterogenetic" past.[24]

The Cultural Consequences of Primary and Secondary Urbanization

The discussion of primary and secondary urbanization above has been a bare outline. It may be filled in by reference to some postulated consequences of each type of process. The most important cultural consequence of primary urbanization is the transformation of the Little Tradition into a Great Tradition. Embodied in "sacred books" or "classics," sanctified by a cult, expressed in monuments, sculpture, painting, and architecture, served by the other arts and sciences, the Great Tradition becomes the core culture of an indigenous civilization and a source, consciously examined, for defining its moral, legal, aesthetic and other cultural norms. A Great Tradition describes a way of life and as such is a vehicle and standard for those who share it to identify with one another as members of a common civilization. In terms of social structure, a significant event is the appearance of literati, those who represent the Great Tradition. The new forms of thought that now appear and extend themselves include reflective and systematic thought; the definition of fixed idea systems (theologies, legal codes) ; the development of esoteric or otherwise generally inaccessible intellectual products carried forward, now in part separate from the tradition of the folk; and the creation of intellectual and aesthetic forms that are both traditional and original (cities of the Italian Renaissance; development of "rococo" Maya sculpture in the later cities).

In government and administration the orthogenesis of urban civilization is represented by chiefs, rulers and laws that express and are closely controlled by the norms of the local culture. The chief of the Crow Indians, in a pre-civilized society, and the early kings of Egypt, were of this type. The Chinese emperor was in part orthogenetically controlled by the Confucian teaching and ethic; in some part he represented a heterogenetic development. The Roman pro-consul and the

[24]D. W. Fryer, "The 'million city' in Southeast Asia," *Geog. Rev.,* Oct., 1953; J. E. Spencer, "Changing Asiatic cities," *Geog. Rev.,* Vol. 41 (1951). This last is a summary of an article by Jean Chesneaux. See also *Record of the XXVIIth Meeting of the International Institute of Differing Civilizations,* Brussels, 1952, esp. papers by R. W. Steel and K. Neys.

Indian Service of the United States, especially in certain phases, were more heterogenetic political developments.

Economic institutions of local cultures and civilizations may be seen to be orthogenetic insofar as the allocation of resources to production and distribution for consumption are determined by the traditional system of status and by the traditional specific local moral norms. The chief's yam house in the Trobriands is an accumulation of capital determined by these cultural factors. In old China the distribution of earnings and "squeeze" were distributed according to family obligations: these are orthogenetic economic institutions and practices. The market, freed from controls of tradition, status and moral rule, becomes the world-wide heterogenetic economic institution.

In short, the trend of primary urbanization is to co-ordinate political, economic, educational, intellectual and aesthetic activity to the norms provided by the Great Traditions.

The general consequence of secondary urbanization is the weakening or supersession of the local and traditional cultures by states of mind that are incongruent with those local cultures. Among these are to be recognized:

1. The rise of a consensus appropriate to the technical order: i.e., based on self-interest and pecuniary calculation, or on recognition of obedience to common impersonal controls, characteristically supported by sanctions of force. (This in contrast to a consensus based on common religious and non-expediential moral norms.) There is also an autonomous development of norms and standards for the arts, crafts, and sciences.

2. The appearance of new sentiments of common cause attached to groups drawn from culturally heterogeneous backgrounds. In the city proletariats are formed and class or ethnic consciousness is developed, and also new professional and territorial groups. The city is the place where ecumenical religious reform is preached (though it is not originated there). It is the place where nationalism flourishes. On the side of social structure, the city is the place where new and larger groups are formed that are bound by few and powerful common interests and sentiments in place of the complexly interrelated roles and statuses that characterize the groups of local, long-established culture. Among social types that appear in this aspect of the cultural process in the city are the reformer, the agitator, the nativistic or nationalistic leader, the tyrant and his assassin, the missionary and the imported school teacher.

3. The instability of viewpoint as to the future, and emphasis on prospective rather than retrospective view of man in the universe. In cities of predominantly orthogenetic influence, people look to a future that will repeat the past (either by continuing it or by bringing it around again to its place in the cycle). In cities of predominantly heterogenetic cultural influence there is a disposition to see the future as different from the past. It is this aspect of the city that gives rise to reform movements, forward-looking myths, and planning, revolutionary or melioristic. The forward-looking may be optimistic and radically reformistic; it may be pessimistic, escapist, defeatist or apocalyptic. In the city there are Utopias and counter-Utopias. Insofar as these new states of mind are secular, worldly, they stimulate new political and social aspiration and give rise to policy.

Consequences for World View, Ethos, and Typical Personality

The difference in the general cultural consequences of primary and secondary urbanization patterns may be summarily characterized by saying that in primary urbanization, all phases of the technical order (material technology, economy, government, arts, crafts, and sciences) are referred, in theory at least, to the standards and purposes of a moral order delineated in the Great Tradition, whereas in secondary urbanization different phases of the technical order are freed from this reference and undergo accelerated autonomous developments. With respect to this development, the moral order, or rather orders, for there are now many competing ones, appears to lag.[25]

There is another way of describing these differences: in terms of the consequences of the two kinds of urbanization for changes in world view, ethos, and typical personality.[26] To describe the consequences in these terms is to describe them in their bearings and meanings for the majority of individual selves constituting the society undergoing urbanization. We now ask, how do primary and secondary urbanization affect mental outlook, values and attitudes, and personality traits? These are in part psychological questions, for they direct our attention to the psychological aspects of broad cultural processes.

[25]Redfield, *The Primitive World and Its Transformations*, pp. 72–83.
[26]For a further discussion of these concepts, see Redfield, *ibid.*, Ch. 4, and Redfield, *The Little Community*, University of Chicago Press (forthcoming), Chs. 5 and 6 on personality and mental outlook.

There are many accounts of the psychological consequences of urbanization. These have described the urban outlook, ethos, and personality as depersonalized, individualized, emotionally shallow and atomized, unstable, secularized, blase, rationalistic, cosmopolitan, highly differentiated, self-critical, time-coordinated, subject to sudden shifts in mood and fashion, "other-directed," etc.[27] The consensus in these descriptions and their general acceptance by social scientists seem great enough to indicate that there probably is a general psychological consequence of urbanization, although it cannot be precisely described and proven. We should, however, like to suggest that the "urban way of life" that is described in the characterizations to which we refer is primarily a consequence of secondary urbanization and of that in a particular critical stage when personal and cultural disorganization are greatest. To see these consequences in perspective, it is necessary to relate them on the one hand to the consequences of primary urbanization and on the other to those situations of secondary urbanization that produce new forms of personal and cultural integration. Most of all it is necessary to trace the continuities as well as the discontinuities in outlook, values, and personality, as we trace the transformation of folk societies into their civilized dimension. The "peasant" is a type that represents an adjustment between the values of the precivilized tribe and those of the urbanite. The "literati" who fashion a Great Tradition do not repudiate the values and outlook of their rural hinterland but systematize and elaborate them under technical specialization. The cosmopolitan "intelligentsia" and "sophists" of the metropolitan centers have a prototype in the "heretic" of the indigenous civilization. And even the most sophisticated urban centers are not without spiritualists, astrologers and other practitioners with links to a folk-like past.[28]

[27]See L. Wirth, "Urbanism as a way of life," and G. Simmel, "The metropolis and mental life," both reprinted in Hatt and Reiss, *Reader in Urban Sociology;* E. Fromm, *Escape from Freedom,* David Riesman and collaborators, *The Lonely Crowd,* and A. Kroeber, *Anthropology,* 1948, sec. 121. For the effects of urban life on time-coordination, see H. A. Hawley, *Human Ecology,* 15, and P. Hallowell, "Temporal orientations in western and non-western cultures," (?), *American Anthropologist,* Vol. 39, 1937.

[28]Redfield, *The Folk Culture of Yucatan,* Ch. 11; R. E. Park, "Magic, Mentality, and City Life," reprinted in Park, *Human Communities;* N. C. Chaudhuri, *The Autobiography of an Unknown Indian,* Macmillan, 1951, gives some interesting observations on the survival of "folk" beliefs and practices among the people of Calcutta, pp. 361–62; P. Masson-Oursel, "La Sophistique. Etude de philosophie comparée," *Revue de métaphysique et de morale,* 23 (1916), pp. 343–62.

The connections between the folk culture, the Great Tradition, and the sophisticated culture of the heterogenetic urban centers can be traced not only in the continuities of the historical sequence of a particular group of local cultures becoming urbanized and de-urbanized, but they also can be traced in the development of two distinct forms of cultural consciousness which appear in these transformations.

Cultural Integration Between City and Country

From what has been said about primary and secondary urbanization it follows that city and country are more closely integrated, culturally, in the primary phase of urbanization than in the secondary phase. Where the city has grown out of a local culture, the country people see its ways as in some important part a form of their own, and they feel friendlier toward the city than do country people ruled by a proconsul from afar. The sterotype of "the wicked city" will be stronger in the hinterlands of the heterogenetic cities than in those of the orthogenetic cities. Many of these are sacred centers of faith, learning, justice and law.

Nevertheless, even in primary urbanization a cultural gap tends to grow between city and country. The very formation of the Great Tradition introduces such a gap. The *literati* of the city develop the values and world view of the local culture to a degree of generalization, abstraction and complexity incomprehensible to the ordinary villager, and in doing so leave out much of the concrete local detail of geography and village activity. The Maya Indian who lived in some rural settlements near Uaxactun could not have understood the calendrical intricacies worked out in that shrine-city by the priests; and the rituals performed at the city-shrine had one high level of meaning for the priest and another lower meaning, connecting with village life at some points only, for the ordinary Indian.

On the other hand, primary urbanization involves the development of characteristic institutions and societal features that hold together, in a certain important measure of common understanding, the Little Tradition and the Great Tradition. We may refer to the development of these institutions and societal features as the universalization of cultural consciousness—meaning by "universalization," the preservation and extension of common understanding as to the meaning and purpose of life, and sense of belonging together, to all the people, rural or urban, of the larger community. Some of the ways in which this universalization takes place are suggested in the following paragraphs. The examples are taken chiefly from India; they probably have considerable cross-cultural validity.

1. The embodiment of the Great tradition in "sacred books" and secondarily in sacred monuments, art, icons, etc. Such "sacred scriptures" may be in a language not widely read or understood; nevertheless they may become a fixed point for the worship and ritual of ordinary people. The place of the "Torah" in the lives of Orthodox Jews, the Vedas among orthodox Hindus, the "Three Baskets" for Buddhists, the thirteen classics for Confucianists, the Koran for Muslims, the stelac and temples of the ancient Maya, are all examples of such sacred scriptures, although they may vary in degree of sacredness and in canonical status.

2. The development of a special class of "literati" (priests, rabbis, Imams, Brahmins) who have the authority to read, interpret, and comment on the sacred scriptures. Thus the village Brahmin who reads the *Gita* for villagers at ceremonies mediates a part of the Great Tradition of Hinduism for them.

The mediation of a great tradition is not always this direct. At the village level it may be carried in a multitude of ways—by the stories parents and grandparents tell children, by professional reciters and storytellers, by dramatic performances and dances, in songs and proverbs, etc.

In India the epics and *puranas* have been translated in the major regional languages and have been assimilated to the local cultures. This interaction of a "great tradition" and the "little tradition" of local and regional cultures needs further study, especially in terms of the professional and semi-professional "mediators" of the process.

3. The role of leading personalities who because they themselves embody or know some aspects of a Great Tradition succeed through their personal position as leaders in mediating a Great Tradition to the masses of people. There is a vivid account of this process in Jawarhalal Nehru's *Discovery of India*, in which he describes first how he "discovered" the Great Tradition of Indian in the ruins of Mohenjo-Daro and other archeological monuments, her sacred rivers and holy cities, her literature, philosophy, and history. And then he describes how he discovered the "little traditions" of the people and the villages, and how through his speeches he conveyed to them a vision of *Bharat Mata*— Mother India—that transcends the little patches of village land, people, and customs.[29]

[29]Jawarharlal Nehru, *The Discovery of India,* John Day, New York, 1946, pp, 37–40, 45–51.

4. Nehru's account suggests that actual physical places, buildings and monuments—especially as they become places of sacred or patriotic pilgrimage—are important means to a more universalized cultural consciousness and the spread of a Great Tradition. In India this has been and still is an especially important universalizing force. The sanctity of rivers and the purifying powers of water go all the way back to the Rig Veda. The Buddhists—who may have started the practice of holy pilgrimages—believed that there were four places that the believing man should visit with awe and reverence: Buddha's birth place, the site where he attained illumination or perfect insight, the place where the mad elephant attacked him, and the place where Buddha died. In the *Mahabharata*, there is a whole book on the subject of holy places (Arareyaka Book). Even a sinner who is purified by holy water will go to heaven. And the soul ready for *moksha* will surely achieve it if the pilgrim dies on a pilgrimage.[30] Today the millions of pilgrims who flock to such preeminent holy spots as Allahabad or Banaras create problems of public safety and urban over-crowding, but they, like Nehru, are also discovering the *Bharat Mata* beyond their villages.

In India "sacred geography" has also played an important part in determining the location and layout of villages and cities and in this way has created a cultural continunity between countryside and urban centers. In ancient India, at least, every village and every city had a "sacred center" with temple, tank, and garden. And the trees and plants associated with the sacred shrine were also planted in private gardens, for the households too had their sacred center; the house is the "body" of a spirit (Varta Purusha) just as the human body is the "house" of the soul.[31]

At each of these levels—of household, village, and city—the "sacred center" provides the forum, the vehicle, and the content for the formation of distinct cultural identities—of families, village, and city. But as individuals pass outward, although their contacts with others become less intimate and less frequent, they nevertheless are carried along by

[30]D. Patil, *Cultural History from Väya Puräna*, Poona, 1946, Appendix B.
[31]C. P. V. Ayyar, *Town Planning in the Ancient Dekkan*, Madras, no date, with an introduction by Patrick Geddes. See also Patrick Geddes in *India*, ed. J. Tyrwhitt, London, 1947; N. V. Ramanayya, *An Essay on the Origin of the South Indian Temple*, Madras, 1930, and Stella Kramrisch, *The Hindu Temple*, Calcutta, 1946; H. Rao, "Rural habitation in South India," *Quarterly Journal of the Mythic Society*, 14; J. M. Linton Bogle, *Town Planning in India*, Oxford University Press, 1929; Mudgett and others, *Banaras: Outline of a Master Plan*, prepared by Town and Village Planning Office, Lucknow.

the continuity of the "sacred centers," feeling a consciousness of a single cultural universe where people hold the same things sacred and where the similarities of civic obligations in village aid city to maintain tanks, build public squares, plant fruit trees, erect platforms and shrines, is concrete testimony to common standards of virtue and responsibility.

Surely such things as these—a "sacred scripture," and a sacred class to interpret it, leading personalities, "sacred geography" and the associated rites and ceremonies—must in any civilization be important vehicles for the formation of that common cultural consciousness from which a Great Tradition is fashioned and to which it must appeal if it is to stay alive. It is in this sense that the universalization of cultural consciousness is a necessary ingredient in its formation and maintenance. Moreover, as the discussion of the role of "sacred geography" in the formation of Hinduism has intimated, this process does not begin only at the point where the villager and the urbanite merge their distinct cultural identities in a higher identity, but is already at work at the simpler levels of family, caste and village, and must play an important part in the formation and maintenance of the Little Tradition at these levels.[32]

The integration of city and country in the secondary phase of urbanization cannot rest on a basic common cultural consciousness or a common culture, for there is none. Rural-urban integration in this phase

[32]See Robert Redfield, *The Little Community*, (ms. to be published 1954) Ch. 8, on the little community "As a community within communities."

In addition to the above factors, it has been usual to single out special items of content of the world view and values of a Great Tradition as explanations of the "Universalization" of Great Traditions. It has been frequently argued, e.g., that religions which are monotheistic and sanction an "open class" social system will appeal more to ordinary people and spread faster than those which are polytheistic and which sanction "caste" systems. (See e.g., H. J. Kissling, "The sociological and educational role of the Dervish orders in the Ottoman Empire," in G. von Grunebaum (ed.), *Studies in Islamic Cultural History.*) F. S. C. Northrop and Arnold Toynbee both attached great importance to the ideological content of cultures as factors in their spread, although they come out with different results. It may be that such special features of content are important in the formation and spread of some particular religions at some particular time, but it is doubtful that they would have the same role in different civilizations under all circumstances. In his recent study of the Coorgs of South India, Srinivas argues with considerable plausibility that the spread of Hinduism on an all-India basis has depended on its polytheism, which has made it easy to incorporate all sorts of alien deities, and on a caste system which assimilates every new culture or ethnic group as a special caste.[28]

Another difficulty about using special features of content of some particular tradition as a general explanation of the formation and maintenance of any

of urbanization rests primarily on the mutuality of interests and on the "symbiotic" relations that have often been described.[33] The city is a "service station" and amusement center for the country, and the country is a "food basket" for the city. But while the diversity of cultural groups and the absence of a common culture makes the basis of the integration primarily technical, even this kind of integration requires a kind of cultural consciousness to keep it going. We refer to the consciousness of cultural differences and the feeling that certain forms of inter-cultural association are of great enough benefit to override the repugnance of dealing with "foreigners." We may call this an "enlargement" of cultural horizons sufficient to become aware of other cultures and of the possibility that one's own society may in some ways require their presence. To paraphrase Adam Smith, it is not to the interest of the (Jewish) baker, the (Turkish) carpet-dealer, the (French) hand laundry, that the American Christian customer looks when he patronizes them, but to his own.

This is the practical psychological basis for admission of the stranger and tolerance of foreign minorities, even at the level of the folk society.[34] In a quotation from the *Institutions of Athens*, which Toynbee has, perhaps ironically, titled "Liberté-Egalité-Fraternité," we are told that the reason why Athens has "extended the benefits of Democracy to the relations between slaves and freemen and between aliens and citizens" is that "the country requires permanent residence of aliens in her midst on account both of the multiplicity of trades and of her maritime activities."[35]

When all or many classes of a population are culturally strange to

---

Great Traditions is that one inevitable selects features that have been crystallized only after a long period of historical development and struggle. These are more relevant as factors in explaining *further* development and spread than they are in explaining the cultural-psychological processes that have accompanied primary urbanization. The "universalization" of universal faiths takes us into the realm of secondary urbanization where diverse and conflicting cultures must be accommodated.

[33] R. E. Park, "Symbiosis and socialization: a frame of reference for the study of society," reprinted in *Human Communities*, Free Press, Glencoe, 1952.

[34] Robert Redfield, *The Primitive World and Its Transformations*, pp. 33–34, for the institutionalization of hospitality to strangers in peasant societies.

[35] Arnold Toynbee, *Greek Civilization and Character*, Beacon Press, Boston, 1950, pp. 48–49. See also David G. Mandelbaum, "The Jewish way of life in Cochin," *Jewish Social Studies*, Vol. I (1939).

each other and where some of the city populations are culturally alien to the country populations, the necessity for an enlarged cultural consciousness is obvious. In societies where social change is slow, and there has developed an adjustment of mutual usefulness and peaceful residence side by side of groups culturally different but not too different, the culturally complex society may be relatively stable.[36] But where urban development is great, such conditions are apt to be unstable. Each group may be perpetually affronted by the beliefs and practices of the other groups. Double standards of morality will prevail, since each cultural group will have one code for its "own kind" and another for the "outsiders." This simultaneous facing both inward and outward puts a strain on both codes. There may then be present the drives to proseletize, to withdraw and dig in, to persecute and to make scapegoats; there may even be fear of riot and massacre. In such circumstances the intellectuals become the chief exponents of a "cosmopolitan" enlarged cultural consciousness, inventing formulas of universal toleration and the benefits of mutual understanding, and extolling the freedom of experiment in different ways of life. But they do not always prevail against the more violent and unconvinced crusaders for some brand of cultural purity.

In primary urbanization when technical development was quite backward, a common cultural consciousness did get formed. The travelling student, teacher, saint, pilgrim or even humble villager who goes to the next town may be startled by strange and wonderful sights, but throughout his journey he is protected by the compass of the common culture from cultural shock and disorientation. In ancient times students and teachers came from all over India and even from distant countries to study at Taxila, just as they came from all over Greece to Athens. In secondary urbanization, especially under modern conditions, technical developments in transportation, travel and communication enormously facilitate and accelerate cultural contacts. The effects of this on common cultural consciousness are not easy briefly to characterize. They make the more traditional cultural differences less important. They provide a wide basis of common understanding with regard to the instruments and practical means of living. It is as least clear that the integration of country and city that results is not the same kind of sense of common purpose in life that was provided to rural-urban

[36]Redfield, "Primitive Merchants of Guatemala."

peoples through the institutions mediating Little and Great Traditions referred to above. At this point the enquiry approaches the questions currently asked about the "mass culture" of modern great societies.

Cities as Centers of Cultural Innovation, Diffusion, and Progress

It is a commonly stated view that the city rather than the country is the source of cultural innovations, that such innovations diffuse outward from city to country, and that the "spread" is more or less inverse to distance from the urban center.[37] The objection to this view is not that it is wrong—for there is much evidence that would seem to support it—but that the limits and conditions of its validity need to be specified. It seems to assume for example that in the processes of cultural change, innovation, and diffusion, "city" and "country" are fixed points of reference which do not have historics, or interact, and are not essentially related to larger contexts of cultural change. Yet such assumptions—if ever true—would hold only under the most exceptional and short-run conditions. It is one thing to say that a large metropolitan city is a "center" of cultural innovation and diffusion for its immediate hinterland at a particular time; it is another to ask how that center itself was formed, over how long a period and from what stimuli. In other words, as we enlarge the time span, include the rise and fall of complex distributions of cities, allow for the mutual interactions between them and their hinterlands, and also take account of interactions with other civilizations and *their* rural-urban patterns, we find that the processes of cultural innovation and "flow" are far too complex to be handled by simple mechanical laws concerning the direction, rate, and "flow" of cultural diffusion between "city" and "country." The cities themselves are creatures as well as well as creators of this process, and it takes a

[37]P. Sorokin and C. Zimmerman, *Principles of Rural-Urban Sociology*, New York, Henry Holt and Co., 1929, Ch. 17, "The role of the city and the country in innovation, disruption, and preservation of the national culture;" Chabot, G., "Les zones d'influence d'une ville." *Congr. int. de Geog.*, Paris, 1931, III, pp. 432–37; Jefferson, Mark, "The law of the primate city," *Geog. Rev.*, 1939, 226–32; Spate, O. H. K., "Factors in the development of capital cities," *Geog. Rev.*, 1942, pp. 622–31; R. E. Park, "The urban community as a spatial pattern and a moral order," "Newspaper circulation and metropolitan regions," both reprinted in Park, *Human Communities;* Hiller, "Extension of urban characteristics into rural areas," *Rural Sociology*, Vol. 6 (1941).

broad cross-cultural perspective to begin to see what its nature is. While this perspective may not yield simple generalizations about direction and rates of cultural diffusion to widen the viewpoint as here suggested may throw some light on the processes of cultural change, including the formation and cultural "influence" of cities.

In a primary phase of urbanization, when cities are developing from folk societies, it seems meaningless to assert, e.g., that the direction of cultural flow is from city to country. Under these conditions a folk culture is transformed into an urban culture which is a specialization of it, and if we wish to speak of "direction of flow" it would make more sense to see the process as one of a series of concentrations and nucleations within a common field. And as these concentrations occur, the common "Little Tradition" has not become inert; in fact, it may retain a greater vitality and disposition to change than the systematized Great Tradition that gets "located" in special classes and in urban centers. From this point of view the spatial and mechanical concepts of direction" and "rate" of flow, etc., are just metaphors of the processes involved in the formation of a Great Tradition. The cultural relations between city and country have to be traced in other terms, in terms of socio-cultural history and of cultural-psychological processes. Physical space and time may be important obstacles and facilitators to these processes but they are not the fundamental determinants of cultural "motion" as they are of physical motion.

Under conditions of secondary urbanization, the spatial and mechanical concepts seem more appropriate because people and goods are more mobile and the technical development of the channels of transportation and communication is such as to permit highly precise measurement of their distributions and of "flows." But here too we may be measuring only some physical facts whose cultural significance remains indeterminate or, at most, we may be documenting only a particularly recent cultural tendency to analyze intercultural relations in quantitative, abstract, and non-cultural terms. The assumption of a continuous and quantitatively divisible "diffusion" from a fixed urban center is unrealistic.

We may see Canton or Calcutta as a center for the diffusion of Western culture into the "East." We may also see these cities as relatively recent metropolitan growths, beginning as minor outliers of Oriental civilizations and then attracting both foreign and also uprooted native peoples, varying in fortune with world-wide events, and becoming at last not so much a center for the introduction of Western ways as a center for nativestic and independence movements to get rid of Western control and dominance. "Everything new happens at Canton," is said in China. We have in such a case not simple diffusion, or spread of urban influence from a city, but rather a cultural interaction which takes place against a background of ancient civilization with its own complex and changing pattern of urbanization now coming into contact with a newer and different civilization and giving rise to results that conform to neither.

The city may be regarded, but only very incompletely, as a center from which spreads outward the idea of progress. It is true that progress, like the ideologies of nationalism, socialism communism, capitalism and democracy, tends to form in cities and it is in cities that the prophets and leaders of these doctrines are formed. Yet the states of mind of Oriental and African peoples are not copies of the minds of Western exponents of progress or of one or another political or economic doctrine. There is something like a revolution of mood and aspiration in the non-European peoples today.[38] The Easterner revolts against the West; he does not just take what can be borrowed from a city; he does sometimes the opposite: the Dutch language is set aside in Indonesia; there, anthropology, because associated with Dutch rule, does not spread from any city but is looked on with suspicion as associated with Dutch rule. Moreover, the influence of the West does not simply move outward from cities; it leap-frogs into country regions; a city reformer in Yucatan, Carrillo Puerto, arouses village Indians to join his civil war for progress and freedom against landowners and townspeople; Marxists discover that revolution can be based on the peasants without waiting for the development of an industrial proletariat.[39]

The conception of progress is itself an idea shaped by and expressive of one culture or civilization, that of the recent West.[40] What Toynbee and others have called the "Westernization" of the world may be the

[38]For further discussion of these concepts of "mood," "aspirations" and "policy" as they might figure in community studies, see Redfield, *The Little Community*, chapter on "Little Community as a History."

[39]David Mitrany, *Marx and the Peasants*.

[40]See A. L. Kroeber, *Anthropology*, Secs. 127, 128; Milton Singer, *Shame Cultures and Guilt Cultures*, for an examination of some of the evidence on this point for American Indian cultures. Also see Redfield, *A Village that Chose Progress*, esp. Chapter 8, "Chan Kom, Its Ethos and Success." Recent material on cross-cultural comparisons of value systems will be found in Daryll Forde (ed.), *African Worlds*, and in the forthcoming publications of the Harvard Values Study Project directed by Clyde Kluckhohn.

spread of only parts of the ideas associated in the West with the word "progress." Not without investigation can it be safely assumed that the spread of Western ideas from cities carries into the countryside a new and Western value system emphasizing hard work, enterprise, a favorable view of social change and a central faith in material prosperity. In the cases of some of the peoples affected by modern urbanization these values may be already present. In other cases the apparent spread of progress may turn out, on closer examination, to be a return to ancient values different from those of the West. Nationalistic movements are in part a nostalgic turning back to local traditional life. We shall understand better the varieties and complexities of the relations today between city and country as we compare the values and world views of the modernizing ideologies, and those of the Little and Great Traditions of the cultures and civilizations that are affected by the modern West. It may be that such studies[41] will discover greater "ambivalence" in the mood to modernize than we, here in the West, acknowledge; that the progressive spirit of Asia and Africa is not simply a decision to walk the road of progressive convictions that we have traversed, but rather in significant part an effort of the "backward" peoples to recover from their disruptive encounters with the West by returning to the "sacred centers" of their ancient indigenous civilizations.

[41]Several such studies have been made. See, e.g., Paul Mus, *Viet-Nam, l'histoire d'une guerre,* Paris, 1952; Shen-Yu Dai, *Mao Tse-Tung and Confucianism,* Doctoral Dissertation, University of Pennsylvania, 1952; E. Sarkisyanz, Russian *Weltanschauung and Islamic and Buddhist Messianism,* Doctoral Dissertation, University of Chicago, 1953. V. Barnouw, "The Changing Character of a Hindu Festival," *American Anthropologist,* February, 1954.